DISCOVER
Physical & Environmental geography

Keith Grimwade

Hodder & Stoughton

A MEMBER OF THE HODDER HEADLINE GROUP

...er

This text is based on the First Edition of Discover Physical Geography but has been completely re-written. It meets the requirements of the new GCSE syllabuses.

Opportunities for developing essential skills have been included, and the way the text is structured makes it easy to select material to support schemes of work. Greater emphasis has been given to the study of specific places. The Enquiries help pupils to record important information and to develop their understanding of the themes covered; ideas for further research and for fieldwork projects are also included. Each section contains an assessment task which allows achievement to be demonstrated at a range of levels.

The style and format of the First Edition has been retained. The aim of the text also remains the same: to provide a thematic approach to GCSE Geography; to explore people-environment relationships; and to present information in an attractive, accessible and varied way.

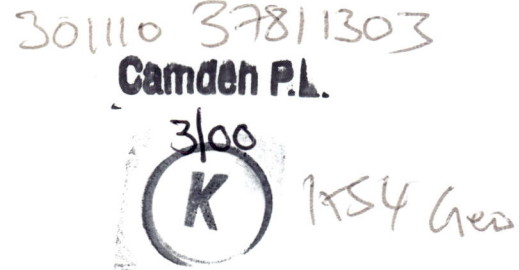

British Librarby Cataloguing in Publication Data
Grimwade, Keith
 Discover Physical and Environmental
 Geography. - 2Rev.ed
 I. Title
 910.02

ISBN 0340 59344 X
First publishred in 1994
Impression number   10 9 8 7 6 5
Year   2002 2001 2000 1999

This impression revised and updated 1995

Copyright © 1994 Keith Grimwade

All rights reserved. No part of this publication may be reproduced or transmitted in any form or by any means, electronic or mechanical, including photocopy, recording, or any information storage and retrieval system, without permission in writing from the publisher or under licences from the Copyright Licensing Agency Limited. Further details of such licences (for reprographic reproduction) may be obtained from the Copyright Licensing Agency Limited, of 90 Tottenham Court Road, London W1P 9HE.

Typeset by Litho Link Ltd, Welshpool, Powys.
Printed for Hodder & Stoughton Educational, a division of Hodder Headline Plc, 338 Euston Road, London NW1 3BH by Colorcraft Ltd, Hong Kong.

To the Pupil

This book covers the themes you need to study for the physical and environmental parts of your syllabus. However, it is important to understand that human and physical geography are closely related: our "human home" is the "physical earth".

The Enquiries will help you to record important information and to develop your understanding of the themes covered. Ideas for your own fieldwork projects are also included. Please be safe: always work with a partner and if you are surveying a stream, for example, it is best if there are at least three of you so that one person can stay on the bank in case of difficulties. Let your parents know where you are going!

There is a glossary at the end of the book for you to use if you come across a word or phrase with which you are unfamiliar. Glossary terms are in **bold** in the main text. Use the index as well to find out where topics are mentioned.

I hope that this book, together with its companion volume *Discover Human Geography*, will make the world — its scenery, weather and climate, environments and people — more interesting and more alive, and that you will want to visit many of the places written about for yourself.

Discover Geography!

EARTH page 4

1.1 *What is the earth like inside?* 5   1.2 *What are volcanoes and earthquakes?* 10
1.3 *What happens as the crust moves around?* 15   1.4 *Why do rocks break down?* 21
1.5 *What shapes the land?* 25   1.6 *What makes up soil?* 30
1.7 *Assessment task: soil survey* 33   1.8 *What is happening to our soil?* 34

WATER page 38

2.1 *What makes up a river system?* 39
2.2 *Why do rivers flood and how do we cope?* 40   2.3 *Where does the water come from?* 43
2.4 *What are the features of a river basin?* 46   2.5 *How does the river system work?* 48
2.6 *River landforms — what are they like and how do they form?* 52
2.7 *Where does our water come from?* 59   2.8 *Assessment task: Rivers on OS maps* 65

ICE page 66

3.1 *What was the ice age?* 67   3.2 *What do glaciers do to the land?* 70
3.3 *How do we make use of glaciated uplands?* 77
3.4 *Assessment task: Glacial features on OS maps* 81

CARBONIFEROUS LIMESTONE

4.1 *Carboniferous Limestone — how should we manage a special landscape?* 83
4.2 *Assessment task: The Malham area of North Yorkshire* 88

SEA page 90

5.1 *What does the sea do to the land?* 91
5.2 *How do changes in sea-level affect the coastline?* 97
5.3 *How do we cope with the threat from the sea?* 99
5.4 *How do we sometimes make things worse?* 101
5.5 *How can we explain a physical landscape?* 103
5.6 *Assessment task: The landforms of the Isle of Purbeck* 107

WEATHER, CLIMATE AND VEGETATION page 108

6.1 *What makes up weather and climate?* 109   6.2 *Assessment task: Weather survey* 113
6.3 *What is the climate of the British Isles like?* 115   6.4 *Why does it rain?* 117
6.5 *Where does Britain's weather come from, and why?* 118
6.6 *How does climate and vegetation vary from place to place?* 124
6.7 *What explains the world pattern of climate?* 129   6.8 *Is climate to blame?* 138

ENERGY page 142

7.1 *Where does our energy come from?* 143
7.2 *Oil — what impact does its use have on the environment?* 146
7.3 *Assessment task: Oil and the environment* 153
7.4 *Hydroelectric power — what impact does it have on the environment?* 154
7.5 *What will we use for energy in the future?* 157

ENVIRONMENTAL ISSUES page 162

8.1 *What are we doing to the land?* 163   8.2 *What are we doing to the sea?* 167
8.3 *What are we doing to the atmosphere?* 171   8.4 *What are we doing to the forests?* 175
8.5 *Can the earth cope?* 180   8.6 *Assessment task: The earth's future* 184

Glossary page 187
Index page 190
Acknowledgements page 192

1.1 What is the earth like inside?

We cannot explore the inside of the earth for ourselves. However, we do have some evidence which tells us what a journey to the centre of the earth could be like. For example, we can study the material which comes out from inside the earth through volcanoes.

The Earth's Crust

The average thickness of the earth's **crust** is 40 km. This is thinner than the Enquiry on this page suggests. Stick a postage stamp on a football and you will get some idea of how thick it really is! The many different types of rock which make up the crust are put into three groups or 'families': **igneous**, **sedimentary** and **metamorphic**.

Fig 1 Journey to the centre of the earth

ENQUIRY

1 Draw a series of circles one inside the other. The outer circle should have a radius of 64 mm; the next circle in should have a radius of 63 mm; the next a radius of 34 mm; and the smallest a radius of 14 mm. This gives you a diagram of the earth's main layers at a scale of 1 mm = 100 km.
2 Add the following labels to your diagram. They are in the correct order starting with the outer layer.
— crust (solid rock)
— mantle (heavy, thick, molten rock)
— outer core (hot, liquid, iron)
— inner core (hot, solid iron)
3 Add a title and the scale to your diagram.

Igneous Rocks

These form when hot, molten rock (known as **magma**) cools down and turns hard. Basalt (Fig 2) forms from magma which has flowed out onto the earth's crust as lava. As a result, it cools down very quickly and crystals do not have time to grow. Its main minerals are dark coloured. Granite (Fig 3) forms from magma which has cooled down inside the earth's crust. As a result, it cools down very slowly and crystals have plenty of time to grow. Its speckled colour is due to the different minerals in it. In Fig 3 the grey crystals are quartz, the black crystals are mica and the cream or pink crystals are feldspar.

Sedimentary Rocks

These are made from fragments of other rocks, the remains of plants and animals, or chemicals which have built up in layers. Sandstone (Fig 4) is made from grains of sand which have been deposited (dumped) in the sea by rivers, or on the land by wind. Chemicals cement the grains together. Shelly limestone (Fig 5) forms when the shells and skeletons of sea creatures pile up and become cemented together. Oolitic limestone (Fig 6) is made up of small spheres of calcium carbonate. They form when a speck of sand or a tiny fragment of shell is rolled backwards and forwards by gentle currents in water which has a lot of calcium carbonate dissolved in it.

Fig 2   Basalt

Fig 3   Granite

Fig 4   Sandstone

Fig 5   Oolitic limestone

Fig 6   Shelly limestone

As the layers of sedimentary rock build up, the bottom ones are compressed. Each layer of rock is known as a bed, and the lines separating it from the bed below and the bed above are known as bedding planes. Together, the layers are known as strata (Fig 7).

Metamorphic Rocks

These are igneous or sedimentary rocks which have been changed by tremendous heat and/or pressure, e.g. by a volcano or in an earthquake. Usually, all traces of the original rock are destroyed. Marble (Fig 8) is metamorphosed limestone. It forms when limestone is heated to great temperatures. Slate (Fig 9) is metamorphosed mudstone, a sedimentary rock made up of fine particles of clay. It forms when mudstone is put under great pressure, perhaps because of earth movements. The minerals in the mudstone are squeezed together and form lines known as cleavage planes. Although slate is a hard rock it splits easily along these cleavage planes.

Fig 7 Layers of sedimentary rock

Fig 8 Marble

Fig 9 Slate

NAME	FAMILY	COLOUR	GENERAL APPEARANCE e.g. crystals? shell fragments?	FORMATION
basalt				
		speckled – white, cream, black		
				grains of sand cemented together
shelly limestone				
			made up of small spheres	
				limestone changed by great heat
slate				

Fig 10 Rock summary table

ENQUIRY

1 Copy and complete the table in Fig 10.
2 Make a sketch of Fig 7. Label onto it two bedding planes and a bed of rock. Give your sketch the title 'Sedimentary strata'.
3 Select one of the igneous, one of the sedimentary and one of the metamorphic rocks mentioned in this section and write about the ways in which we make use of them.

Fig 11 The earth's plates

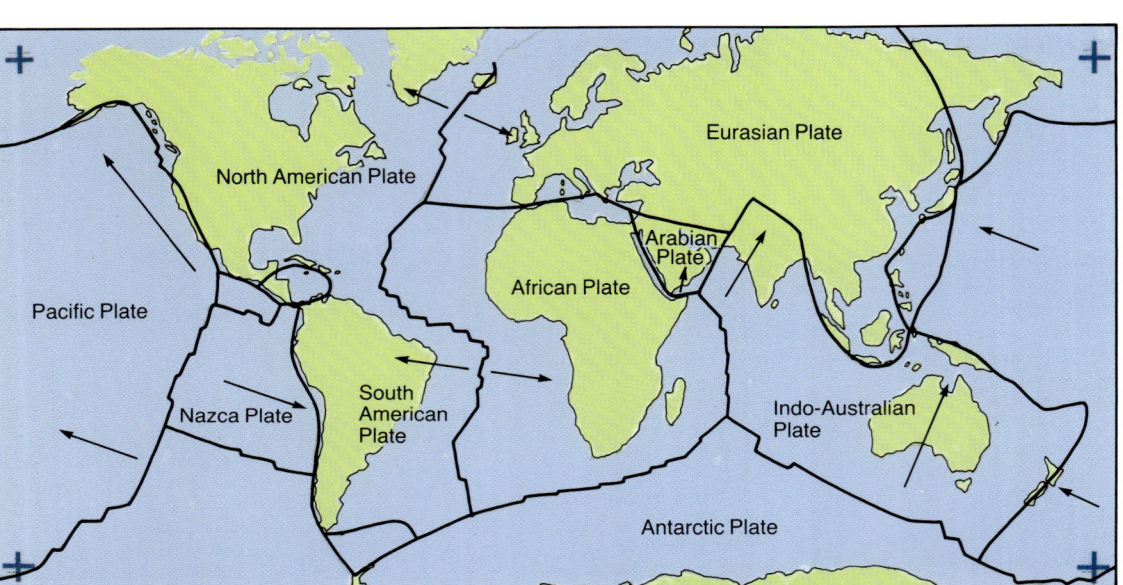

The Earth's Plates

The earth's crust is broken up into a number of pieces by deep cracks. Each of these pieces is known as a **plate** and they are all moving very slowly, towards, away from, or alongside each other (Fig 11). Why they move is not certain but it could be the result of giant convection currents in the mantle dragging them along (Fig 12).

The continents are passengers on these plates. As the plates move the continents have to move with them. It has been discovered that between about 350 and 200 million years ago, today's continents were joined together to form a single "super continent", known as Pangaea. About 200 million years ago Pangaea began breaking up and since then the continents have been drifting apart.

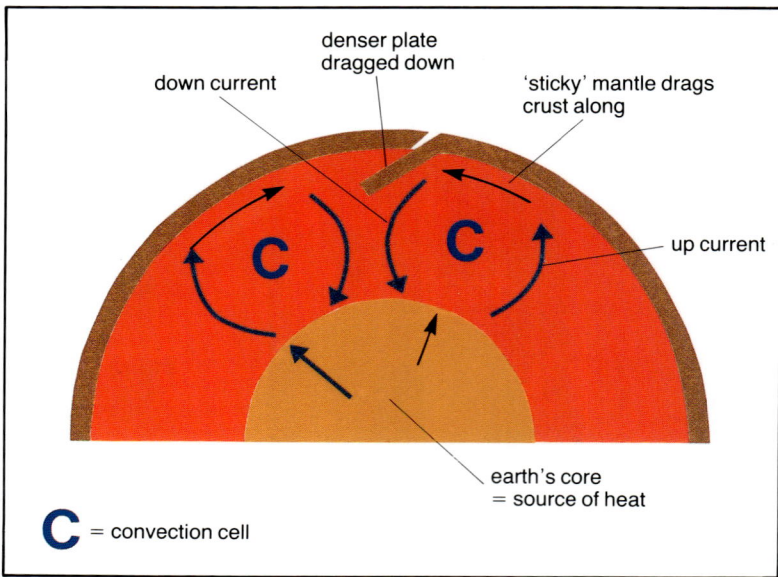

Fig 12 Convection currents in the mantle

EARTH 1.1

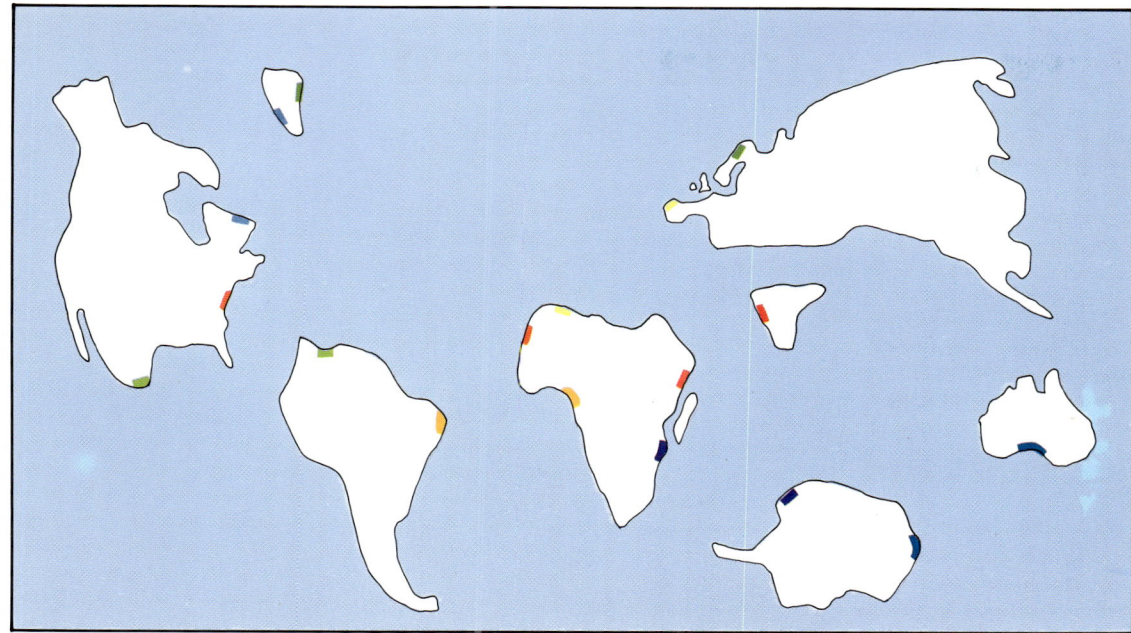

Fig 13 Pangaea

1 Mark onto an outline map of the world the details shown in Fig 11. Label one place where the plates are moving together, one where they are moving apart and one where they are moving alongside each other.
2 Write a paragraph to explain the convection current theory of plate movement.
3 Trace the outlines of the continents in Fig 13 onto a sheet of plain paper. Cut them out and stick them together by lining up the coloured strips – blue with blue, green with green etc. This gives you the shape of Pangaea. Add a suitable title and write a brief explanatory account.

1.2 What are volcanoes and earthquakes?

Volcanoes

A volcano is a crack in the earth's **crust** out of which comes lava (hot, molten rock), ash, steam and gas. There are many different types of volcano. Some erupt gently while others erupt in great explosions. A volcanic eruption is one of the most spectacular sights on earth.

The hot rock under the surface is called **magma** and it usually collects in a large chamber. The crack or pipe leading up to the surface is called the vent. The hole at the top of the vent is called the crater. The hill or mountain made by the volcano is called the **cone**. These features are shown on Fig 14.

There are two main types of lava: basic and acid. Basic lava is thinner than acid lava and it flows more quickly. This makes volcanoes with gentle slopes, known as shield volcanoes; Fig 14 shows this shape. Mauna Loa in Hawaii (see Fig 34, page 19) is an example of a shield volcano. It is, in fact, the largest volcano on earth with a diameter of 200 km at its base on the sea floor and a height of 10 km, 4 km of which is above sea level. Acid lava flows slowly because it is so thick and this makes volcanoes with steep slopes e.g. Ngauruhoe in New Zealand (Fig 15).

Some volcanoes, called composite cones (Fig 16), are made up of layers of lava and ash, one on top of the other. They form when thick, acid lava cools and forms a hard plug of rock in the vent of the volcano. Pressure from gas and magma builds up until it is great enough to blast the plug out of the vent. The plug is

Fig 15 Ngauruhoe, New Zealand

shattered by the explosion and the fragments settle as a layer of ash. With the plug out of the way the lava flows freely and forms a layer on top of the ash. When the eruption has finished the lava hardens to form another plug and the process begins again.

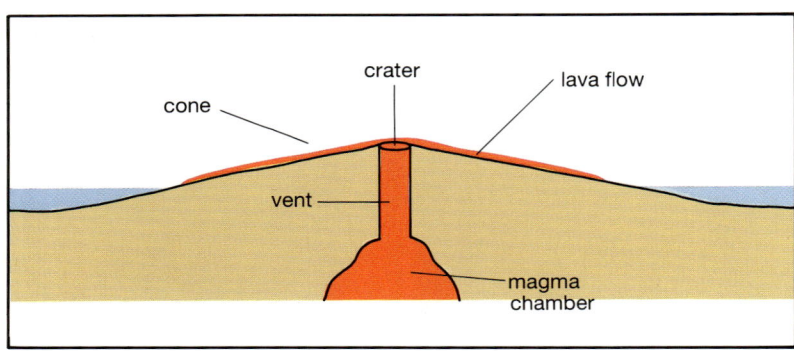

Fig 14 A shield volcano

Mount Etna on the island of Sicily in Italy is an example of a composite cone (Fig 17). It has been erupting for thousands of years. Its cone is 3340 metres high and it covers a very large area. In 1983 the lava from an eruption slowly destroyed the village of Sapienza, a skiing resort on the slopes of the volcano. To stop it causing more damage barriers of rock were built to divert the flow. It took four months and cost £3 million but the scheme was a success. The volcano erupted again in 1992 and this time the Italian army and the United States Air Force managed to divert and to stop the lava by blasting channels and by dropping slabs of concrete into the lava flow.

Mount Etna erupts slowly, so although it can do a great deal of damage people have time to get out of the way. It provides benefits as well: it attracts tourists; local people make souvenirs, such as ash trays, out of the lava; and the lava makes a very fertile soil which is excellent for farming.

When volcanoes erupt quickly they are much more of a hazard. For example, when Nyeragongo in Zaire, in Africa, erupted in 1977, the lava flowed at between 60 and 70 km per hour and over 100 people were killed because they could not get out of the way in time.

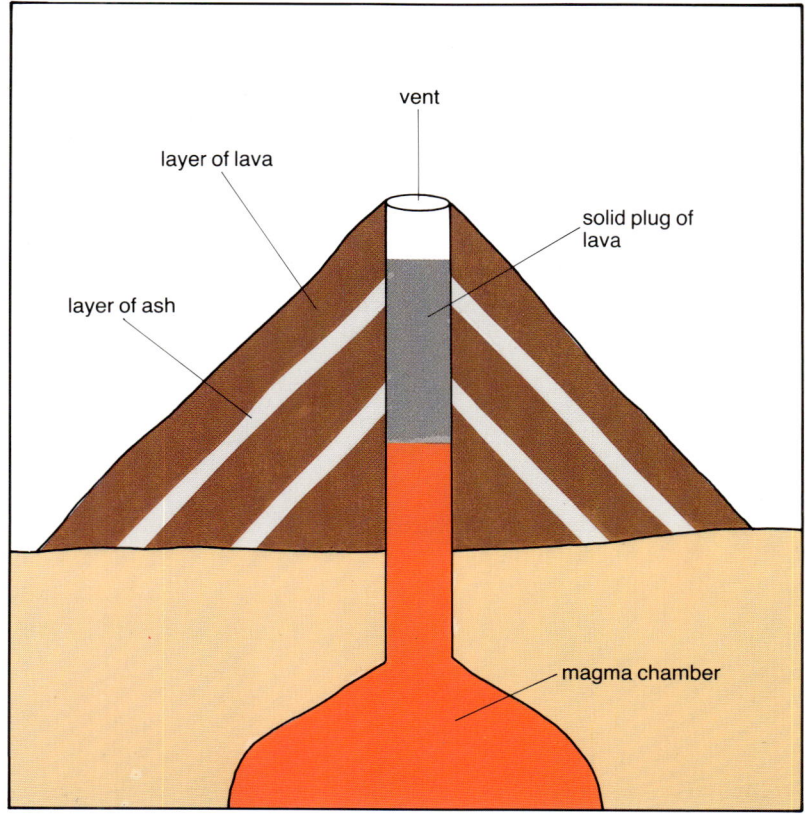

Fig 16 A composite cone

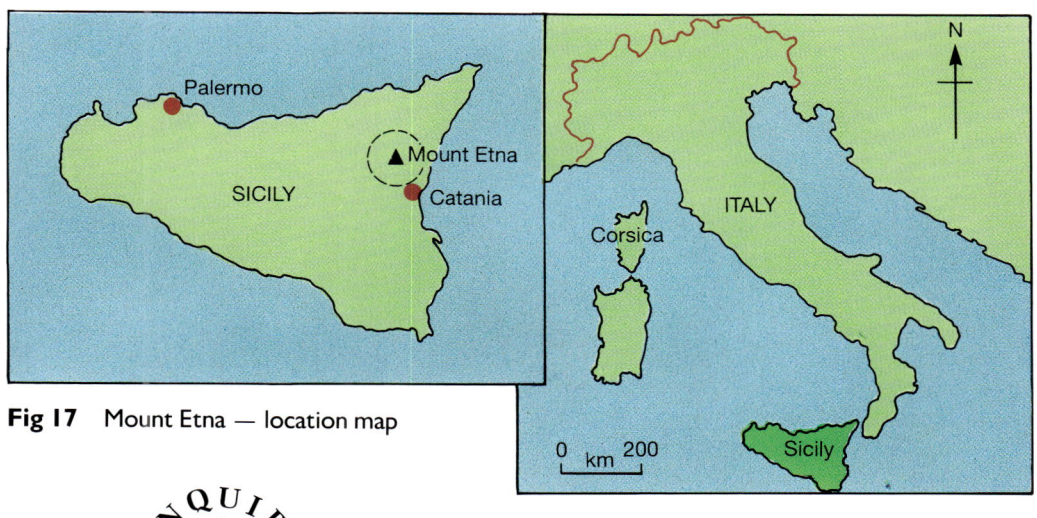

Fig 17 Mount Etna — location map

ENQUIRY

1 Copy Fig 14. Label onto your diagram definitions of the terms crater, cone and lava flow.

2 What are the differences between a basic cone and an acid cone? Name an example of each.

3 Draw a diagram of a composite cone volcano. Add labels to explain how this type of volcano forms.

4 How do volcanoes affect people? (Mention good and bad points in your answer.)

Earthquakes

An **earthquake** is when the ground shakes because a piece of the earth's crust has suddenly moved. The place in the crust where an earthquake starts is called the **focus**. The place on the surface above the focus is called the **epicentre**. The shock waves get weaker as you move away from the epicentre (Fig 18). The strength of an earthquake is measured on either the Mercalli scale or the Richter scale (Fig 19).

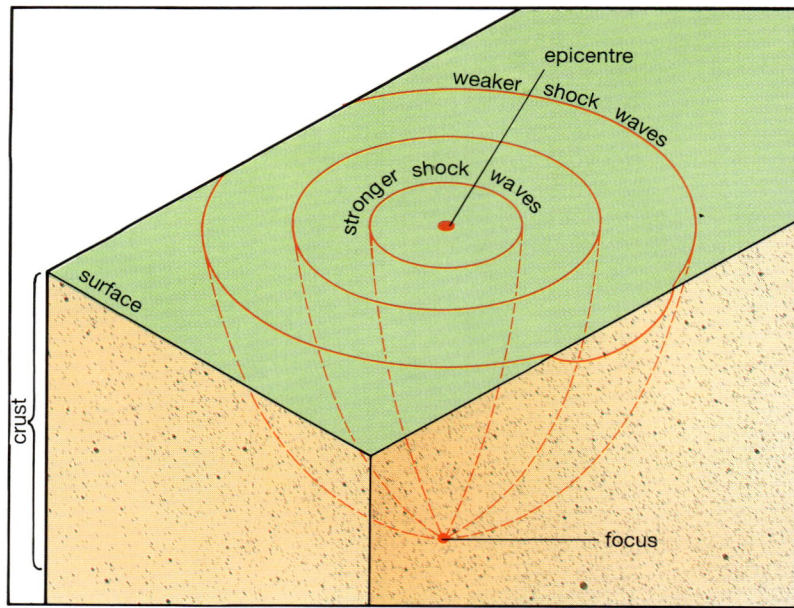

Fig 18 Focus, epicentre and earthquake strength

Mercalli	Description	Richter
1	felt only by measuring instruments	0.0
2	felt sitting down in a quiet room	3.5
3	feels like a lorry going past	4.2
4	ornaments and windows rattle	4.3
5	the ground noticeably shakes	4.8
6	trees sway, furniture falls over	4.9
7	walls crack	5.5
8	chimneys fall, roads crack	6.2
9	houses collapse	6.9
10	many buildings, roads, railways destroyed; ground cracks badly	7.0
11	very little remains standing	7.4
12	total destruction	8.9

Fig 19 Richter and Mercalli scales

Fig 20 San Francisco

Fig 21 Earthquake damage: Bay Bridge, San Francisco, 1989

On 17 October 1989 an earthquake measuring 9 on the Mercalli scale happened 60 miles to the south of San Francisco in California, USA. The vibrations lasted for 15 seconds. Buildings and bridges collapsed (Fig 21), fires started because the earthquake broke gas pipes, and water and electricity supplies were cut off. Over 270 people were killed, many of them when the upper deck of a two-storey highway collapsed onto the lower deck, crushing over 100 cars and lorries.

Given the amount of damage — it cost $10 billion to repair — it seems incredible that so few people lost their lives. However, San Francisco has had earthquakes in the past (see page 14 for the reason) and many of the buildings have been designed to cope with all but the biggest tremors. Also, it was easy for the government to fly in troops to help San Francisco's well-equipped emergency services.

San Francisco will have earthquakes in the future and no building can stand up to a really big tremor. Why do people carry on living in such a dangerous place — is it because it is such a beautiful city (Fig 20), is it because people think "it will never happen to them", or are there other reasons?

Ten months earlier on 7 December 1988 an earthquake had happened near Leninakan in Armenia, which used to be part of the former USSR and is now part of the CIS (Fig 22). Roads, railways and bridges were destroyed. Three-quarters of the city of Leninakan was destroyed. Some smaller towns and villages were completely wiped out. 80 000 people were killed and the same number were injured.

This earthquake was almost exactly the same strength as the one in California, so why was its effect so much worse? Firstly, the epicentre of the Armenian earthquake was closer to the city of Leninakan than the Californian earthquake was to the city of San Francisco. Secondly, Armenia is much poorer than San Francisco, so the houses are not built so well and the emergency services are not so well-equipped. Thirdly, the lack of money meant that President Gorbachev of the former USSR had to ask for help from other countries and although it was sent straight away, it obviously took some time to arrive. Fourthly, when help did arrive in Leninakan, they still had the problem of getting it to the villages which had been cut off by the earthquake.

When earthquakes happen in the crust under the sea they can cause giant waves called **tsunamis**. These waves do more damage than the earthquake themselves e.g. tsunamis were responsible for most of the 115 deaths in the Alaskan earthquake in 1964 (Fig 23).

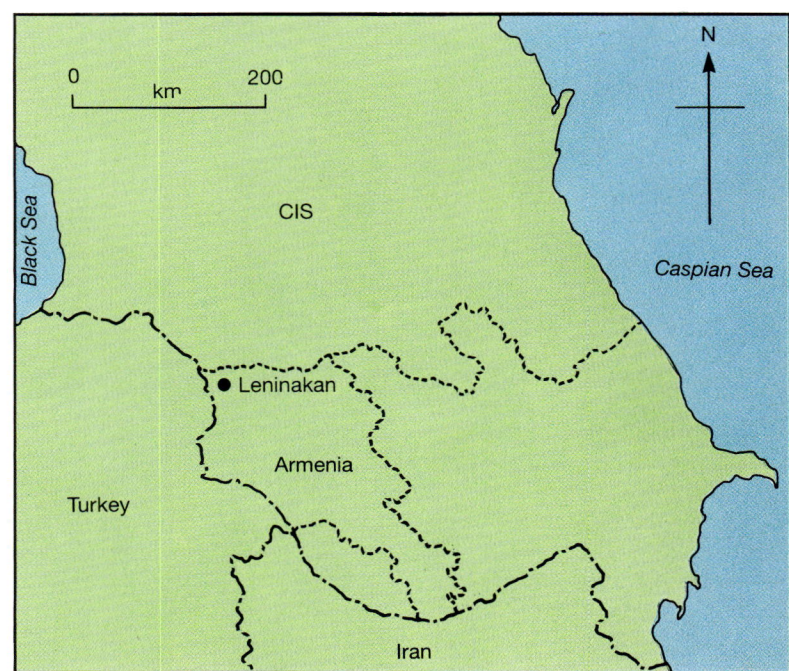

Fig 22   Leninakan, Armenia: location map

1   Copy Fig 18. Add labels to explain what is meant by the focus and the epicentre of an earthquake.
2   Draw pictures to show what happens at the following points on the Mercalli earthquake scale — 2, 4, 6, 9, 11. What number is each of these points on the Richter scale?
3   What were the effects of **a)** the 1989 San Fransisco earthquake and **b)** the 1988 Armenian earthquake on people, buildings and services, e.g. roads and electricity? Why were the effects of the Armenian earthquake so much worse?
4   What are tsunamis? Try to find out which country the word "tsunami" comes from — it has a lot of earthquakes.
5   Compare a map of world population density in an atlas with the distribution of earthquakes shown on Fig 27, page 15 Name five countries with areas of high population density which are likely to have earthquakes. Choose one of these countries and find out why so many people live in the parts of it which are likely to have earthquakes. Also, find out about the major earthquakes it has suffered. Why do you think people carry on living in such dangerous places?

Fig 23   Ships swept ashore by Alaskan earthquake, 1964

Predicting Volcanoes and Earthquakes

Fig 24 Mount Aso (Kumamoto), Japan

We cannot stop volcanic eruptions and earthquakes but we can try to predict when they are going to happen so that the people who live near them can be given a warning.

For example, Japan has 70 active volcanoes and it uses the latest technology to monitor their progress. Sensitive instruments measure earth tremors caused by magma pushing its way up to the surface. The ground often bulges as the magma tries to push its way out and this is also measured with special equipment. Pressure pads are placed round a volcano and if anything lands on them, like ash or lava at the start of an eruption, alarms in nearby settlements are set off and video cameras are switched on so that the eruption can be watched.

By studying the rocks on either side of the San Andreas fault in California scientists have worked out that the Pacific plate and the North American plate are moving past each other at an average speed of 3 cm a year (Fig 25). In some places this movement happens slowly and causes only small earthquakes, but in other places the rocks lock together and the stress builds up until they snap apart causing a large earthquake. Lasers are used to measure the amount of movement so that the "at risk" places where stress is building up — the places which have not moved for a long time — can be pin-pointed. Earth tremors, the amount of stress building up in the rocks, the level of water in wells — all of these can be monitored with special equipment and can warn of the start of an earthquake.

The potential damage of an earthquake in California is so great that scientists are also exploring ways of preventing strain from building up along the line of the fault. One idea is to pump water down the fault in order to lubricate it. Another idea is to use explosions to relieve the stress in a controlled way.

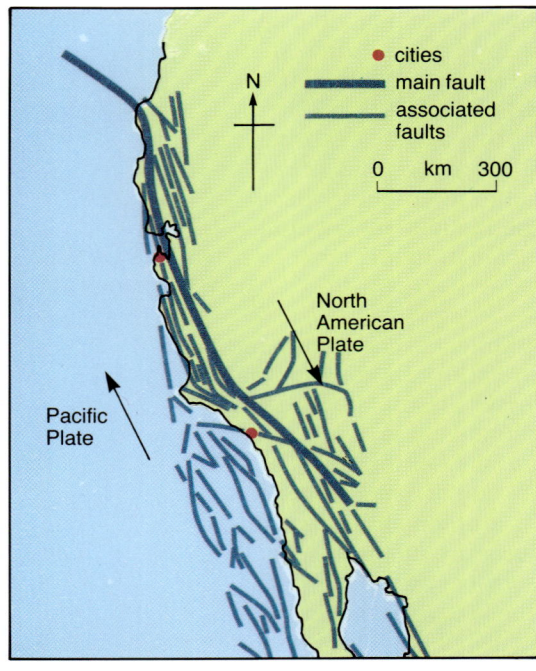

Fig 25 The San Andreas fault, California: location map

1 Why does a rich country like Japan stand a better chance of predicting a volcanic eruption than a poor country like Indonesia? (Indonesia has the largest number of active volcanoes in the world.)
2 Mark Los Angeles and San Fransisco onto a copy of Fig 25. How long will it take (at the current average rate of movement) for the San Andreas fault to move the distance between these two cities?
3 The map suggests one of the reasons why predicting earthquakes in California is so difficult? What is it?
4 "Pumping water down the fault line in Los Angeles may stop an earthquake there but may start one in San Fransisco". Explain this statement.

1.3 What happens as the crust moves around?

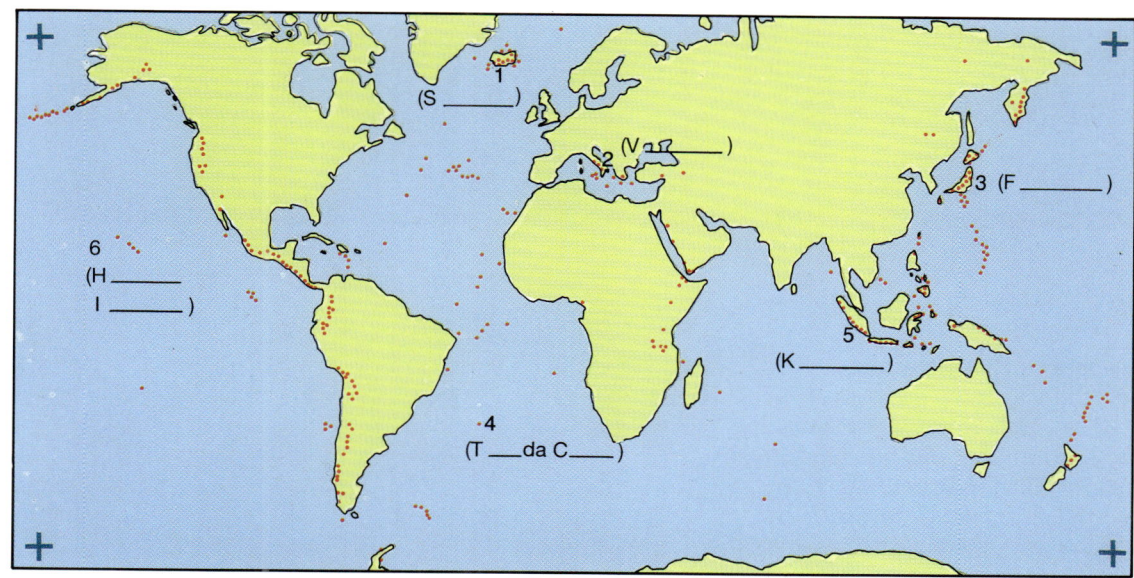

Fig 26 World distribution of volcanoes

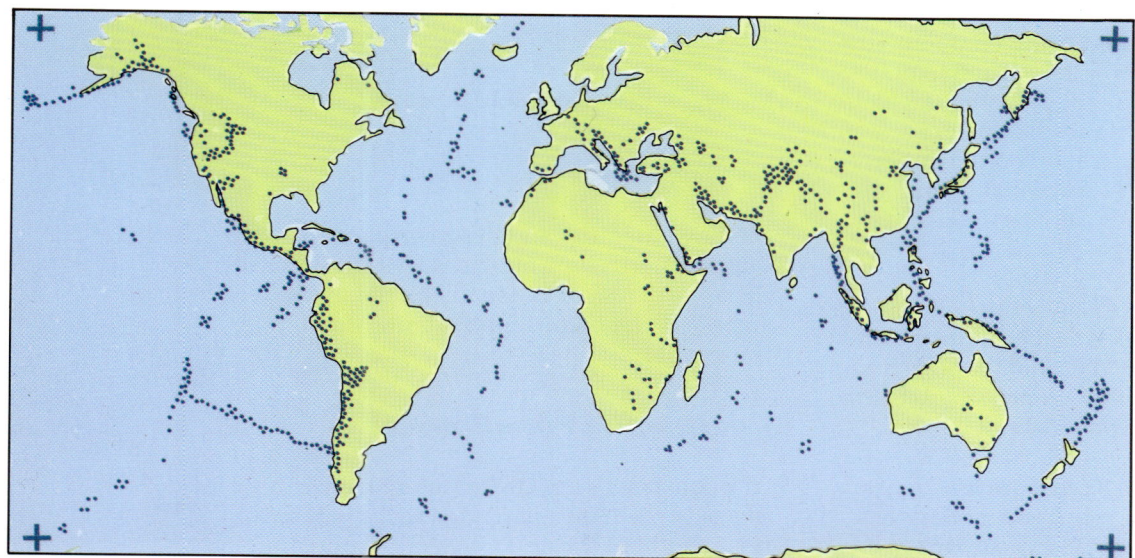

Fig 27 World distribution of earthquake

Fig 28 Surtsey, Iceland

ENQUIRY

1 Mark onto a piece of tracing paper the distribution of volcanoes shown in Fig 26. Place your tracing paper over Fig 11, page 8 which is drawn at the same scale. (The blue crosses will help you to line up the tracing paper correctly). What is the relationship between the distribution of volcanoes and the plate boundaries? Use an atlas to name the famous volcanoes labelled 1-5. The volcanic islands labelled 6 are an exception to the general pattern. What is their name?

2 Carry out the same exercise for the distribution of earthquakes shown in Fig 27. What relationship exists between earthquakes and plate boundaries?

3 Why is the UK free from volcanic eruptions and major earthquakes?

Destructive Plate Boundaries

The Enquiry on this page shows that most volcanoes and earthquakes happen close to plate boundaries. This is because there are cracks in the crust going down towards the molten rock below the surface, and because the slabs of crust rub together as they move.

In areas where the earth's plates are moving together, the denser plate moves under the less dense plate and is swallowed up into the **mantle**; this is known as a destructive plate boundary (Fig 29). The place where the plate disappears is known as a subduction zone and it is marked by a deep trench on the ocean floor; an example is the Marianas Trench in the north-west Pacific which is the deepest place on earth.

The temperature increases as the plate moves down into the mantle. At a depth of 100 km the temperature is 1000°C and the plate has already begun to melt. Evidence suggests that it finally melts at a depth of about 700 km.

The rocks of the earth's crust are less dense than the mantle. As a result the molten rock from the melting plate rises back to the surface. If the plate is moving under the ocean this material erupts as a line of volcanoes which may rise above the surface to form an island arc; an example is the Aleutian Islands in the north Pacific. If it is moving under a continent the material may become stuck, forming an "intrusion", or it may be able to follow a line of weakness to the surface and erupt as a volcano. The lava at this type of boundary tends to be of the acid type and, as has been mentioned, it results in volcanoes with steep slopes.

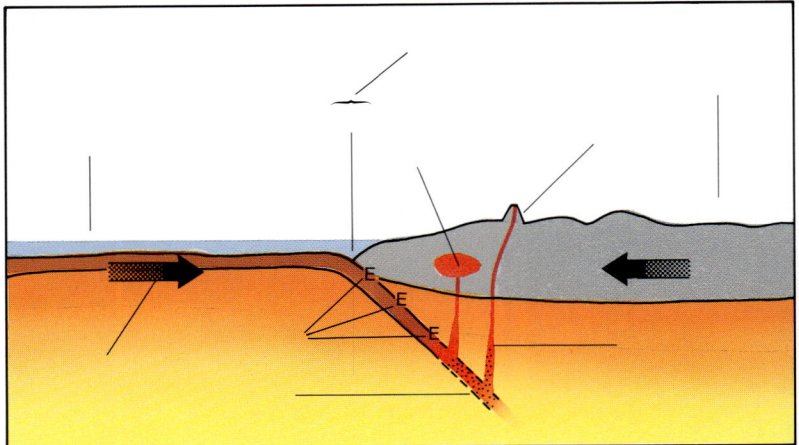

Fig 29 A destructive plate boundary

Shallow, medium and deep earthquakes happen at this type of boundary. The focus of these earthquakes is usually on the upper surface of the plate which is going down into the mantle.

Constructive Plate Boundaries

At a constructive plate boundary the earth's plates are moving apart and cracks, known as faults, form in the crust. Magma rises to the surface along these faults. It plugs the gap and may add new material to the sea-floor, forming an ocean ridge, and/or it may erupt to form a volcano, e.g. Surtsey which rose out of the sea 100 km south of Iceland in 1963 (Fig 28). The lava at this type of boundary tends to be of the basic type and produces volcanoes with gentle slopes.

Earthquakes happen as the crust pulls apart and their focus tends to be at quite a shallow depth.

Conservative Plate Boundaries

There is very little volcanic activity where the earth's plates are moving alongside each other (a conservative plate boundary) because the plates are not being destroyed, nor is a gap being opened up: one plate is simply sliding past the other.

However, this movement does not happen smoothly. Thick sections of rock get stuck when they are dragged past each other. The stress builds up to a point and then the rocks jerk apart causing an earthquake. The San Andreas fault, which is responsible for the earthquakes in San Francisco described in Section 1.2, is an example of such a plate boundary.

Fold Mountains

All the time, sediment is being washed into the seas and oceans by rivers. This builds up on the sea floor as sedimentary rock. These deposits are less dense than the rocks of the oceanic crust or the mantle. As a result, they crumple up like folds in a blanket instead of being dragged down into the mantle along a subduction zone.

1   Copy Fig 29. Label onto it the following terms in their correct place — igneous intrusion, melting plate, direction of plate movement, subduction zone, acid cone, ocean trench, less dense material rises to surface, ocean, continent, earthquake focus.
2   Go back to the copy you made of Fig 11, page 8. Use an atlas to help you work out the plate movements involved in the formation of the Marianas Trench and the Aleutian Islands. Note this information and mark these places onto your map. What is the maximum depth of the Marianas Trench?
3   Copy Fig 30. Label onto it the following terms in their correct place — crust, volcano, direction of plate movement, new material is added to the crust as the plates move apart, ocean floor, earthquake focus.
4   Go back to the copy you made of Fig 11, page 8. Find out from an atlas the names of three ocean ridges and add these to your map.
5   Why are deep-seated earthquakes found at destructive plate boundaries while only shallow earthquakes are found at constructive plate boundaries?
6   Why do you get earthquakes but not volcanoes at conservative plate boundaries?

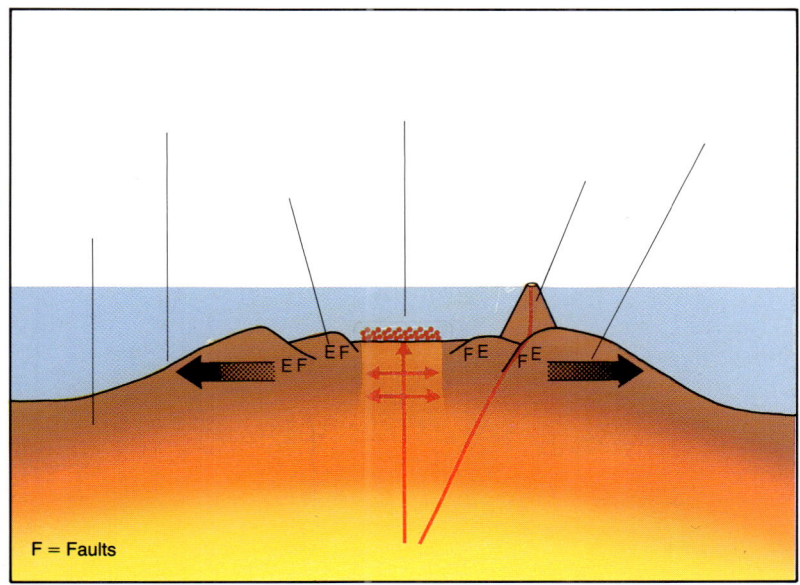

Fig 30   Sea-floor spreading at a mid-ocean ridge

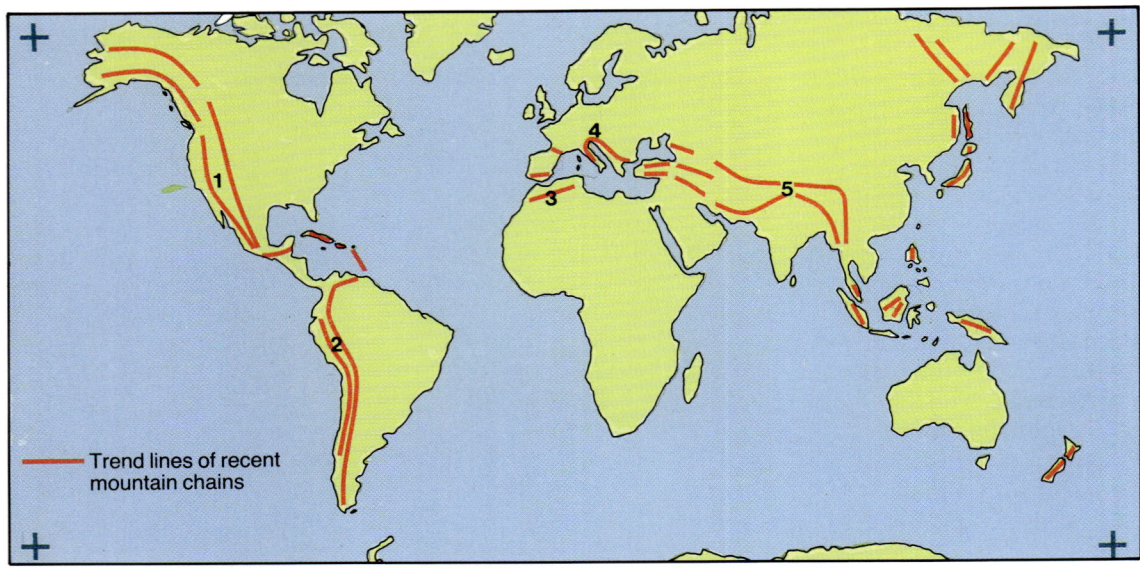

Fig 31 World distribution of recent fold mountain chains

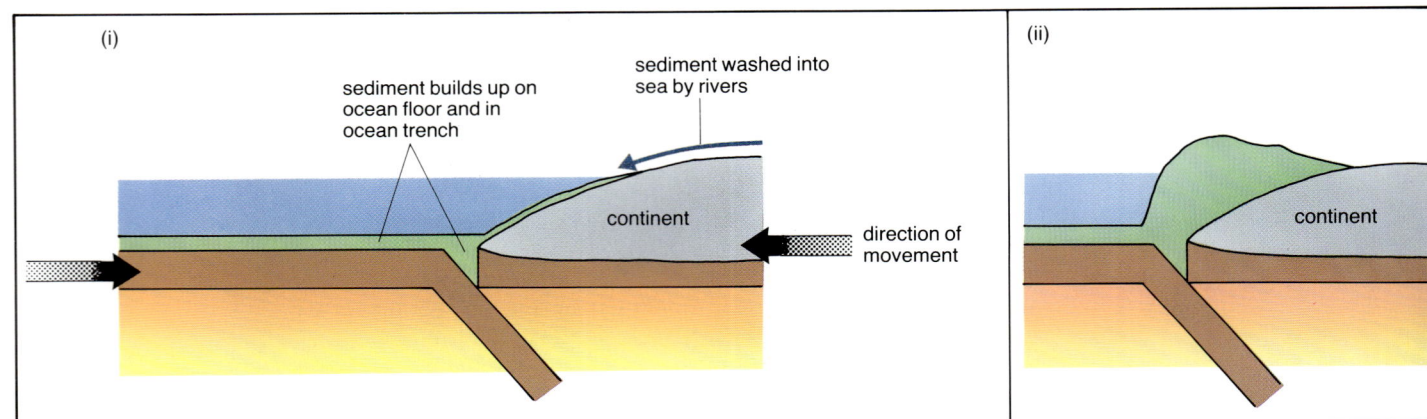

Fig 32 Fold mountains (one continent)

If two plates are moving towards each other and one of them has a continent as a passenger, these sediments may pile up as a chain of fold mountains along the edge of the continent (Fig 32).

If two continents are moving towards each other the sediments are crumpled up between them. Eventually, the continents themselves may collide and this makes the folding even more intense (Fig 33).

Fig 33 Fold mountains (continental collision)

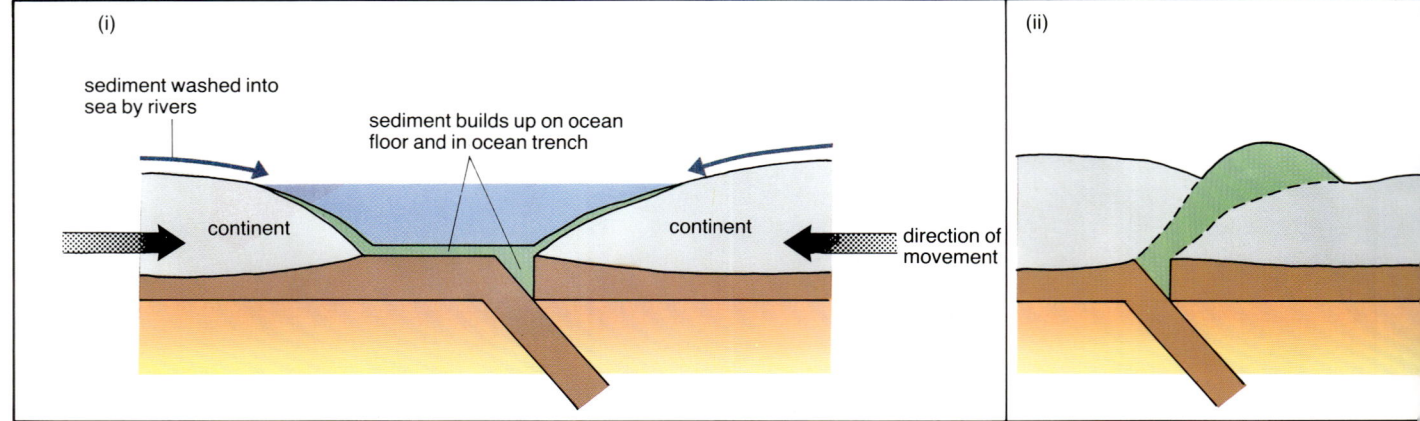

Hot Spots

You learnt from the Enquiry on page 16 that not all volcanoes are found near plate boundaries, e.g. the Hawaiian islands. These exceptions to the general pattern are found at places known as hot spots.

The cause of these hot spots is far from clear, but pools of very hot, active magma are found beneath the surface. Also, it would seem that although the earth's plates are moving, the hot spots themselves stay in the same place. This explains the chain of extinct volcanoes running to the north and west of Hawaii (Fig 35).

Fig 34 An eruption on Mauna Loa, Hawaii

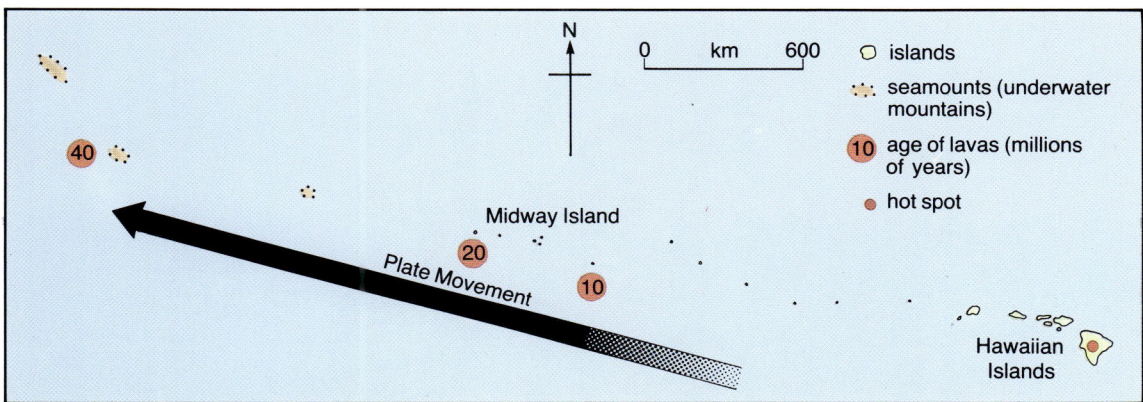

Fig 35 The Hawaiian hot spot

1   Copy Fig 32 (ii) and Fig 33 (ii). Add labels to these diagrams to explain why fold mountains have formed.
2   Name the fold mountain chains 1-5. Compare Fig 31 with Fig 11, page 8. Name one example of mountains which have formed because of two plates moving towards each other, one carrying a continent. Name one example of mountains which have formed because of a collision between two continents.
3   How far does "hot spot evidence" suggest that the Pacific plate has moved in the last 40 million years? Does the plate seem to be moving at a steady speed? Explain your answer.

1.4 Why do rocks break down?

Weathering is when rocks break down because they have come into contact with the earth's atmosphere. There are three types of weathering — physical, chemical and biological — and in the end all rocks crumble away because of this process, even the hardest: no wonder Wilfred is worried!

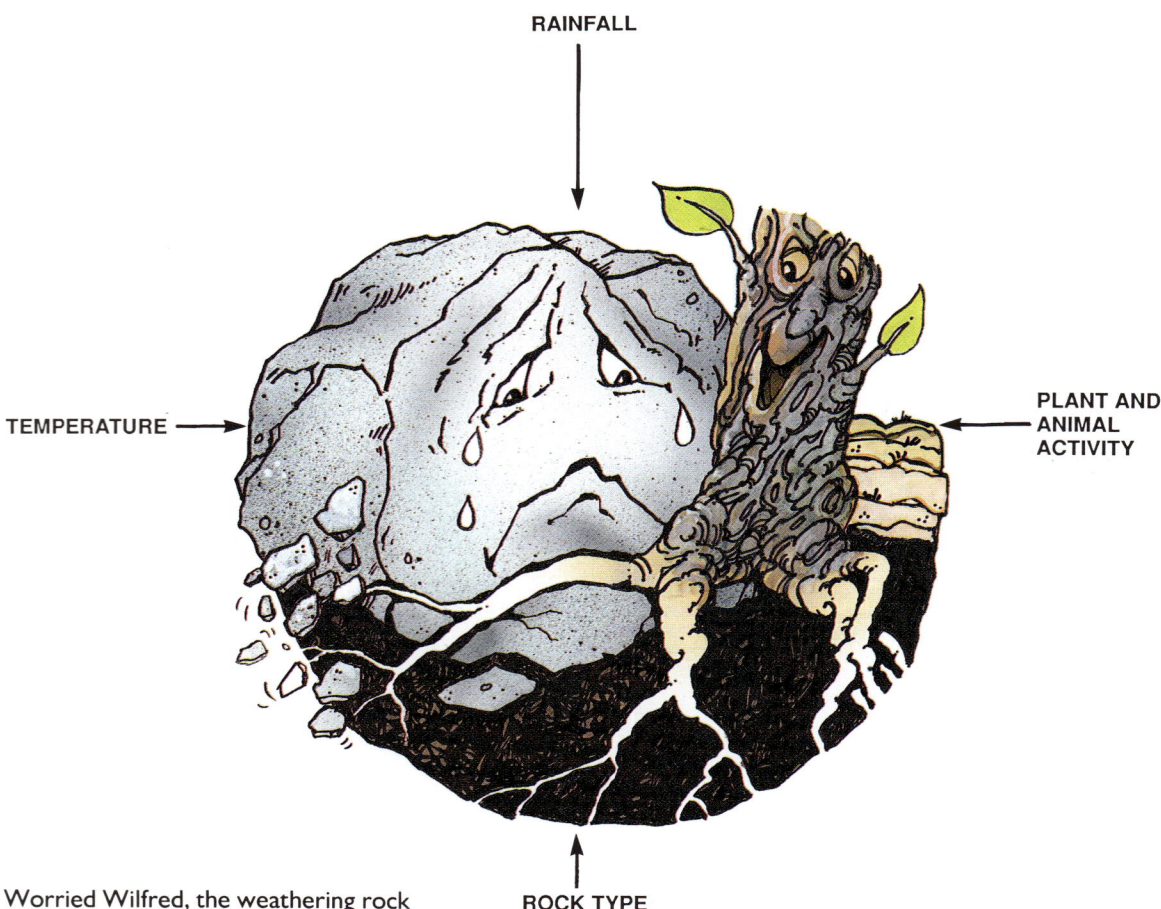

Fig 36 Worried Wilfred, the weathering rock

Physical Weathering

Physical weathering is the mechanical breakdown of rocks, usually because of changes in temperature; two examples are freeze-thaw weathering and onion-skin weathering.

Freeze-thaw weathering happens when water gets into a crack in a rock and freezes. As the water turns to ice it expands in volume by about 9%. This puts a strain on the rock which may be enough to split it. When the ice melts, the water trickles into another crack: if it then freezes and turns to ice the process is repeated (Fig 37). This type of weathering happens a lot in places where the temperature hovers around freezing point, such as mountains in the UK in the winter.

Onion-skin weathering (or exfoliation) happens when a rock is heated and cooled

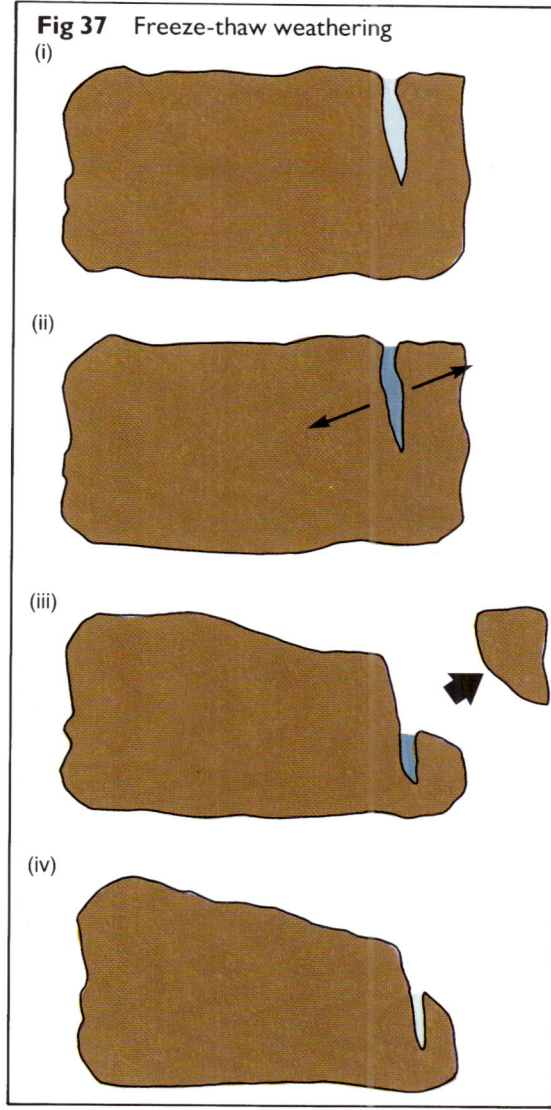

Fig 37 Freeze-thaw weathering

Fig 38 Onion-skin weathering, California

Fig 39 Scree slope, Wast Water, Lake District

many times. This type of weathering is important in the hot deserts where there is a big difference between daytime and night-time temperatures. As it is heated the outer layer of the rock expands slightly and as it is cooled it contracts. This puts a strain on the rock and its surface begins to split away in layers (Fig 38).

The angular rock fragments which result from physical weathering are known as scree. They can build up to form a scree slope (Fig 39).

Chemical Weathering

Chemical weathering is mainly the result of rocks dissolving in rainwater. This happens because as rainwater passes through the atmosphere and the soil, it picks up carbon dioxide and becomes a weak carbonic acid.

Fig 40 Chemical weathering of limestone

RAINWATER + CARBON DIOXIDE = WEAK CARBONIC ACID
H_2O CO_2 H_2CO_3

+LIMESTONE (CALCIUM CARBONATE) = CALCIUM BICARBONATE
$CaCO_3$ (this dissolves in water)
         $Ca(HCO_3)_2$

Carbonic acid reacts with some rocks more than others. Its effect on limestone is dramatic. Fig 40 shows the chemical reaction which takes place: the rock is dissolved completely.

Fig 41 A Norber rock

Fig 42 Roots breaking up rock

Fig 43 Animal burrow

However, the process happens very slowly. Fig 41 shows a sandstone boulder resting on a block of Carboniferous Limestone at Norber in North Yorkshire. The boulder is impermeable and has protected the limestone underneath it from the rain. The limestone around it has been dissolved away: 45 cm in 100 000 years.

Biological Weathering

Biological weathering is when plants and animals help to break down rocks.

The roots of plants and trees can get into cracks in a rock. As they grow they put pressure on the rock which can be enough to split it (Fig 42). Animals burrowing into soil and rock have the same effect (Fig 43).

Rotting vegetation lets out acids which dissolve rock. Also, some animals let out acids which attack rock; limpets, for example, help to break down rocks on the sea shore.

1 Copy the diagrams in Fig 37. Add labels to explain freeze-thaw weathering.
2 Make a sketch of Fig 38. Add labels to explain onion-skin weathering.
3 Explain how and why rainwater dissolves limestone. What has been the average rate of weathering of the limestone in the Norber area of North Yorkshire in the last 100 000 years?
4 How do plants and animals help to break down rocks?
5 What type(s) of weathering would you expect to find in the following places and why?
— a tropical rain forest;
— a hot desert;
— the Lake District in England;
— the arctic region of Scandinavia.

Weathering Surveys

Weathering is not an easy topic for a survey because its tell-tale signs are difficult to spot and because it happens very slowly. However, even in a town or city there are things that you can do.

What different types of weathering did you find? Which type of weathering was most common? Were any of the buildings in your area badly damaged by weathering? Did some types of building material seem to be more easily damaged than others? Were older buildings more damaged than younger buildings?

1 Buildings Survey

Weathering attacks buildings in the same way that it breaks down rocks. Choose a small area, preferably one which includes old and new buildings. Draw a sketch map of the area. Carry out a survey of the area and mark onto your map any signs of weathering e.g.
- damage to brickwork (Fig 44) is a sign of physical weathering;
- chemical weathering attacks statues (Fig 45);
- old walls often show signs of damage by plants and animals = biological weathering (Fig 46);
- physical weathering can cause cracks in houses (Fig 47);
- tree roots (biological weathering) can crack pavements (48).

Sketch an example of each of the different types of weathering that you find. Make a note of how bad the weathering is and what type of building material has been damaged. Try to find out how old the buildings are.

Fig 44   Freeze-thaw weathering damaging brickwork

Fig 46   A wall damaged by tree roots

Fig 45   A statue damaged by weathering

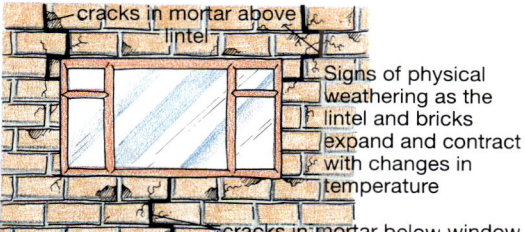

Fig 47   Cracks caused by physical weathering

Fig 48   Path damaged by tree roots

2 Gravestones Survey

Another idea is to look at the weathering of gravestones. Get permission from the people in charge of the graveyard before carrying out this survey. Many different types of rock are used for gravestones, such as marble, limestone, sandstone, granite. Find two gravestones made of different types of rock but with the same date, and compare the quality of the lettering — this will tell you which type of rock has weathered more quickly. Find two gravestones made from the same rock but with different dates and compare the quality of the lettering — this will tell you how quickly the rock weathers.

Fig 49 Weathered gravestones

1.5 What shapes the land?

Fig 50 The power of running water

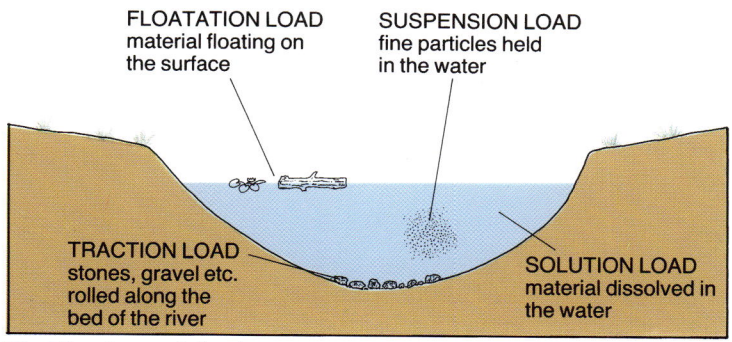

Fig 51 A river's load

The land is shaped by three main processes: **erosion** (rock and soil being worn away); **transportation** (rock and soil being moved from one place to another); and **deposition** (rock and soil being dumped). The agents of erosion which carry out this work are water (rain, rivers and sea), ice and wind.

Water

Water erodes in a number of ways. Heavy rain can dislodge particles of soil. Moving water can undermine the foundations of a river bank or pound away at the face of a cliff; this is known as **hydraulic action** (Fig 50). Rivers and waves can roll or hurl rock fragments and pebbles against the land which is chipped and scratched away as a result; this is known as **abrasion**. As the rock fragments and pebbles knock into each other they break up into smaller pieces — a process known as **attrition**; this provides more material for abrasion.

Water transports material if it has enough energy. Rain can wash the soil off a slope in sheets. The different parts of a river's load are shown in Fig 51. Tides and currents move sand and pebbles along the shore. However, the most important way in which the sea transports material is the process of **longshore drift**. It is the result of wave action and gravity (Fig 52). In order to stop this movement of material, wooden fences called **groynes** have been built across many of our beaches (Fig 53). This is being done to protect the coast and/or to stop a valuable tourist attraction from being washed away!

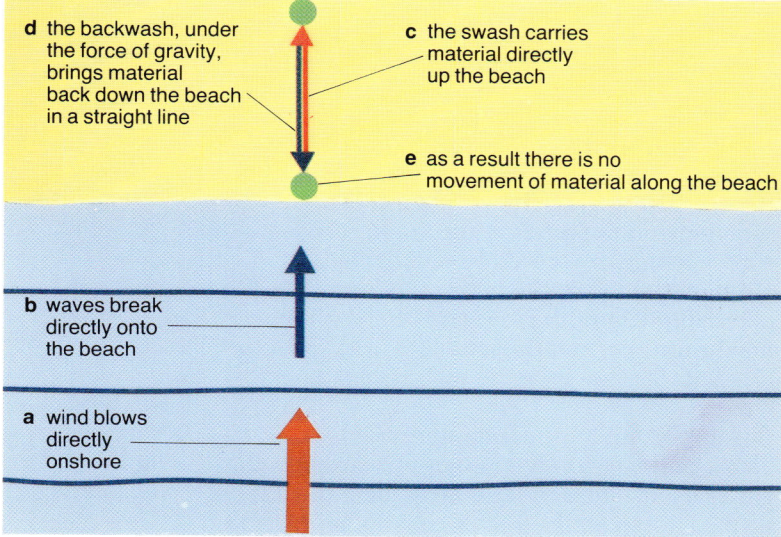

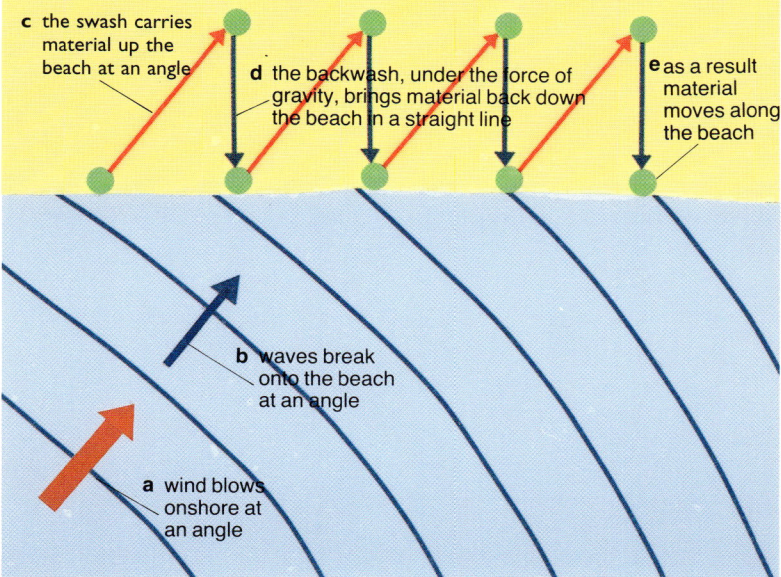

Fig 52 Longshore drift

Water deposits its load when it runs out of the energy it needs to carry it along. Soil washed from the side of a valley is often deposited on the flatter slopes at the bottom of the valley where its rate of flow slows down. Features of deposition are more common in the lower section of a river where the gradient is gentler. As a very rough guide, if less than eight waves break on the coastline per minute, deposition is likely to be the main process.

Waves

The importance of waves to the processes of erosion, transportation and deposition has already been mentioned, but it is worth having a more detailed look.

Most waves are the result of friction between the wind and the sea. However, it is important to remember that waves can be caused in other ways, e.g. by submarine volcanic eruptions and/or earthquakes (see page 13).

The size of a wave depends on the strength of the wind, how long the wind has been blowing and the **fetch** — the amount of sea across which the wind has blown. The stronger the wind, the bigger the wave, but it takes about 24 hours for waves to reach their maximum size and the fetch is a critical factor (Fig 55).

It is important to understand that it is the shape of the wave that moves forward, not the water itself. This explains why sea-gulls bob up and down on the waves without appearing to move. The wave is the way in which the energy transferred from the wind to the sea by friction is moved forward. As a complete wave passes a particular point each particle of water moves round in a circle. However, when a wave moves into shallow water the particles cannot complete their circle because they come into contact with the sea bed, and the height of the wave increases. Eventually, the wave breaks and topples over. The wave breaking up a beach is known as the swash. The water coming back down the beach is known as the backwash (Fig 56).

Fig 53 Beach with groynes, Southend-on-Sea, Essex

Fig 54 River deposition: Wharfedale, North Yorkshire

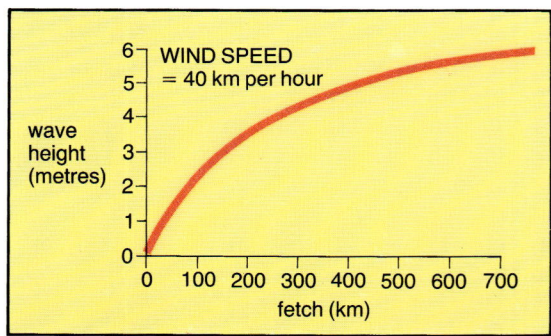

Fig 55 The relationship between wave height and fetch

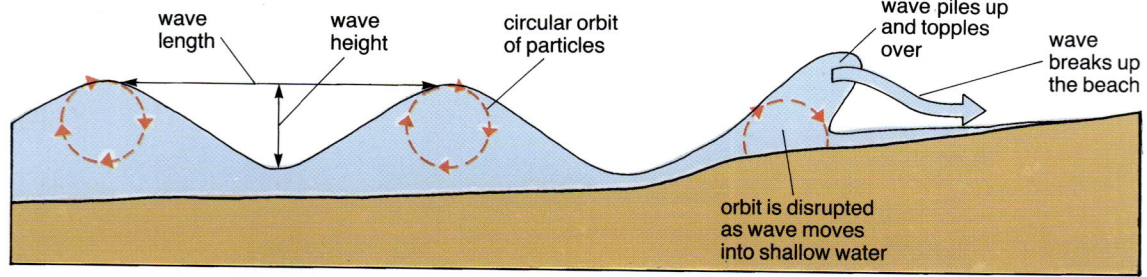

Fig 56 Wave forms

Another change which happens as waves move into shallow water is that they slow down and alter direction — a process known as wave refraction. If, for example, a wave is moving onto a coastline with a series of bays and headlands, the section of the wave moving into the deeper water of the bay will move at a faster speed than the section of the wave moving into the shallow water off the headland. The result is that the wave front is bent as it moves into the bay and this has the further consequence of concentrating wave energy on the headlands (Fig 57).

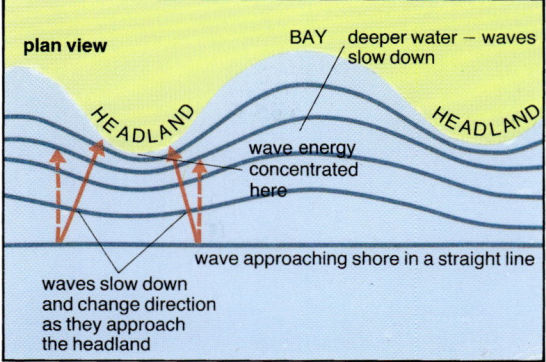

Fig 57 Wave refraction

Ice

Glaciers — slow moving rivers of ice — carry out the same eroding processes as water but in slightly different ways.

Fig 58 Plucking

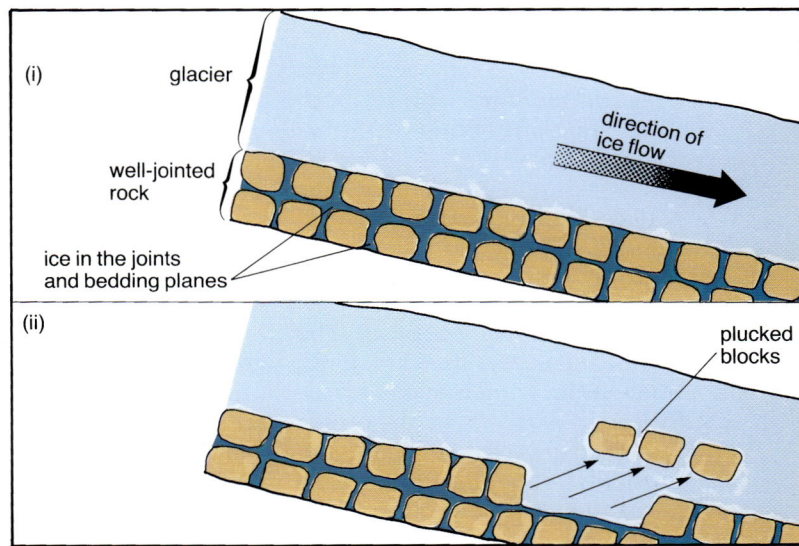

They erode the land in three main ways:
- **Abrasion**. This is when glaciers pick up rock fragments and drag them against the bed and sides of the valley which are scratched away as a result.
- **Bulldozing**. This is when the sheer power of the glacier breaks off rocks from the bed and sides of the valley, or when it moves already shattered material.
- **Plucking**. If the ice freezes onto a rock, the glacier will pull it away when it moves. This is known as plucking and it is common in rocks with lots of cracks or joints.

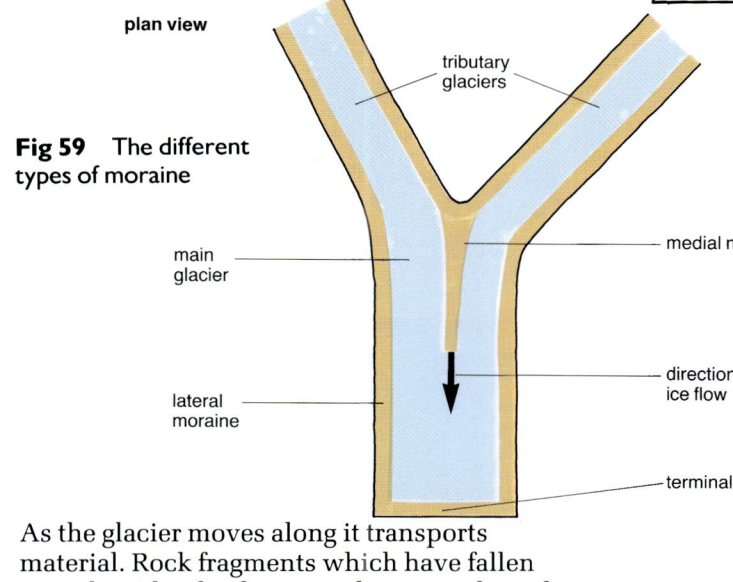

Fig 59 The different types of moraine

As the glacier moves along it transports material. Rock fragments which have fallen onto the side of a glacier are known as lateral **moraine**. A line of fragments in the middle of a glacier is known as a medial moraine. The fragments which collect at the snout of a glacier pile up to form a terminal moraine.

Fig 60 Moraine on the Fox Glacier, New Zealand

Rock fragments can also be carried along within the ice (e.g. material which has fallen into a crevasse) or at the base of a glacier.

When the ice melts it deposits its load. The rock fragments cover the ground or form a line of hills with a variety of different shapes (see Section 3.2).

Wind

The wind is an important agent of erosion. It can remove dry and unprotected soil from fields. In deserts it can literally sand-blast the landscape; most erosion takes place near the surface because the wind cannot lift sand particles very high off the ground (Fig 61).

The wind can carry small particles for hundreds of miles; for example, loess is a wind-blown deposit of fine silt or dust which covers large areas of northern China, central Europe and central USA. Sand is more likely to be rolled along, or carried for short distances, as in the formation of barchans. These are crescent-shaped dunes which vary between 2 and 30 metres in height and 20 to 200 metres in width and breadth. They form when the wind always blows from the same direction. As the wind blows sand particles over the hump of the dune, the dune migrates downwind; speeds of up to 20 metres a year have been recorded. The curved horns are the result of sand being blown around the side of the dune.

Fine particles can be washed out of the sky when it rains. In the desert sand is deposited when the wind drops or when it comes up against an obstacle and loses energy; many sand dunes begin to form in this way.

Fig 61 Mushroom rock, Death Valley, California

1 Describe the evidence you can see in the photographs in this section for the processes of erosion, transportation and deposition.
2 What is the main difference between these processes and the process of weathering?
3 In what ways are the processes of glacial erosion **a)** similar and **b)** different to the processes of river erosion?
4 Explain, with the help of diagrams, **a)** the process of longshore drift and **b)** the formation of a barchan.
5 Describe and explain the relationship between wave height and fetch.
6 Explain why **a)** waves break when they move into shallow water and **b)** why wave energy is concentrated on headlands?

Fig 62 The formation of a barchan

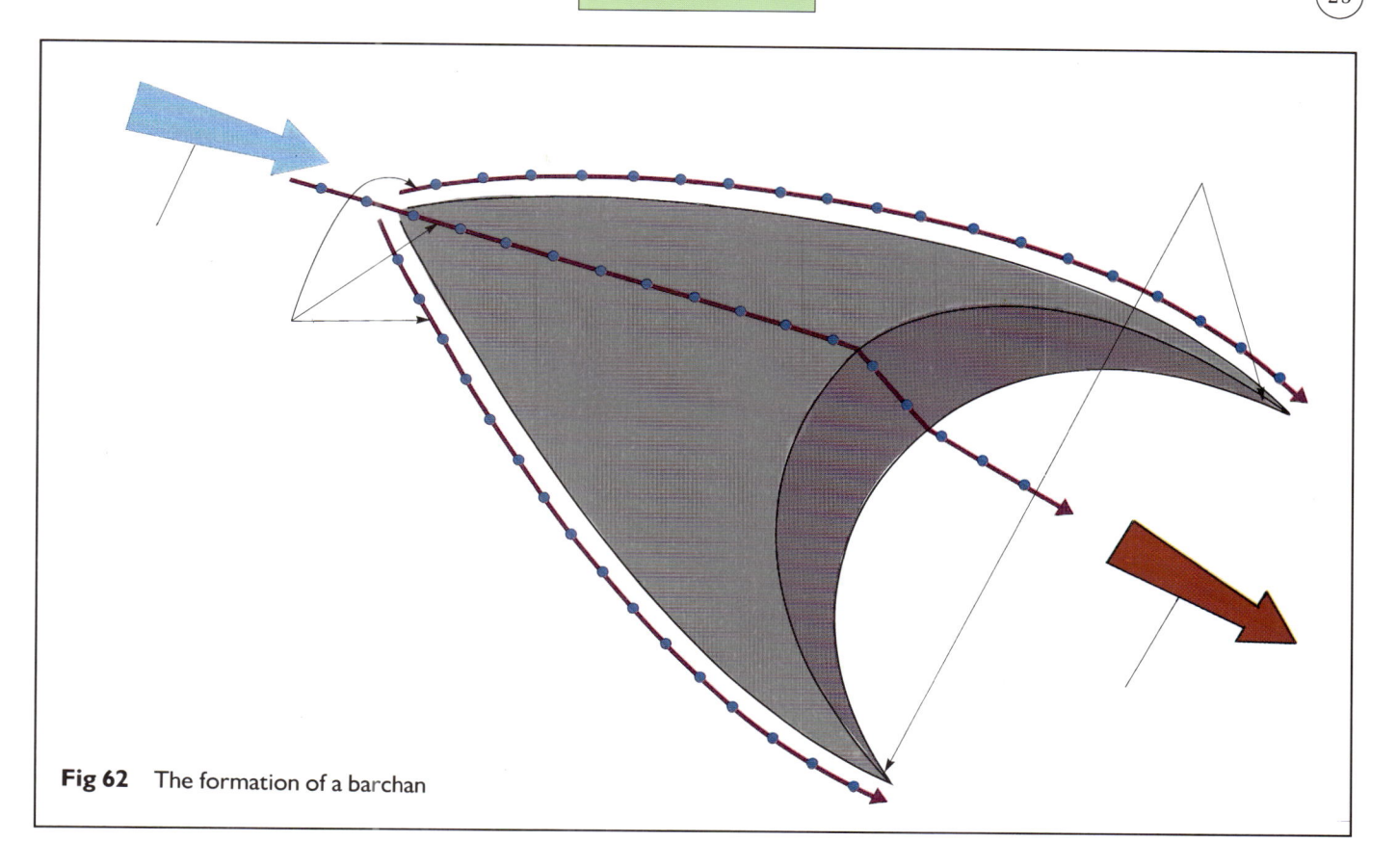

Fig 63 Sand dunes, Death Valley, California

1.6 What makes up soil?

Soil is a mixture of mineral matter (made by rocks being weathered), organic matter (made by vegetation rotting down), air and water (Fig 64).

There are many different types of soil. Some of the main differences are:
1 **Texture** — this depends on the particles in the soil. Moisten a small sample of soil and rub it between your fingers.
- if it feels gritty it has a sandy texture (easy to work but it dries out quickly so lack of water can be a problem);
- if it feels sticky it has a clayey texture (difficult to work because it is very sticky when it is wet and very hard when it is dry);
- if it feels smooth and silky it has a loamy texture (easy to work and holds the right amount of water – the best for farming).

2 **Colour.** You can learn important facts about a soil from its colour (Fig 65) e.g. compare the dark brown peat soil in the Fens with the red laterite soil found in many parts of the tropics.

3 **Depth.** Some soils are very shallow and contain many fragments of rock e.g. the thin, chalky soils of East Anglia (Fig 68) while other soils can be several metres deep. Most soils can be divided into two main layers (Fig 69).

4 **Acidity.** This is measured on the pH scale (Fig 70). It is important because most plants like neutral or slightly acid soils.

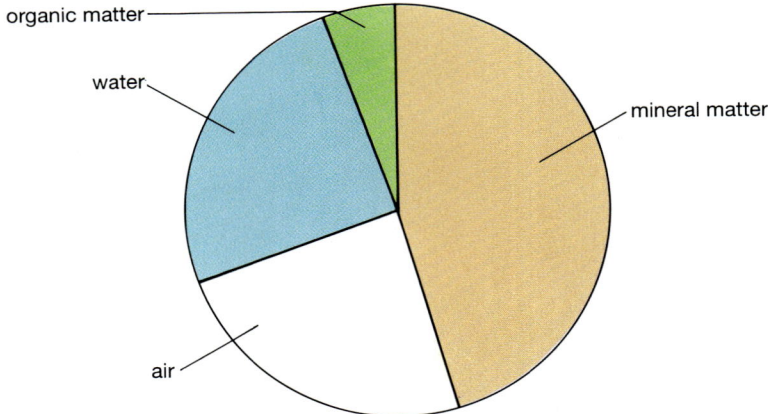

Fig 64 A typical soil

Colour	What it tells us
Dark Brown	rich in organic matter
Light Brown or Yellow	much of the goodness has been washed out of the soil
Red	chemical weathering has left it stained by iron
Grey	bad drainage

Fig 65 Soil colour chart

Fig 66 Peat soil, the Fens

Fig 67 Laterite soil, Kenya

Fig 68   Chalky soil, East Anglia

Fig 69   Soil profile

pH	Colour	Acidity	Examples of Plants
8	Green	alkaline	sugar beet, lettuce,
7	Yellow Green	neutral	wheat, barley, turnip, most garden plants
6	Yellow	slightly acidic	potatoes, cabbage oats, rye
5	Orange	acid	grass
4	Red	very acid	heather

Fig 70   Soil and the pH scale

1   Copy Fig 64. Add labels to explain what is meant by mineral matter and organic matter.
2   What are the three main types of soil texture? Which is best for farming, and why?
3   What does their colour tell us about peat and laterite?
4   Sketch and label Fig 69.
5   Why is soil acidity important?

Investigating Soils

Soils can vary a great deal even in a small area. Some easy ways of investigating these differences are described below. You could use these ideas in a local fieldwork project, like the soil survey in the next section.

1   **Looking at soils**. You can tell a great deal about a soil by looking at it carefully. You will need a ruler, a spoon or trowel, a margarine tub or something similar, a small plastic container of water and a magnifying glass.
• Take a soil sample from a depth of about 5 cm. Fill your margarine tub with this soil.
• Smear a piece of soil onto your chart (see Fig 71) and write down its colour.
• Look for mineral matter — can you see grains of sand or bits of rock?

FEATURES / SITE	SOIL FEATURES							GENERAL FEATURES			
	Colour	Mineral matter	Organic matter	Animal matter	Texture	Acidity	Other Points e.g. bed rock/depth	Land use	Slope	Other Points e.g. recent weather	Infiltration: the depth of water after ___ minutes (10 cm at start)
① Locks Wood GRID REF 243 382	brown	some small stones and grains of sand	some bits of leaf and twig	none seen	sandy	neutral	sandstone	woodland	flat	dry for last fortnight	1 min 5 6 min ___ 2 min 3 7 min ___ 3 min 2 8 min ___ 4 min 1 9 min ___ 5 min — 10 min ___
② ___ GRID REF											1 min ___ 6 min ___ 2 min ___ 7 min ___ 3 min ___ 8 min ___ 4 min ___ 9 min ___ 5 min ___ 10 min ___
③ ___ GRID REF											1 min ___ 6 min ___ 2 min ___ 7 min ___ 3 min ___ 8 min ___ 4 min ___ 9 min ___ 5 min ___ 10 min ___
④ ___ GRID REF											1 min ___ 6 min ___ 2 min ___ 7 min ___ 3 min ___ 8 min ___ 4 min ___ 9 min ___ 5 min ___ 10 min ___
⑤ ___ GRID REF											1 min ___ 6 min ___ 2 min ___ 7 min ___ 3 min ___ 8 min ___ 4 min ___ 9 min ___ 5 min ___ 10 min ___

Fig 71 Soil survey — data collection sheet

- Look for organic matter — can you see any pieces of root or rotting vegetation?
- Animal life — can you see any worms or other burrowing creatures?
- Moisten a piece of soil and decide on its texture (see page 30).
- Put the soil back and fill in the hole. Leave the place neat and tidy.

2 Testing soil acidity.
- At school in the laboratory: Put about 2 cm³ of barium sulphate powder in a test tube. Add about 3 cm³ of soil. Add distilled water to ⅔ of the way up the tube. Add several drops of indicator solution. Put a cork in the top of the tube, shake well and allow the mixture to settle for ten minutes. Check it against the colour chart (Fig 70).
- At home: pH soil testing kits can be bought at garden centres. A kit for ten tests costs about £3.00, so it is a good idea to share it with some friends. The instructions are easy to follow but you should get an adult to help you with the first test you do. The kits come with their own colour chart. Garden centres also sell soil probes for testing acidity but these are quite expensive – you may be able to borrow one from a keen gardener.

3 Testing soil infiltration. Infiltration means how quickly water soaks into a soil. This is very important to the farmer or gardener. If water drains away too quickly it will have to be added. If soil becomes waterlogged it will have to be drained.

You will need to make an infiltration ring. The one in Fig 72 is simply a large tin can with the top and bottom removed. Jagged edges can be a problem, so be careful. Alternatively, a length of plastic pipe with a diameter of about 15 cm could be used. Draw a line around the inside of the ring 3 cm from the bottom. Then, draw and number a scale line 10 cm long. A piece of white sellotape can make this job easier. You will also need a hammer, a water container and a watch.

Knock the infiltration ring into the ground down to the 3 cm mark. Fill it with water to the top of the scale. Note the depth of water in the infiltration ring at the end of every minute. Carry on until the water has drained away or until it has stopped sinking in (the saturation point).

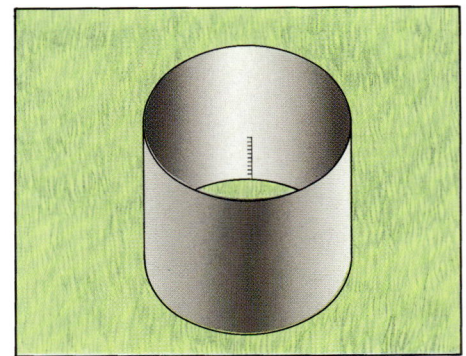

Fig 72 An infiltration ring

1.7 Assessment task: Soil survey

Aims

- to test the idea that soils vary a great deal even in a small area;
- to compare local soils with the general pattern of soils in the home region.

Method

Choose a number of different sites to investigate. If you live in a town they could be different places within a park (Fig 73). If you live in the countryside you could include farmland as part of your study. Your garden or the school grounds could be a good place to start.

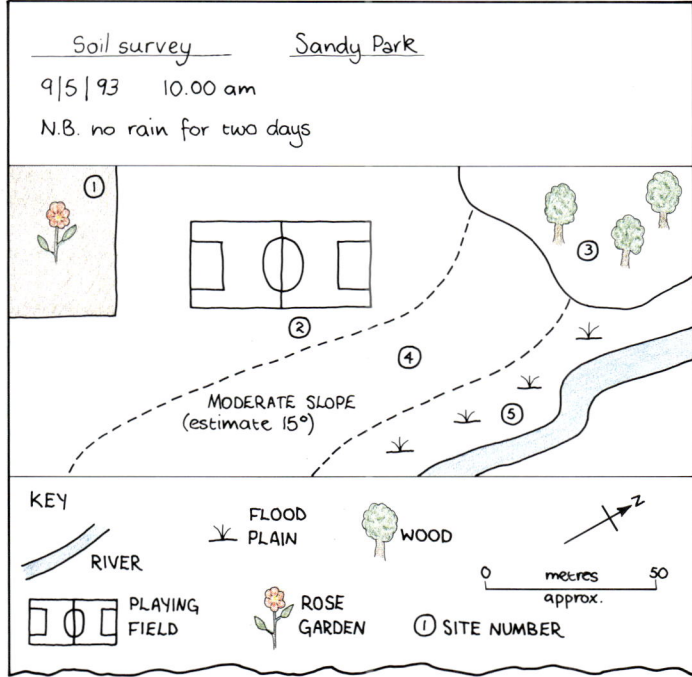

Fig 73 Sites for a soil survey

Draw up a data collection sheet like the one in Fig 71. Sort out the equipment you will need; this should include an OS map of the area. Also, remember to get permission before you take any soil samples!

Draw a sketch map and a field sketch of your survey area, and then carry out your data collection carefully and accurately.

Writing up your Results

- State the aims of the survey.
- Describe the area where you carried out the survey.
- Explain how you carried out the survey.

Presentation of Results

- Make best copies of your sketch map, field sketch and results table.
- Draw a line graph like the one in Fig 74 to show the infiltration rates.

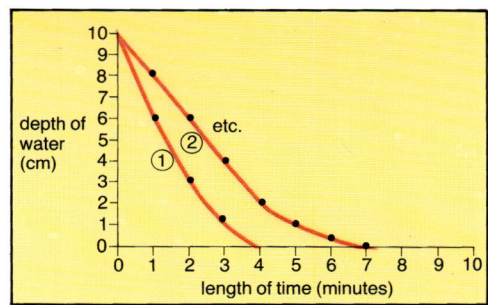

Fig 74 Infiltration graph

Interpretation and Explanation

- Describe **a)** the differences and **b)** the similarities between your soil samples.
- Identify any relationships between the soil characteristics you have described and the general factors you noted down: for example, is there a relationship between soil texture and infiltration rate, or between organic matter and type of use? Try to explain these relationships.

Conclusion and Limitations

- Summarise your main findings.
- Find out about what you would expect soils to be like in your area. Do your results fit in with the general pattern? Try to explain any differences.
- Did you have any problems carrying out this investigation? If you were to repeat this study are there any ways in which you would try to improve it?

1.8 What is happening to our soil?

Farming places a burden on soils, but as long as the land is managed carefully, for example by replacing the nutrients and organic matter which crops take out, its stays in good condition. However, if the land is managed badly soil erosion can become a major problem.

The four main causes of soil erosion are summarised in Fig 75. It is estimated that 35% of the world's cropland is affected by soil erosion. The problem exists in **MDCs** and **EDCs**. However, farmers in MDCs have generally been able to maintain crop yields by using fertiliser, whereas in many EDCs soil erosion has caused a decrease in land production.

Dust Bowl, USA

In the 1930s soil erosion began to affect millions of hectares of land in the centre of the USA. This region became known as the "Dust Bowl" and it is shown in Fig 76.

Settlers moved westwards into this region at the turn of the century in search of cheap, fertile land. The physical environment was very different to the forests and temperate climate they had been used to in a number of ways:
1. It was an area of grassland. The soil of such regions is fertile but it relies on the grass to bind it together with its roots.
2. The climate is characterised by long dry periods with rain falling as heavy showers.
3. There is a tendency for rain to be above or below average for a number of years at a time. At the start of this century the settlers gained a false impression of the climate because the years were generally wetter than normal.
4. Strong winds are common.

The settlers were totally unprepared for dealing with these conditions. They cleared the natural vegetation and let the land lie fallow over the winter, as they were used to doing. However, the soil dried out quickly and without the grass to bind it together the strong winds blew it away.

The most disastrous practice was "dust mulching". This involved breaking up the surface of a ploughed field until it was a fine powder. The idea was to make it easier for the soil to collect moisture. The result was that the wind found it even easier to blow the soil away.

Cause	Definition	Result
wrong ploughing methods	ploughing in the autumn ploughing up and down the slope	fields are left bare and exposed to winter winds rain is channelled along the furrows and erodes gullies
overgrazing	too many animals eating and trampling the vegetation	the soil is left bare and its structure is damaged
monoculture	always growing the same crop	the soil becomes exhausted and its structure is damaged
deforestation	cutting down trees	the soil is left unprotected

Fig 75 The causes of soil erosion

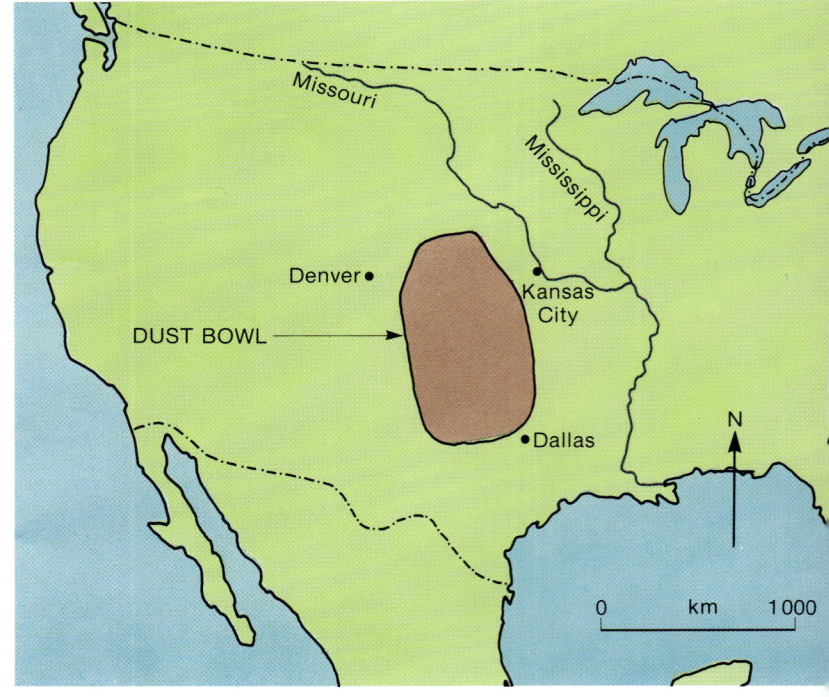

Fig 76 The Dust Bowl, USA

Fig 77 A dust storm in America's mid-west, early 1930s

The problem came to a head in the drought years of 1934 and 1936. Millions of tonnes of top soil were blown away in dust storms. Many farmers had to leave their land which had become all but useless (Fig 77).

In 1936 the US government set up the Soil Conservation Service. Its job was to find out about more appropriate methods of farming. As a result, a series of measures are now taken to prevent soil erosion in this region. The amount of arable land has been reduced; windbreaks of trees have been planted; fields are divided up so that only strips of land rather than whole fields are left fallow at any one time and a protective layer of straw is scattered over fields which are left fallow.

Soil Erosion in Kenya

Only 10% of Kenya's land area is suitable for growing crops. Much of this is used for cash crops for export, such as tea and coffee, which means that there is very little land available for its people to grow food on. This small amount of land has been under tremendous pressure in recent years because Kenya has one of the fastest growing populations in the world — between 1970 and 1990 it more than doubled from 11 million to 25 million.

As a result, farming has expanded into the dry bushland (Fig 78). In the past, crops on this type of land were grown for only a few years and then the land was left to recover. Large areas were used by nomads for grazing their cattle and the animals' dung helped to fertilise the soil.

However, the recent practice of growing crops on this bushland without a break has exhausted the soil. Its structure has been destroyed and consequently it has been eroded by the wind and the heavy tropical rains; gulleys 4 or 5 metres deep are not uncommon. The problem has been made worse by the search for fuel — trees and bushes have been cleared, leaving the soil unprotected, and animal dung is mixed with straw and burnt, instead of being returned to the land.

Some things can be done to help this problem. Villagers have joined forces to build dams in gulleys to prevent further erosion and to trap water and soil. Terraces have been built to stop the rain from washing the soil down a slope. Trees have been planted to act as windbreaks and to provide a source of fuel for the future. These methods are successful, but they need to be repeated many thousands of times if Kenya's soil is to be saved.

ENQUIRY

1 What were the causes of soil erosion in the Dust Bowl?
2 How has the problem been dealt with?
3 Why isn't it fair to blame the settlers for the problems of the dust bowl?
4 What are the causes of soil erosion in Kenya?
5 Copy the diagrams in Fig 79 and add labels to explain how soil erosion can be prevented.
6 Why might Kenya find this a more difficult problem to deal with than did the USA?

Fig 78 Kenya's bushland

EARTH 1.8

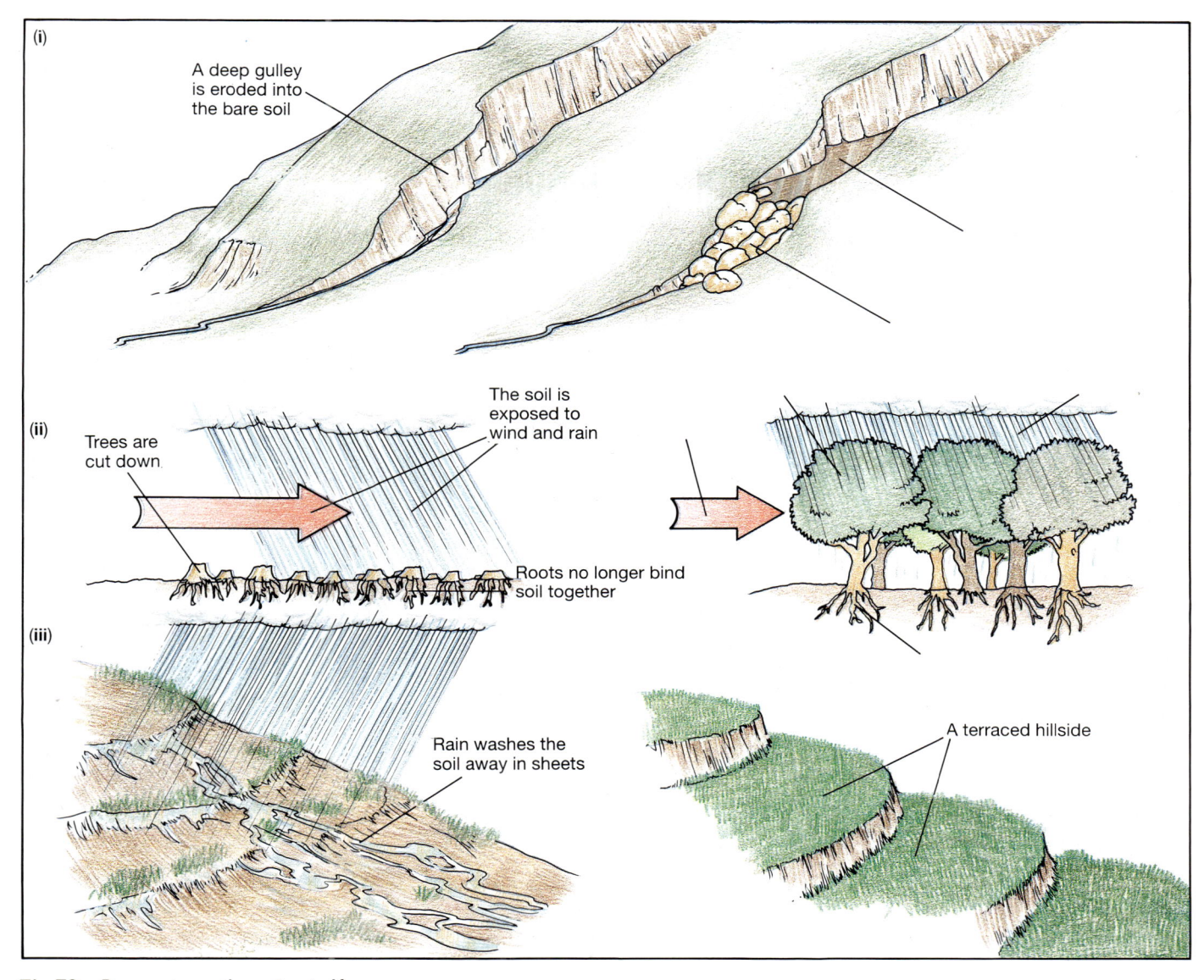

(i) A deep gulley is eroded into the bare soil

(ii) Trees are cut down. The soil is exposed to wind and rain. Roots no longer bind soil together

(iii) Rain washes the soil away in sheets

A terraced hillside

Fig 79 Preventing soil erosion in Kenya

WATER

2.1 What makes up a river system?

The place where a stream or river begins is called its **source**. As it flows down towards the sea it is joined by other streams or rivers called **tributaries**. The place where it enters the sea is called its **mouth**. A main river and its tributaries can cover a very large area and this is known as the **river basin**. The land separating one river basin from another is known as the watershed.

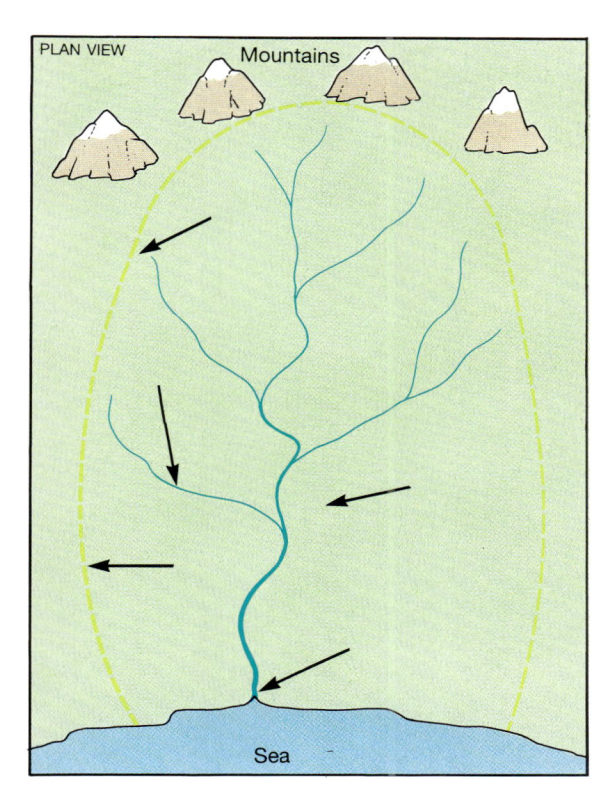

Fig 80 The river system

Investigating the River System

Here are two different ways of making a working model of a river. They are a good way of finding out what a river does.

1 Outdoors Choose a bare, dry slope, or one with short grass (Fig 81). If you scatter sand, gravel and stones over the area you will get an even better result. Pour water steadily down the slope. Watch the route the water takes. Watch what happens to the soil, sand, gravel and stones as the 'river' travels down the slope. Watch what happens at the bottom of the slope.

Was any of the material you scattered picked up (eroded)? Was any of it moved (transported)? Was any of it dumped (deposited)? Did the water flow in a straight line? If not, why not? (e.g. did it flow round large stones?) Did it pick up all the soil, sand, gravel and stones or only some of these? Try to explain your answer. Did it carry all the material to the bottom of the slope, or did it deposit some of it on the way down? If so, which material did it deposit and why? What happened to the water and the material at the bottom of the slope? Why?

Note down what happened on a large sketch.

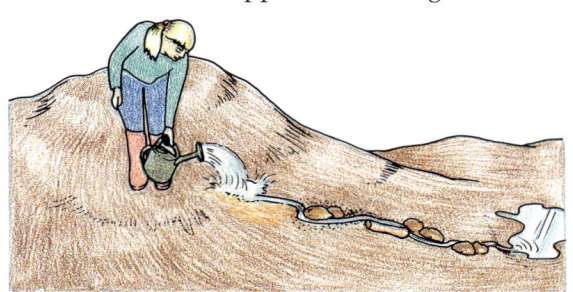

Fig 81 Modelling a river

2 Indoors Fill one half of a large tray with damp sand, gravel and small stones. Raise the sand-filled end by about 10 cm. Supply water at a steady rate at the top end of the tray with a hose from a tap. Make sure there is a drain hole and bucket at the bottom of the tray.

Try to answer the same questions as above. Again, note down what happened on a large sketch.

ENQUIRY

1   Make a copy of Fig 80. Label it using terms from the paragraph at the top of the page.
2   Mark onto an outline map of the British Isles the rivers Trent, Severn and Thames. For each of the rivers name
a) the hills/mountains or place at its source and **b)** the estuary or channel at its mouth.

2.2 Why do rivers flood and how do we cope?

A river flood occurs when a river bursts its banks. This usually happens when there has been heavy rainfall, but Fig 82 shows that the way people use the land can make floods more likely.

Floods do not always cause problems for people. For example, Fig 84 shows the River Nile's annual **hydrograph** (a line graph which shows how much water is in the river in each month of the year). The huge increase in water in August and September is mainly the result of heavy rain in the Ethiopian Highlands moving down one of the Nile's tributaries, the Blue Nile. Before 1960 the river burst its banks every August, irrigating (watering) its flood plain and leaving a layer of fertile silt. In 1960 the Egyptians built the Aswan High Dam and downstream of the dam the yearly flood is completely under control. However, Fig 83 shows that dams cannot stop floods upstream.

A sudden thaw may cause meltwater to flow off the hills.

If this happens, perhaps because of an earthquake, the water in the reservoir will pour down the valley.

When this happens there is nothing left to catch the water or to soak it up.

This stops the rain from soaking into the soil – instead, it rushes to the river in storm drains.

The soil cannot soak up the rain quickly enough so it rushes straight into the river.

Fig 82 River floods, causes and explanations

Flood aid 'a drop in the ocean'

Reuter in Khartoum

A SUDANESE government minister said at the weekend that foreign aid to help nearly two million people made homeless by the flooded Nile amounted to "a drop in the ocean".

The finance minister, Mr Omar Nour al-Dayem, said "relief has so far been little. It is a drop in the ocean compared to the problem.

"It is true that many people have not received assistance. What we have here is nearly two million people made homeless."

He said that foreign countries were widening their participation in relief operations. At least a dozen countries are sending aid, including Egypt, Saudi Arabia, Libya, Turkey, Britain, and the US.

The Nile has continued to rise inexorably, fed by heavy rains in the headwaters of the White and Blue Nile tributaries, since a 13-hour downpour last week washed away thousands of Khartoum's mud huts.

The official Sudan News Agency said the Nile in Khartoum had reached nearly 53 feet, just below the level of the 1946 flood which was the worst in living memory. Government officials have said they expect the flood to peak in Khartoum in the next two to three weeks.

The government, which has declared a six-month state of emergency, last week put the death toll at 39. But relief officials and diplomats reckoned the figure was higher.

Suna said central Sudan had now been declared a disaster area and the governor was on his way to Khartoum to discuss the situation with the Prime Minister, Mr Sadeq al-Mahdi.

Mr Nour al-Dayem rejected reports of differences between the government and donor countries.

"Donor countries wanted to widen their participation in the relief operation and that is what they are doing. But the government of Sudan does not accept any interference in its internal affairs," he said.

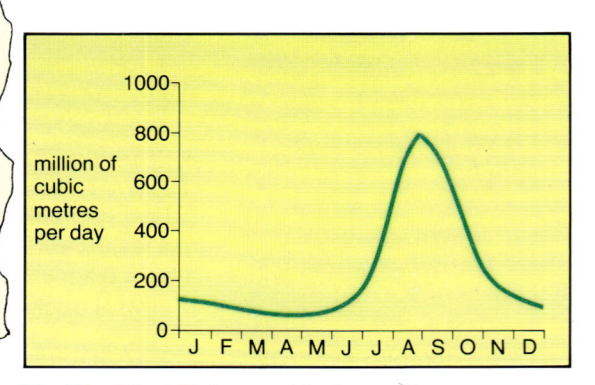

Fig 83 The Nile flood, 1988

Fig 84 The Nile's annual hydrograph

Floods become a hazard (threat or problem) when farmland, buildings and people are at risk. The worst river flood in recorded history was when the Hwang-Ho (Yellow River) in China burst its banks in August 1931; 3.7 million people lost their lives. Every year floods make the headlines in the newspapers (Fig 85).

It is possible to cut down the risk from floods. Building dams has already been mentioned. Trees can be planted to catch (intercept) water and to soak it up. Dams should not be built in places which might have earthquakes, nor houses in places which are likely to flood. Rainfall records and measuring the amount of water in the rivers helps to predict when a flood is likely. However, it will never be possible to prevent all floods because very little can be done to cope with unusually bad (freak) weather.

Also, flood protection schemes are very expensive, and in England and Wales the National Rivers Authority (NRA) will only carry out a scheme if it costs less than the damage the flood would cause. In the Fens (Fig 86), for example, the NRA is faced with a difficult problem. Although the region has a low rainfall, it is very low-lying. The problem has become worse because as the Fens have been drained their peat soils have dried out and shrunk by as much as 3 metres. As a result much of the Fenland is below the level of the rivers.

14th September 1992
Floods kill 3000 and threaten fertile Punjab

24th September 1992
FLOODS KILL 29 AS "MONSOON" STORMS SWEEP PROVINCE

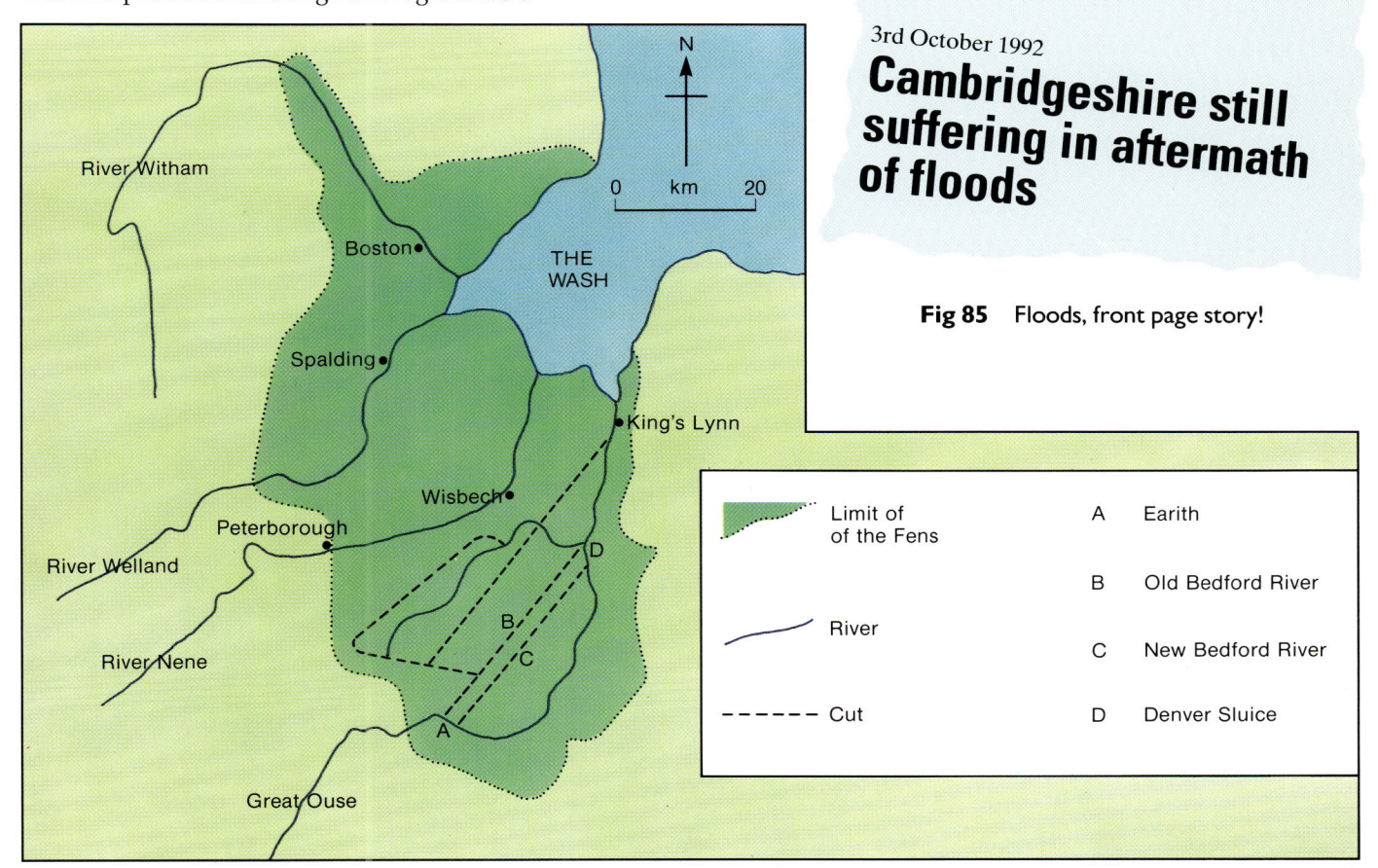

3rd October 1992
Cambridgeshire still suffering in aftermath of floods

Fig 85 Floods, front page story!

Fig 86 River management in the Fens

Flooding is controlled in a number of ways. River banks are built up. River channels are kept clear of silt, debris and other blockages. At Earith, sluice gates control the entrance of the Old and New Bedford Rivers (Fig 87). These rivers, known as "cuts", were dug in the seventeenth century as part of the scheme to drain this area of the Fens. Their job is to carry water more quickly to the Denver Sluice where they re-join the River Ouse.

If there is too much water in the river the sluice gates are opened and it flows into the cuts. If the cuts become too full the water is allowed to spill over into the area of "washland" between them. This prevents

Fig 87 The sluice gates at Earith

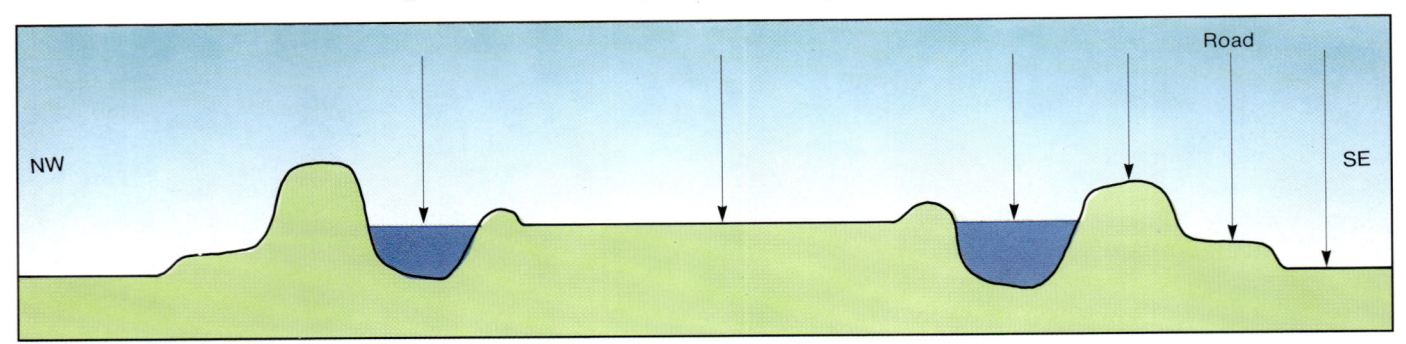

Fig 88 The Ouse Washes

flood problems downstream of the Denver Sluice. The washland is used for grazing cattle in the summer and it is also cut for hay. In the winter, when it is under water for much of the time, it is home for thousands of migratory birds.

ENQUIRY

1 Look at Fig 82. Write out the causes of river floods and match them up with their explanation.
2 Which of the causes in Fig 82 are natural and which are the result of human actions?
3 What is the difference between the amount of water in the River Nile at the start of July and the amount of water at the start of August? What is the highest amount of water in the Nile?
4 Use an atlas to help you to draw a sketch map of Egypt and Sudan. Mark on the places mentioned in the text and in Fig 83. Add captions about:
— the Nile floods before 1960;
— how the floods have been controlled;
— the 1988 flood in Sudan.

5 What is the straight line distance from Earith Sluice to Denver Sluice? What is the distance between these two places by the River Great Ouse? How many kilometres do the cuts save?
6 Explain how the NRA control flooding in the Fens.
7 Make a copy of Fig 88. Complete it by adding these labels in the correct place — Old Bedford River; New Bedford River; embankments; Fenland; Washland; arable farming; pastoral farming. (You can work the answers out from the map and text.)
8 Make a list of the things mentioned in this section which can cut down the risk of river floods.

2.3 Where does the water come from?

The Hydrological Cycle

If water was a **non-renewable resource** — one that cannot be replaced — the world would run out of it in about four weeks. Fortunately, nature recycles water. Energy from the sun evaporates water from the oceans and the land. Plants also release water into the **atmosphere** in a process known as **transpiration**. Water exists in the atmosphere in the form of water vapour. It is moved about by winds and may return to the surface as one of the many types of **precipitation** e.g. rain, snow, dew. Nature's recycling process is known as the **hydrological cycle** (Fig 89).

Our need for water is vital. We take water from the natural system, use it and put it back. You could think of our use of water as a sub-system or loop within the hydrological cycle.

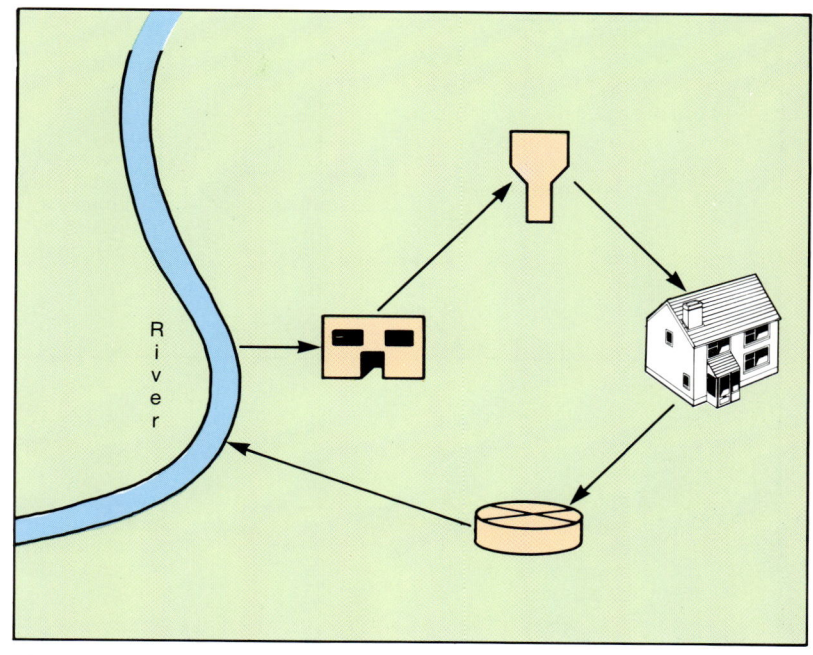

Fig 90 The human water cycle

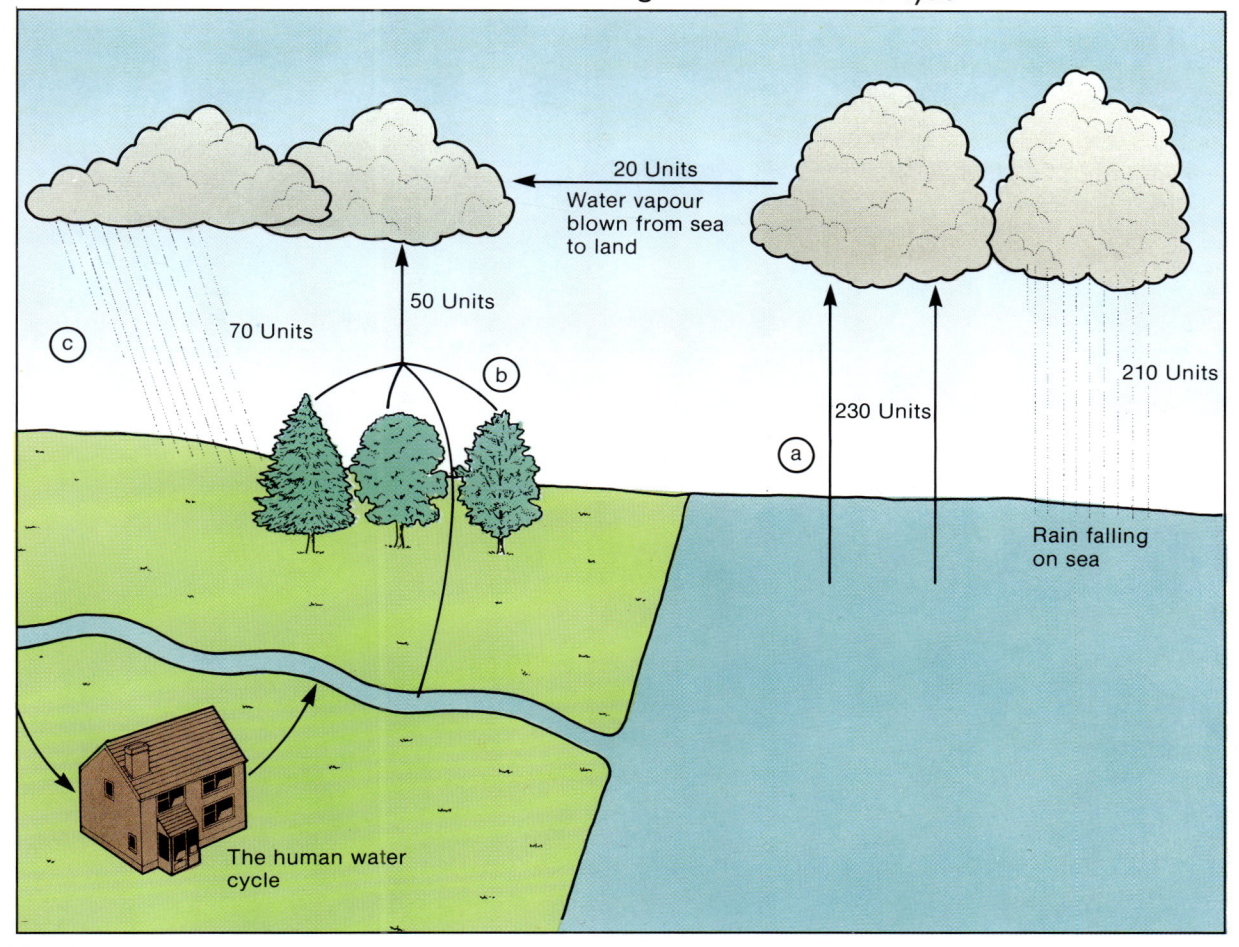

Fig 89 The hydrological cycle

However, our human water cycle is quite complicated. It begins with taking water from the natural environment. The source may be a river, lake, reservoir, spring or well. The water is then treated (Fig 91). From the treatment works it is either pumped to a water tower (Fig 92) from where it reaches our homes under the force of gravity, or it is kept

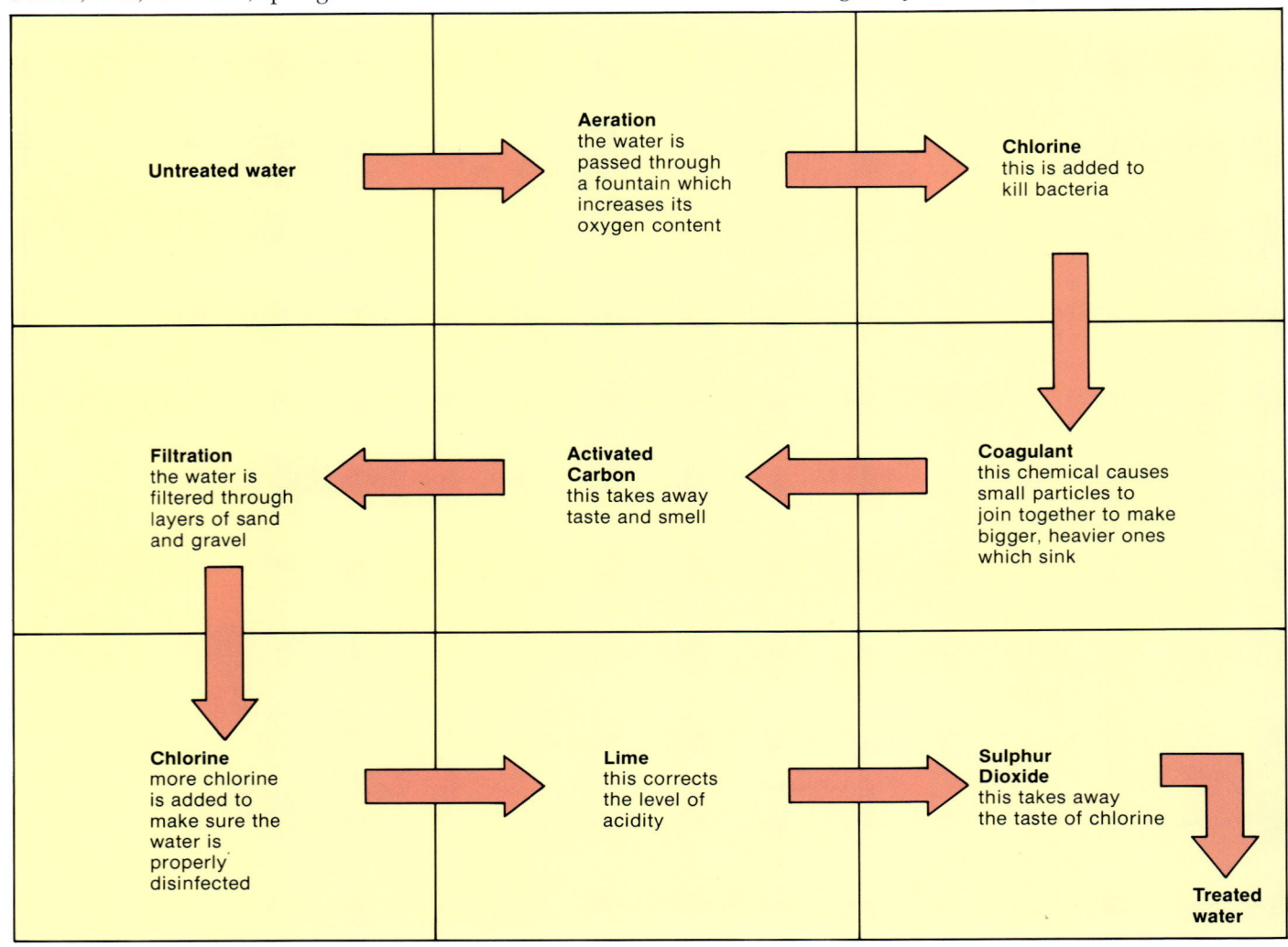

Untreated water → **Aeration** the water is passed through a fountain which increases its oxygen content → **Chlorine** this is added to kill bacteria

↓

Filtration the water is filtered through layers of sand and gravel ← **Activated Carbon** this takes away taste and smell ← **Coagulant** this chemical causes small particles to join together to make bigger, heavier ones which sink

↓

Chlorine more chlorine is added to make sure the water is properly disinfected → **Lime** this corrects the level of acidity → **Sulphur Dioxide** this takes away the taste of chlorine → **Treated water**

Fig 91 Water treatment

Fig 92 Water tower

Fig 93 A sewage treatment works

WATER 2.3

in a storage reservoir and pumped to our homes direct. Of course, when we use the water we pollute it with, for example, household or industrial waste so we cannot put it straight back into the natural system. It is therefore necessary to treat the water again and this is done at the sewage works (Figs 93 and 94).

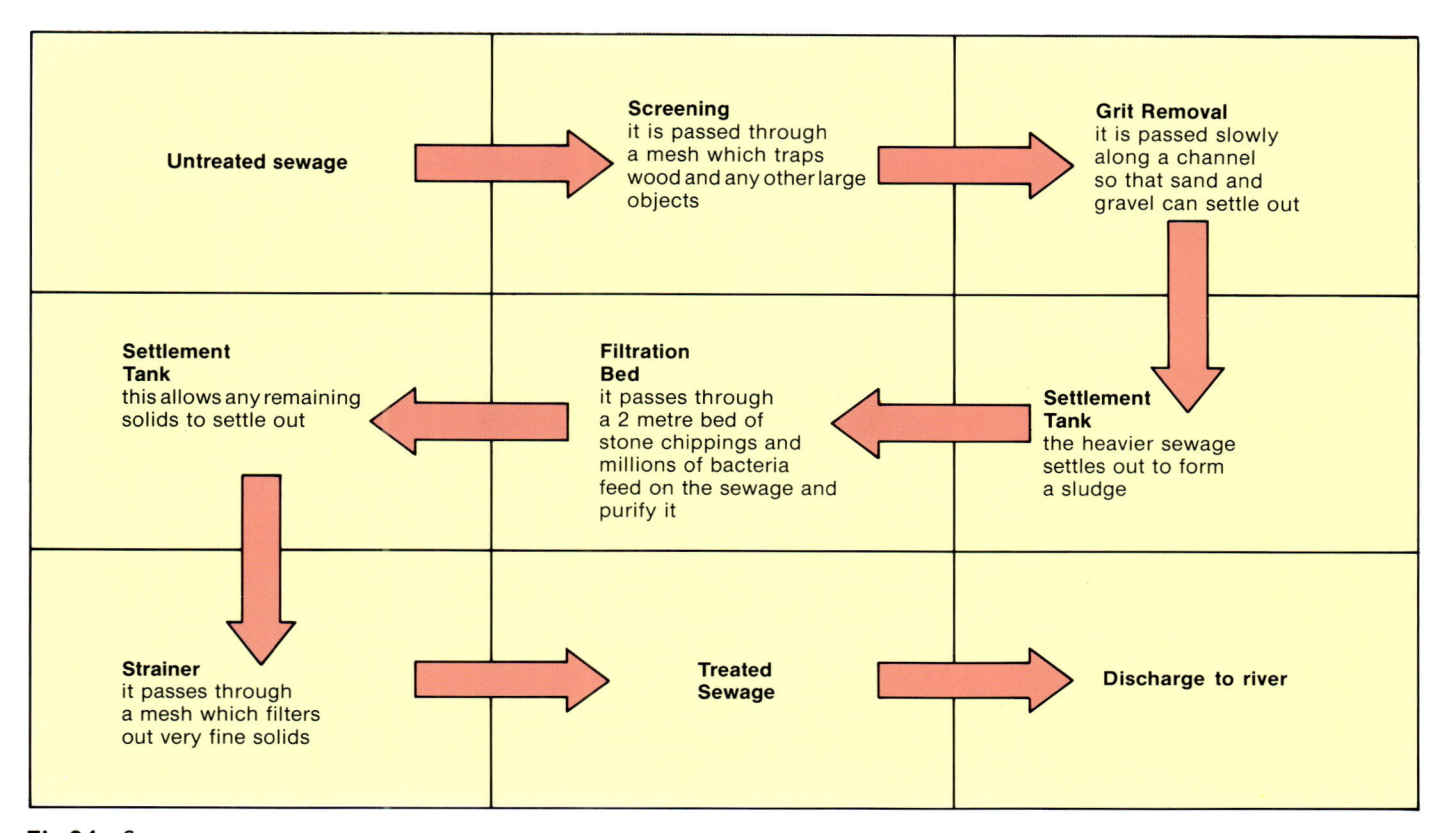

Untreated sewage → **Screening** it is passed through a mesh which traps wood and any other large objects → **Grit Removal** it is passed slowly along a channel so that sand and gravel can settle out ↓

Settlement Tank this allows any remaining solids to settle out ← **Filtration Bed** it passes through a 2 metre bed of stone chippings and millions of bacteria feed on the sewage and purify it ← **Settlement Tank** the heavier sewage settles out to form a sludge

↓ **Strainer** it passes through a mesh which filters out very fine solids → **Treated Sewage** → **Discharge to river**

Fig 94 Sewage treatment

ENQUIRY

1 Draw a column 100 mm in height and 10 mm in width. Mark off 97 mm, shade this part of the column in and label it "water in the oceans (too salty for direct use)". Carefully mark off the next 2 mm, shade this section in and label it "water frozen in the polar ice-caps". The remaining 1 mm represents all the water in the atmosphere, in the ground and in the world's lakes and rivers. The water we use comes from these sources — in other words we depend on only 1 per cent of the earth's water budget. Add a suitable label to this part of the column.
2 Make a copy of Fig 89. Write suitable labels for a), b), and c).
3 Make a copy of Fig 90. Use the information given in this section to help you work out suitable labels for this diagram.
4 Describe the stages water goes through in a treatment works.
5 Describe the stages water goes through in a sewage works.

2.4 What are the features of a river basin?

Stream Order

Section 2.1 introduced you to the ideas that a river basin is the total area drained by a river and its tributaries, and that the line separating one river basin from another is known as the watershed.

River basins can cover thousands of square kilometres and a main river can have many tributaries. Stream ordering is a way of describing a river basin so as to make it seem less complicated.

A stream flowing away from its source is known as a first order stream. If two first order streams join together the result is a second order stream. If two second order streams join together the result is a third order steam, and so on.

It is important to remember that it is only when two streams of the same order join together that the stream order goes up, e.g. if a first order stream joins a second order stream, it remains a second order stream.

The place where two streams join together is known as the confluence.

Drainage Density

This is worked out by adding up the length of all the streams in a river basin and dividing by its area. It is a useful measurement for comparing river basins.

Drainage Patterns

The patterns made by a river system vary from basin to basin, largely because of differences in rock type and structure. Four main patterns can be identified and these are shown in Fig 95.

A *dendritic* pattern is like the shape of a tree — the main river is the trunk and the tributaries are the branches and twigs. This pattern develops in areas of uniform rock type and structure.

A *trellised* drainage pattern has the tributaries arranged roughly at right angles to each other.

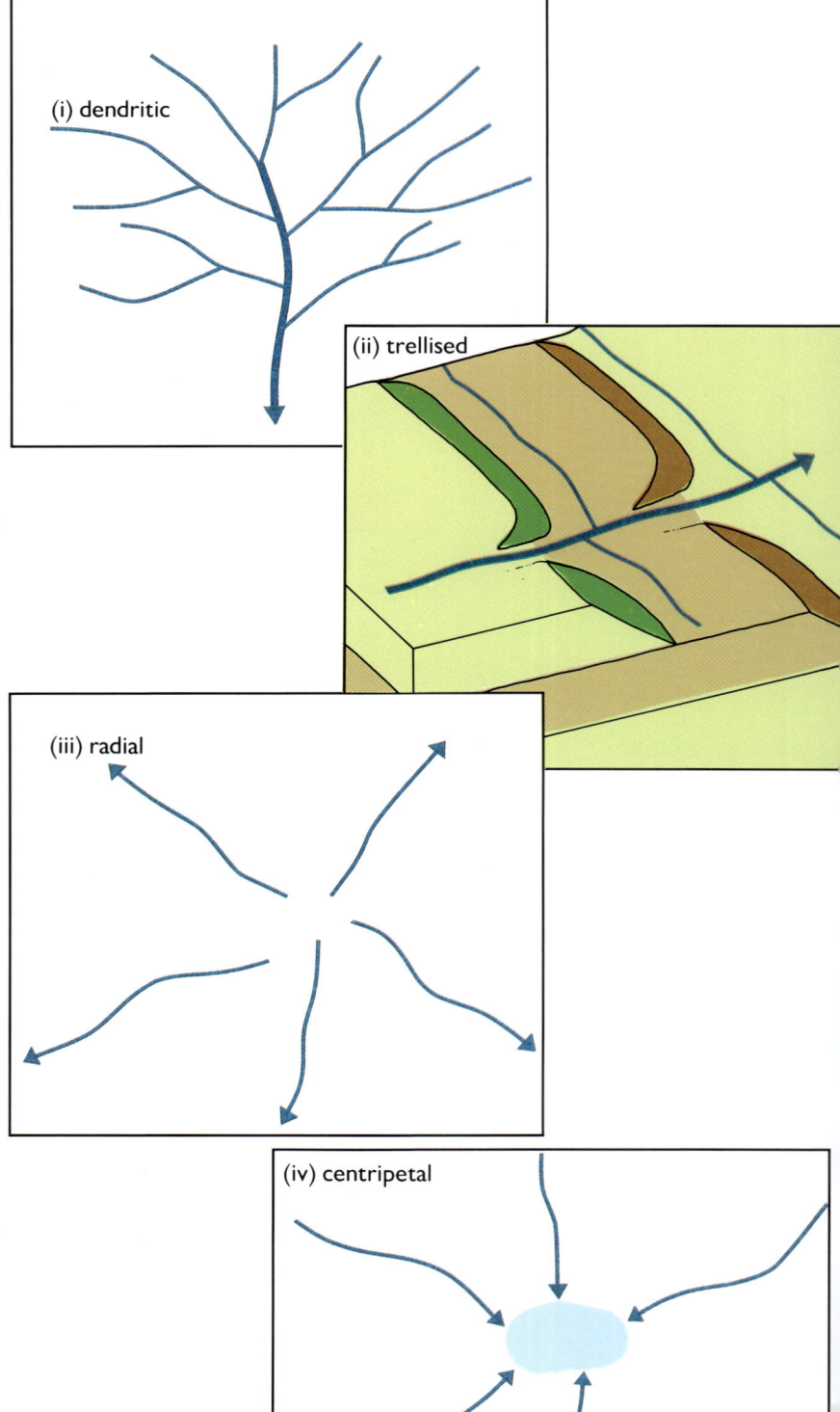

Fig 95 Drainage patterns

WATER 2.4

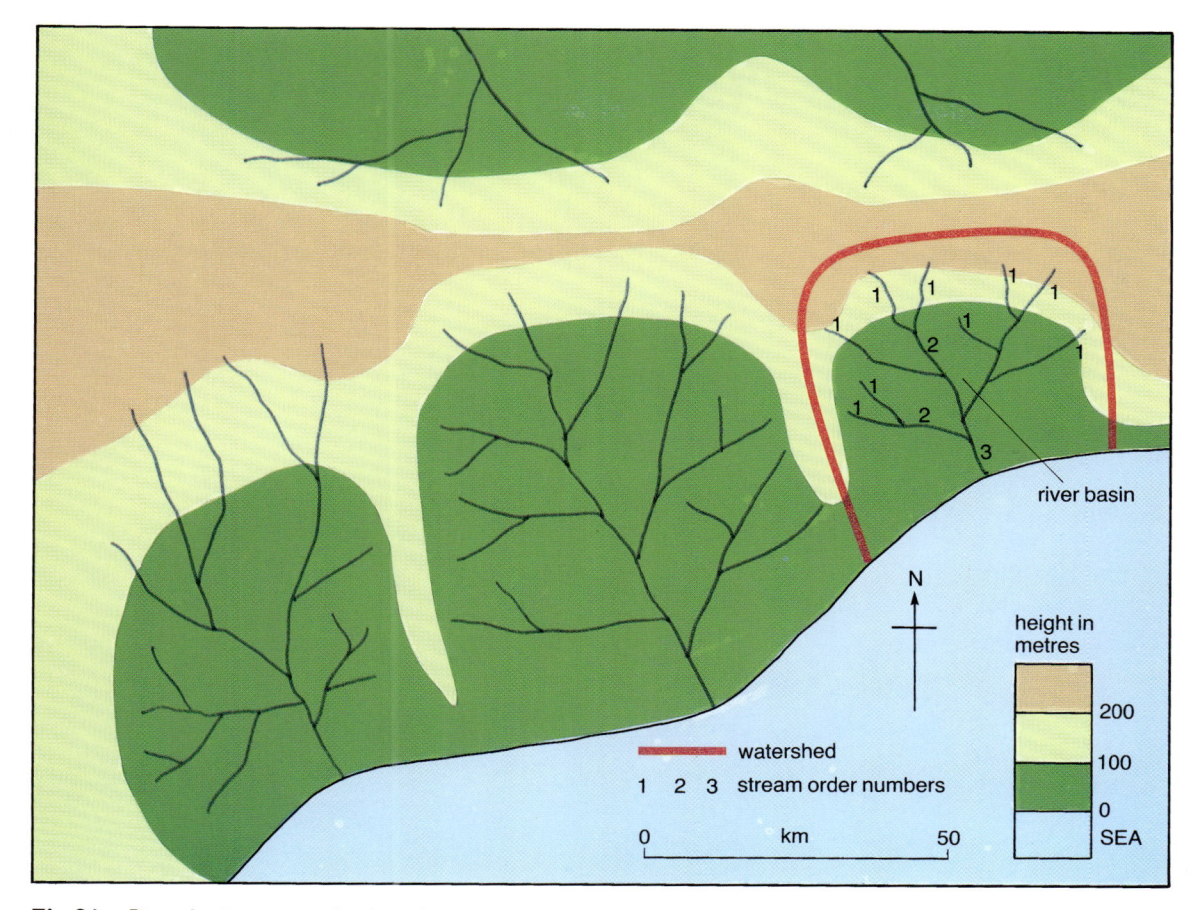

Fig 96 River basins, watersheds and stream ordering

This pattern develops in areas where bands of hard and soft rock are next to each other and all dip in the same direction. A river flowing in the direction of dip is known as a consequent river; one flowing at right angles to the dip is known as a subsequent river.

A *radial* drainage pattern has the rivers flowing outwards from a central point. This pattern develops in areas where the rocks form a dome or cone.

A *centripetal* drainage pattern has the rivers flowing inwards to a central point. This pattern develops in areas where the rocks form a basin.

ENQUIRY

1 Make a copy of Fig 96. Show any other river basins you can identify by drawing on their watersheds. Choose one of these river basins and carry out a stream ordering exercise. Work out its drainage density.

2 How do you think the following factors will affect drainage density — **a)** rock type (permeable/impermeable); and **b)** climate (wet/dry)?

3 Draw sketch maps of the river systems listed below. (You will find them on the physical maps in your atlas.) For each river system, state the type of drainage pattern.
— the River Amazon (Brazil);
— the River Thames between Slough and Cirencester;
— the rivers of the Lake District;
— the rivers of the Aral Sea (CIS).

2.5 How does the river system work?

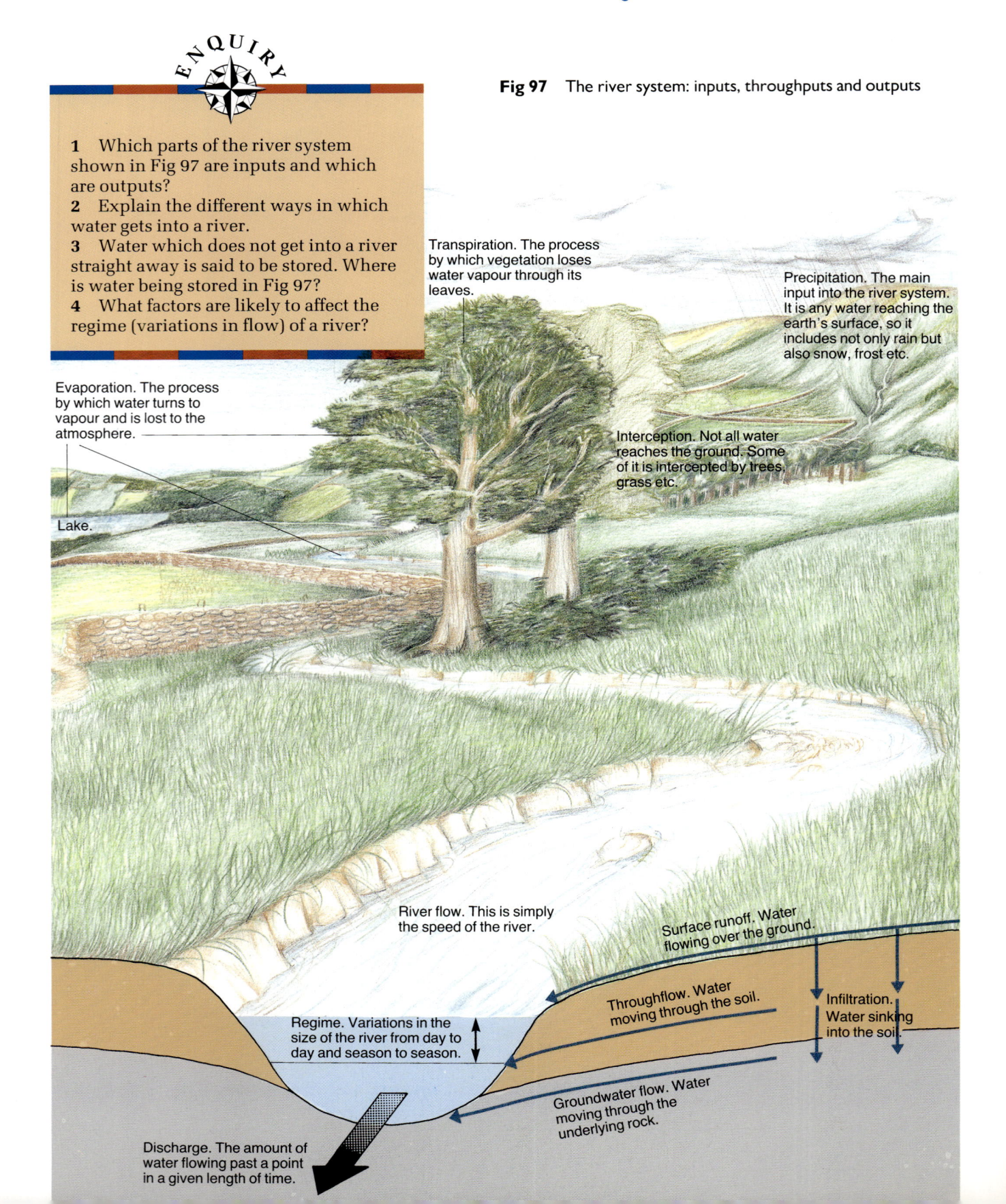

Fig 97 The river system: inputs, throughputs and outputs

ENQUIRY

1. Which parts of the river system shown in Fig 97 are inputs and which are outputs?
2. Explain the different ways in which water gets into a river.
3. Water which does not get into a river straight away is said to be stored. Where is water being stored in Fig 97?
4. What factors are likely to affect the regime (variations in flow) of a river?

Transpiration. The process by which vegetation loses water vapour through its leaves.

Precipitation. The main input into the river system. It is any water reaching the earth's surface, so it includes not only rain but also snow, frost etc.

Evaporation. The process by which water turns to vapour and is lost to the atmosphere.

Interception. Not all water reaches the ground. Some of it is intercepted by trees, grass etc.

Lake.

River flow. This is simply the speed of the river.

Surface runoff. Water flowing over the ground.

Throughflow. Water moving through the soil.

Infiltration. Water sinking into the soil.

Regime. Variations in the size of the river from day to day and season to season.

Groundwater flow. Water moving through the underlying rock.

Discharge. The amount of water flowing past a point in a given length of time.

River Surveys

A wide range of surveys can be carried out on a river. Three ideas are explained below. They could be investigated separately or they could be combined.

Begin your survey by drawing a sketch map of the study area. Locate the site accurately with a six-figure grid reference. Draw a field sketch to show the relationship between the site and the surrounding area.

Once you have collected your results you will need to present, interpret and explain them. Include a section about the survey's limitations. In your conclusion you should return to the aims of your survey and summarise your main findings.

Although the following studies are called river surveys, small streams are much easier and safer to investigate. Always be careful and never work alone.

1 TO STUDY THE SPEED OF A RIVER

Three ideas which could be tested are:

- does speed vary as you move downstream?
- does speed vary across the width of a stream?
- does speed vary with depth?

A simple way of finding out the speed of a river is as follows:

1 Measure out a 10 metre section of river.
2 Place a small dog biscuit in the main current of the river and time how long it takes to cover the 10 metres. (The advantages of a dog biscuit are that it is cheap, it floats and it is biodegradable.)
3 Do this three times and work out the average.
4 The speed of the river in metres per second is simply 10 metres divided by the average time in seconds.

Another way of finding out the speed of a river is to use a flow meter. The one in Fig 98 has a dial which gives you a reading in metres per second. Measurements across the width of a stream can be taken quickly and easily and it is possible to study variations in speed with depth. However, flow meters are very expensive and borrowing one may be difficult.

2 TO STUDY THE SHAPE OF A RIVER'S CHANNEL

A river's channel is made up of its bed and banks. To study its shape you will need a tape measure and a long ruler.

1 Stretch the tape measure across the river.
2 Measure and record the depth of the water at 30 cm intervals. (Always begin with the left bank looking downstream.)
3 Use your results to plot a cross-section on graph paper like the one in Fig 100.

Fig 98 Flow meter

Fig 99 Surveying a river's cross section

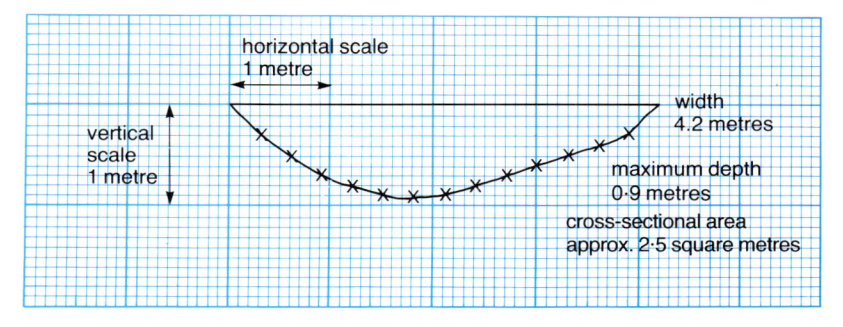

Fig 100 Plotting a river's cross-section

width 4.2 metres
maximum depth 0.9 metres
cross-sectional area approx. 2.5 square metres
horizontal scale 1 metre
vertical scale 1 metre

3 TO STUDY A RIVER'S DISCHARGE

A river's **discharge** is the amount of water flowing past a given point in a certain amount of time. It is usually measured in cumecs (cubic metres per second) and a simple formula is used to calculate it:

discharge = speed (metres/second) × cross sectional area (square metres)

It is therefore necessary to measure the speed of the river and to survey its cross section. Its cross sectional area can be worked out from a graph like the one in Fig 100. In this example 100 small squares make up a square metre. So, all you have to do to get the cross sectional area is to count up the number of small squares and divide by 100.

It is interesting to see what happens to a river's discharge as you move downstream.

Hydrographs

A **hydrograph** is a line which shows river discharge over a given period of time. Flood hydrographs show a river's discharge after a period of heavy rain (Fig 101). The flood appears as a peak above the base (normal) flow. The height of the peak and the time the river takes to reach this peak both depend on a number of factors which vary considerably from one river to another. However, floods have such a major impact on our activities that a thorough knowledge of these factors is important in order that we may predict floods and decide how best to control them.

Factors Affecting River Hydrographs

As a general rule, the greater the rainfall the greater is the discharge from the river. However, the distribution and type of rainfall is important to the shape of the hydrograph; for example, occasional heavy storms produce distinct peaks in discharge, whereas well-distributed rainfall produces a more gentle hydrograph.

Impermeable rocks and soils with low **infiltration** rates result in rapid surface runoff and therefore higher peaks in discharge, in comparison with **permeable** rocks and soils with high infiltration rates.

Interception by vegetation slows down the time it takes for rain to get into the river system; consequently, a lack of vegetation results in peaked hydrographs.

Low drainage densities mean greater peaks because it takes less time for water to get into the main channel. For the same reason, the smaller the **river basin** the greater the peaks. The shape of the basin is important because it affects the distance and therefore the time it takes for water to reach the main channel. The steeper the slope of the basin the greater are the peaks because surface runoff is more rapid.

The most obvious way in which we affect hydrographs is through river management schemes such as dam construction. However, surface runoff is greater in towns and cities compared with the surrounding countryside because of the impermeable nature of roads and pavements etc. As a result, peaks in the hydrograph become much greater and this can lead to flooding downstream of a settlement. There are also many ways in which farming can increase surface runoff, e.g. by leaving fields bare in winter.

ENQUIRY

1 Explain the difference between an annual hydrograph and a flood hydrograph.
2 Complete a copy of Fig 102 by using words and/or phrases from the following list — heavy storms, well-distributed rainfall, permeable, impermeable, low, high, dense, little, high, low, large, small, long and thin, short and round, steep, gentle, flood control schemes, no river management, open countryside, urban settlement, pastoral, arable.
3 On a graph outline like the one in Fig 103 plot the rainfall statistics and the two river hydrographs. Describe the different ways in which the rivers responded to the storm. River A is in an area of impermeable rock used for sheep grazing while River B is in an area of permeable rock used for forestry. How does this information help to explain the different response of the rivers to the storm.
4 Why do you think predicting floods is difficult?

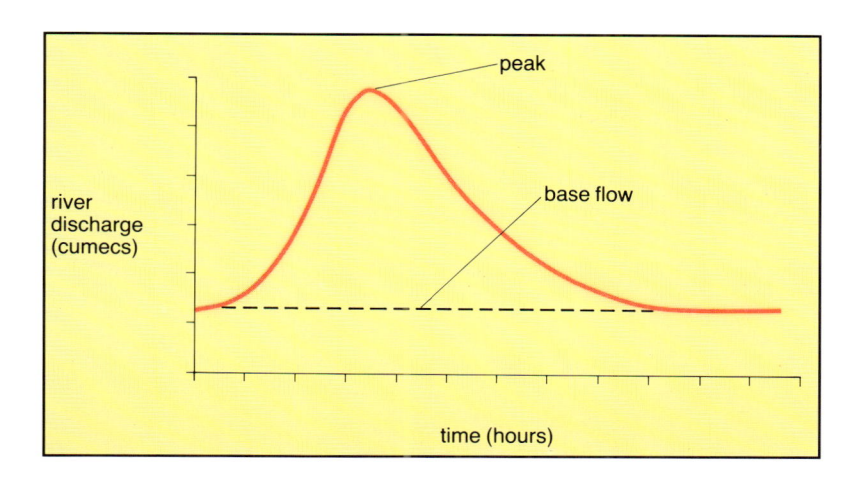

Fig 101 A flood hydrograph

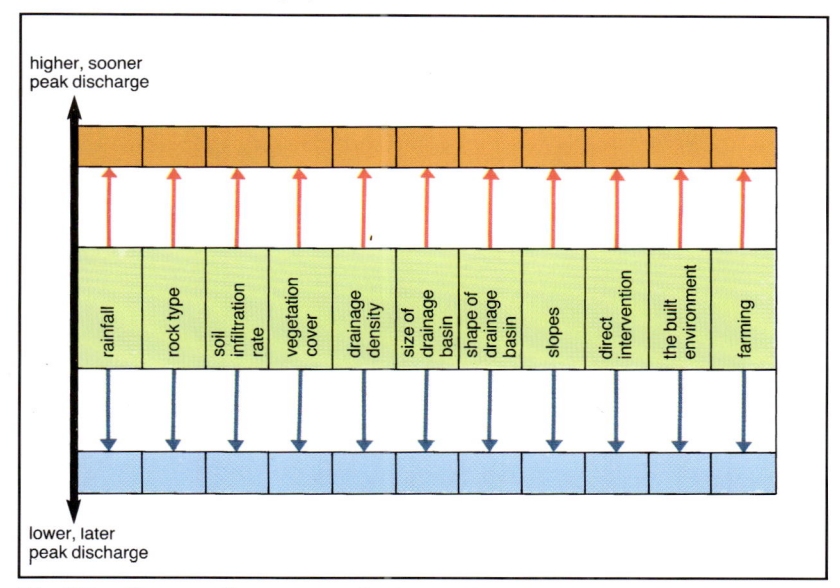

Fig 102 Factors affecting river hydrographs

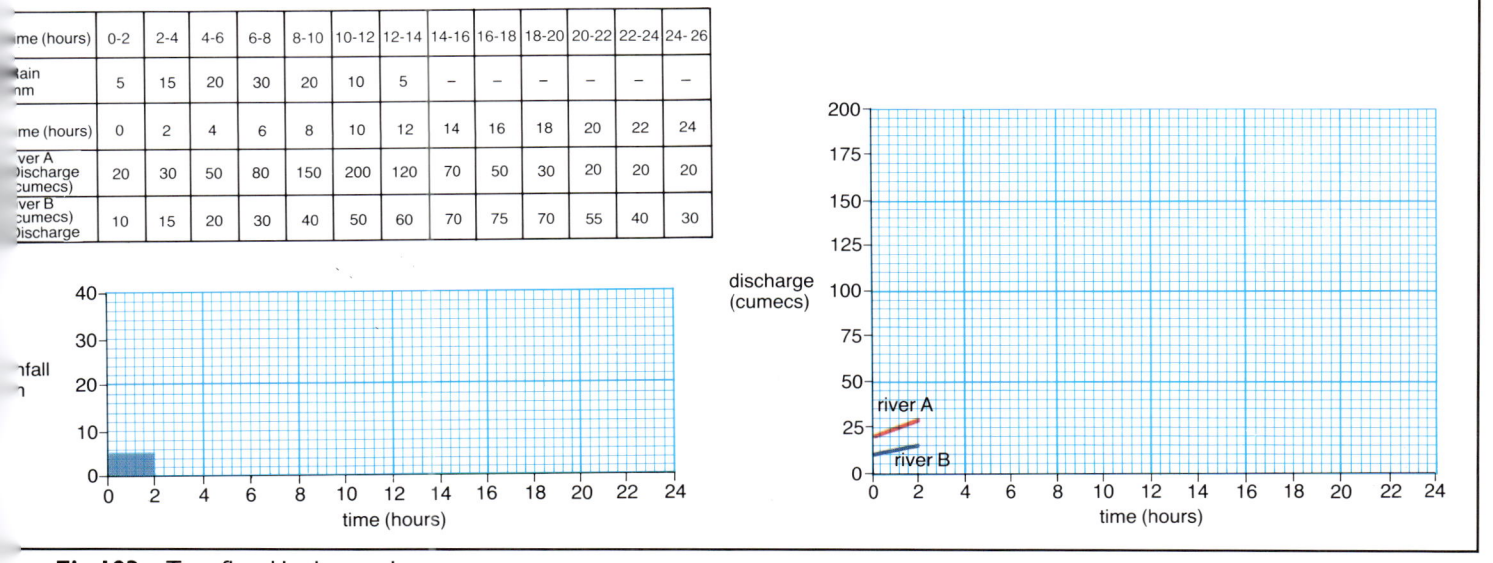

Factors (from higher, sooner peak discharge to lower, later peak discharge): rainfall, rock type, soil infiltration rate, vegetation cover, drainage density, size of drainage basin, shape of drainage basin, slopes, direct intervention, the built environment, farming

time (hours)	0-2	2-4	4-6	6-8	8-10	10-12	12-14	14-16	16-18	18-20	20-22	22-24	24-26
Rain mm	5	15	20	30	20	10	5	–	–	–	–	–	–

time (hours)	0	2	4	6	8	10	12	14	16	18	20	22	24
river A discharge (cumecs)	20	30	50	80	150	200	120	70	50	30	20	20	20
river B discharge (cumecs)	10	15	20	30	40	50	60	70	75	70	55	40	30

Fig 103 Two flood hydrographs

2.6 River landforms — what are they like and how do they form?

The main aim of a river is to cut an efficient course from its source to its mouth. The ideal long profile is a smooth curve like the one in Fig 104. The balance between erosion and deposition varies along this profile. Features of erosion are more common in the upper section where the river's gradient (slope) is greater and where the river has more energy. Features of deposition are more common in the lower section where the river's gradient is gentle and where it has less energy. In the middle section erosion and deposition are more evenly balanced.

However, rates of erosion vary considerably from day to day and season to season. In dry weather rivers in their upper section may have to deposit their load in order to keep flowing. On the other hand, when the river is full erosion can be the most important process even in the lower section.

River Features — the Upper Section

V-shaped Valleys

V-shaped valleys like the one in Fig 105 are a characteristic feature of the upper section of a river. They are the result of rapid downward erosion combined with weathering on the valley sides.

Fig 105 V-shaped valley

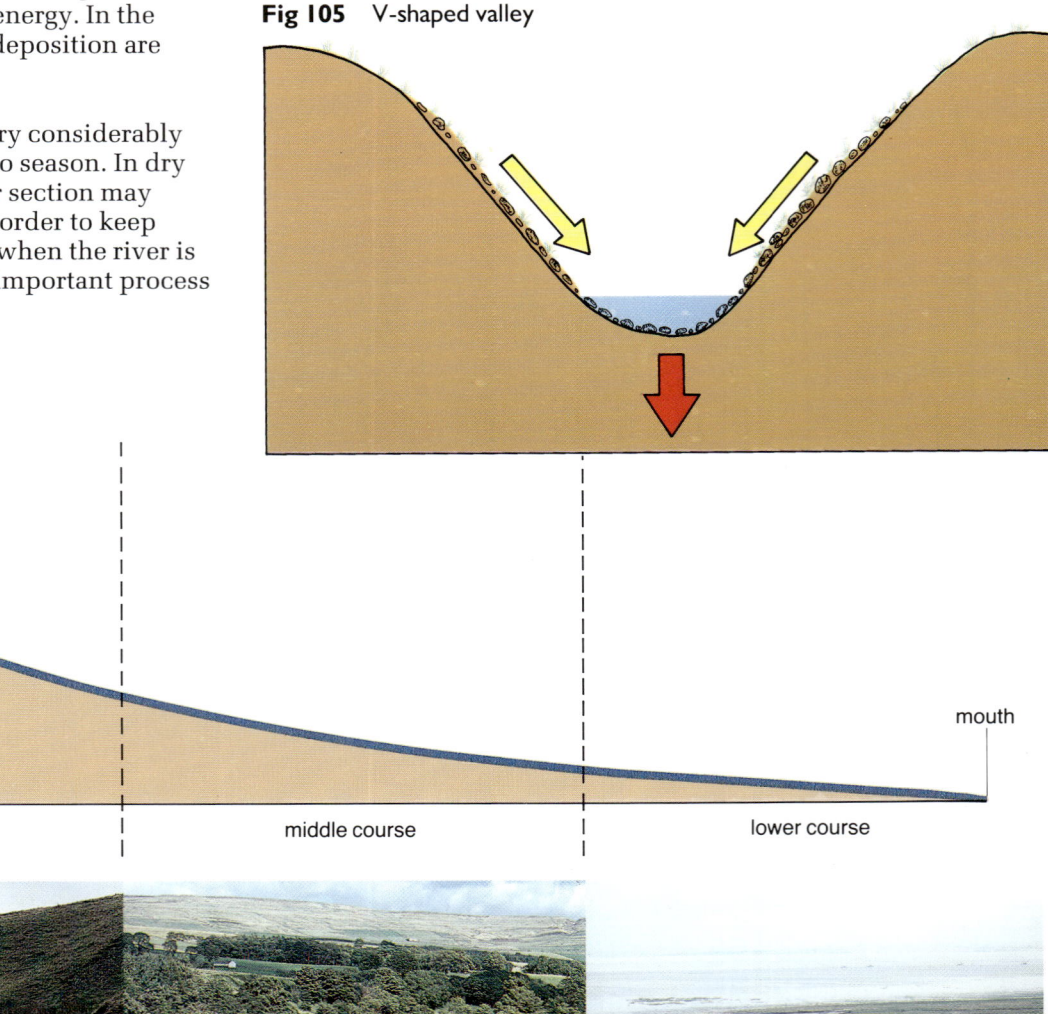

Fig 104 The long profile of a river

Gorges

If there is little or no weathering, or if the rate of downward erosion is very much faster than the rate of weathering, the sides of a valley remain vertical; the result is a gorge.

Interlocking Spurs

As the river flows away from its source it begins to swing from side to side. Of course, it is still rapidly cutting downwards. The result is a series of hills (spurs) which fit together (interlock) like the pieces of a jigsaw puzzle (Fig 106).

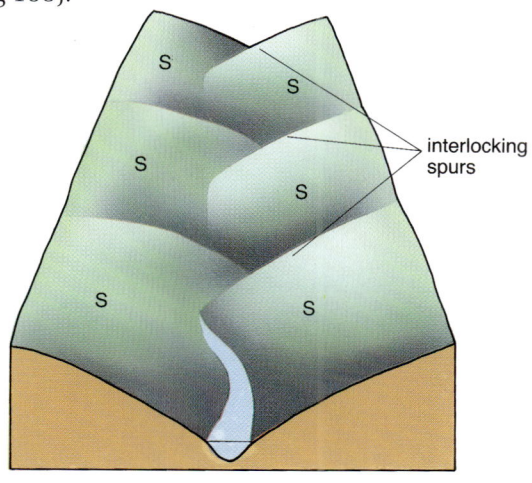

Fig 106 Interlocking spurs

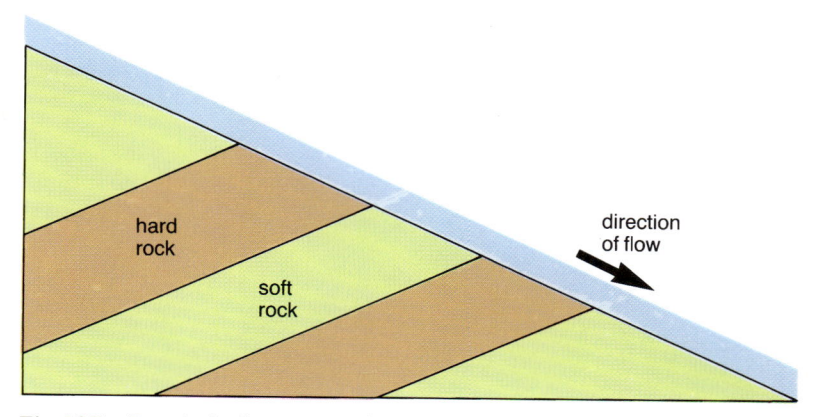

Fig 107 Rapids (before erosion)

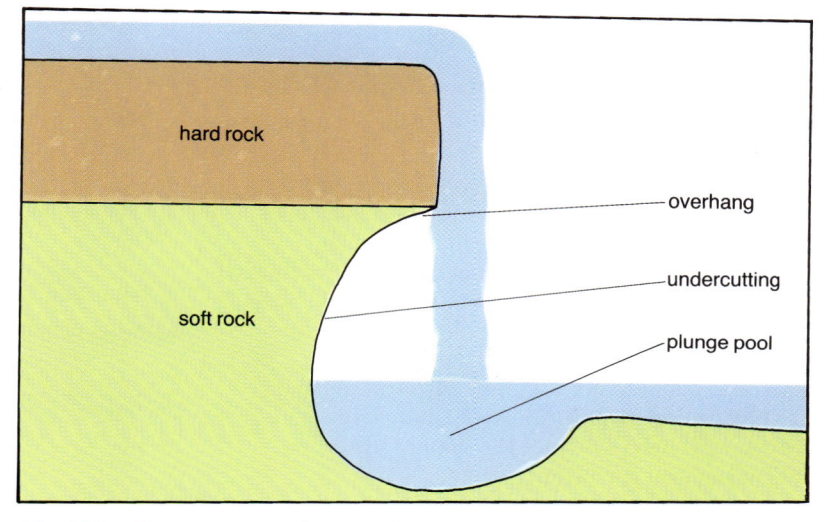

Fig 108 Cross-section of a waterfall

Rapids

Rapids are areas of fast-flowing, turbulent water. They form when the bed of a river is made up of hard and soft rocks (Fig 107). The soft rocks are worn away more quickly leaving the hard rocks sticking up into the river channel.

Waterfalls

These sudden falls of water can be formed in a number of different ways — for example, they could be the result of water plunging over the side of a glaciated valley (see page 71). However, many waterfalls are the result of a bed of hard rock overlying a bed of soft rock. They begin as rapids but as more and more of the soft rock is eroded the drop becomes steeper until it is vertical. At the base of the waterfall hydraulic action erodes a deep plunge pool (Fig 108).

The river continues to erode the soft layer of rock as it goes over the fall. As a result, the

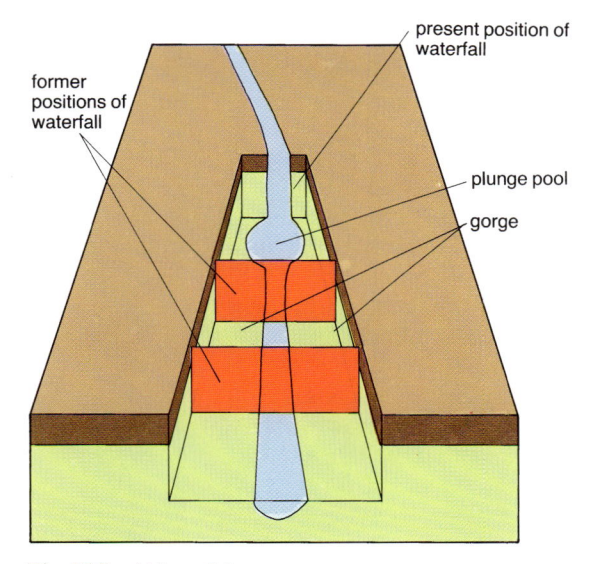

Fig 109 Waterfall retreat

hard layer of rock is undercut. Eventually, the overhang collapses and the process repeats itself. In this way waterfalls retreat upstream leaving a gorge downstream (Fig 109).

Pot-holes

Fig 110 Pot-hole, River Wharfe, North Yorkshire

Geographers use the term pot-hole to describe small depressions found in the bed of a river (Fig 110). However, the term is also used by underground cavers to describe swallow holes (see page 84). Pot-holes form when rock fragments get caught up in eddies (circular currents). As they are swirled round, the process of abrasion "drills" into the rocks. They are often found downstream of a waterfall because here the water is fast flowing and turbulent.

Meanders, Bluffs and Slip-off Slopes

Meanders — the loops and curves in the course of a river — are found in all three section of a river's long profile. In the upper section they are relatively small but they already show a range of features.

As the river flows round the meander the current is swung to the outside of the bend. This means that the erosive power of the river is concentrated on the outside bend. The river's channel is eroded more deeply and the banks are undercut, leaving an overhang. When this overhang eventually collapses a small river cliff, known as a bluff, is formed. On the inside of the bend the current is much weaker and deposition takes place. The small beach which results is known as a slip-off slope (Fig 111).

ENQUIRY

1. Label each of the features found in the upper section of a river onto a large copy of Fig 104, page 52. Add a brief definition for each feature and state whether it is caused by erosion or deposition.
2. Explain, with the help of a diagram, how a V-shaped valley forms.
3. Why do you think gorges are often associated with **a)** rivers flowing across arid (dry) regions (such as the Colorado River flowing through the Grand Canyon in the USA) and **b)** waterfalls?
4. Re-draw Fig 107 to show what the bed of the river would like after a period of erosion.
5. Explain, with the aid of diagrams, how waterfalls are formed and why they retreat upstream.
6. Make a sketch of Fig 112. Label onto it a meander, a bluff and slip-off slope.

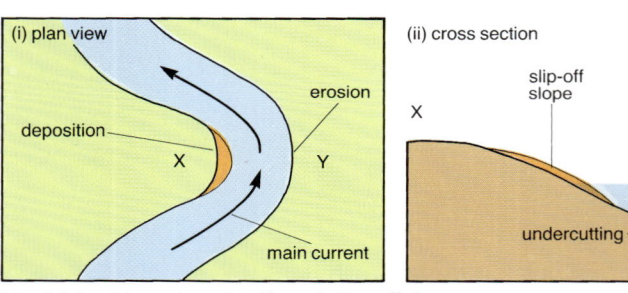

Fig 111 Meanders, bluffs and slip-off slopes

Fig 112 Cowside Beck, near Arncliffe, North Yorkshire

WATER 2.6

River Features – the Middle Section

Some of the features found in the upper section of a river are also found in its middle section. Rapids and waterfalls are still present but they are less common. Meanders are a larger and more important feature, and bluffs and slip-off slopes are still found. However, there are some important differences as well.

Open V-shaped Valleys and Narrow Flood Plains

The most striking difference is that the narrow V-shaped valley and the interlocking spurs of the upper section are no longer there. Instead, the sides of the valley are parallel and the bottom of the valley is flat. The river itself has brought about these changes. In the upper section its erosive power is concentrated on the spurs and eventually the process of undercutting and collapse leads to their removal (Fig 113).

The flood plain forms when the river spills out onto the flat valley bottom and deposits a layer of silt and alluvium.

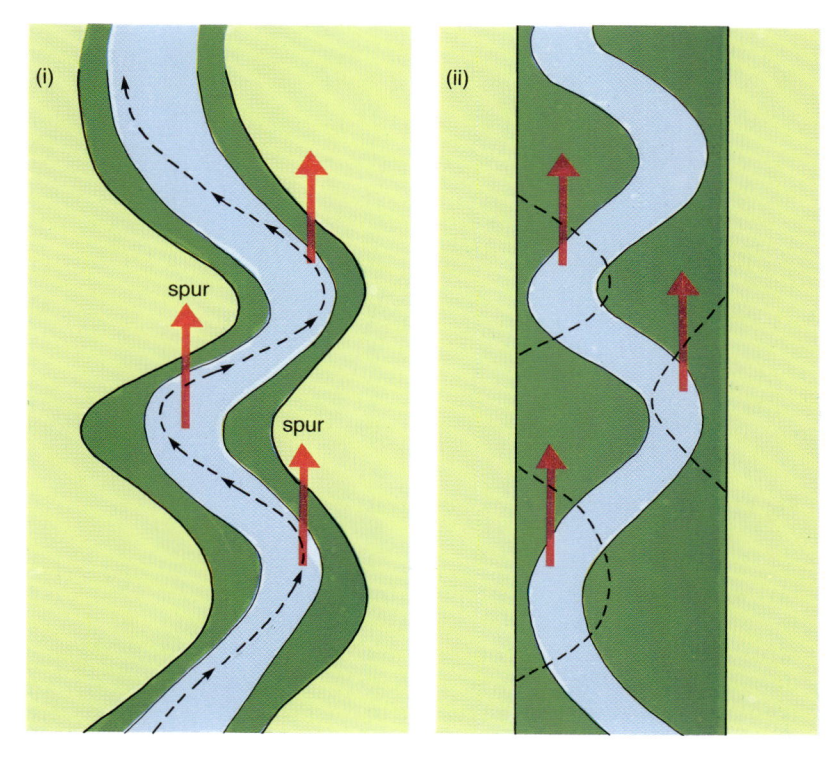

Fig 113 The removal of interlocking spurs

ENQUIRY

1 Copy the diagrams in Fig 113 and add labels to them to explain how the river removes its interlocking spurs.
2 Complete Fig 104, page 52 for the middle section of a river in the same way as you did for the upper section in the previous Enquiry.

River Features — the lower section

This section of a river's course has a number of characteristic features. The sides of the valley have often been completely eroded and the river meanders across a wide flood plain. Deposition has become the major process.

Ox-bow Lakes

These are crescent shaped lakes found on the river's flood plain. They get their name from the U-shaped yoke (the collar which attaches animals to a plough or cart) worn by oxen.

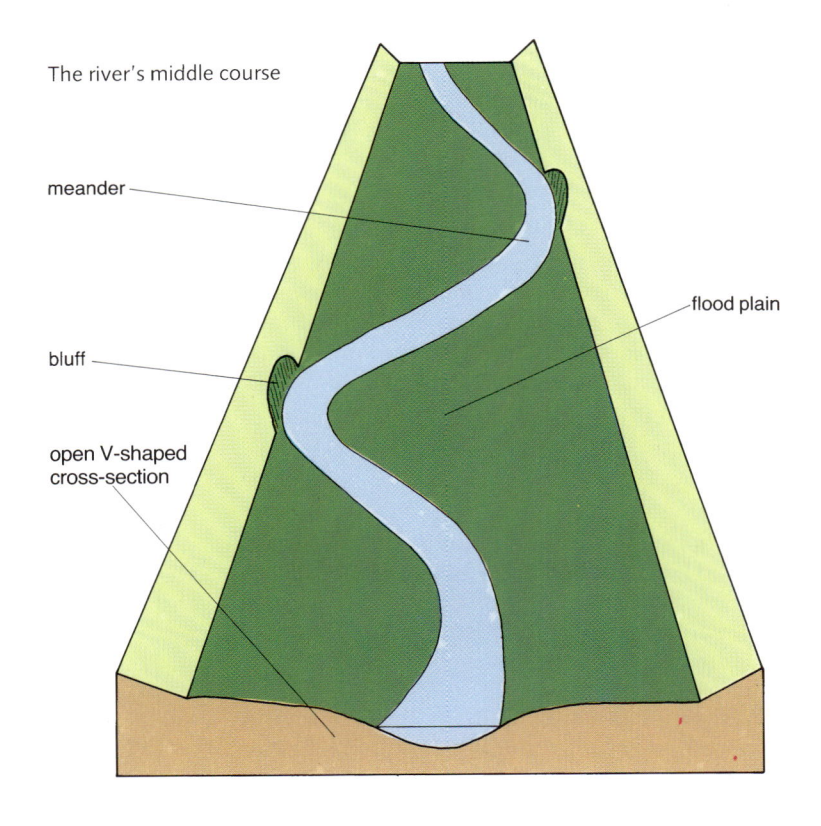

Fig 114 The river's middle course

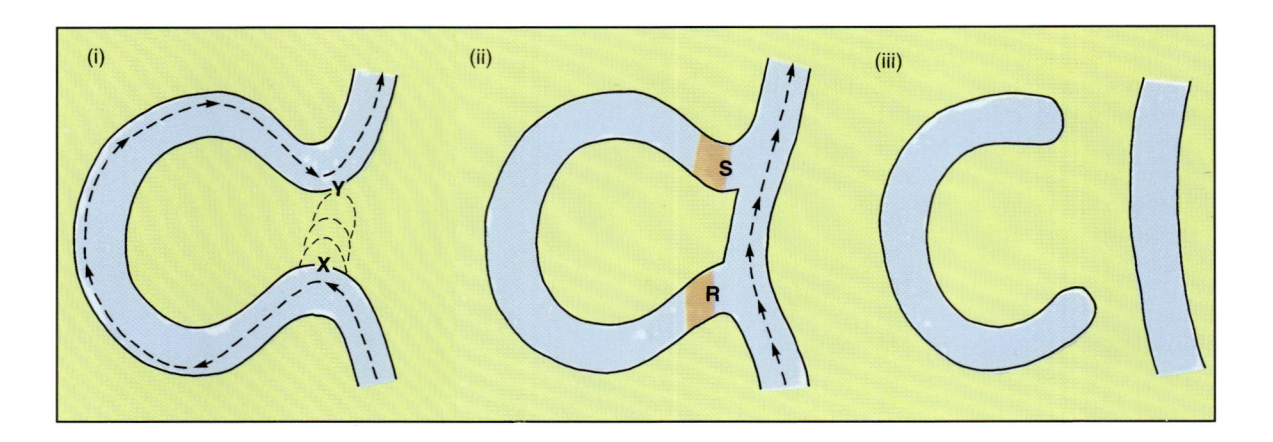

Fig 115 The formation of ox-bow lakes

Ox-bow lakes are another feature formed by the work of meanders (Fig 115). As we have already seen, erosion is concentrated on the outside bend of the meander at place X. Undercutting and collapse results in the neck of the meander becoming narrow until it is breached at place Y. The river can then flow straight across the neck of the meander instead of flowing round it. With no current, the water at the entrance to, and the exit from, the meander at places R and S loses energy and deposits its load. This blocks off the meander completely, forming the ox-bow lake. Eventually, the ox-bow lake itself may silt up and become vegetated.

Braiding

Braiding is the process by which a river channel splits into two or more parts which then join up again. It does this when it is no longer able to carry its load. By depositing material it is able to regain energy and keep flowing. Examples of braids as well as ox-bow lakes can be seen in Fig 116.

Levées

Rivers in their lower section are often lined by raised banks. These may have been built deliberately to prevent flooding or they may have formed naturally, as **levées**, at least in the first instance.

When the river spills onto its flood plain the water loses energy quickly and deposits its load. Larger, heavier material is deposited first, nearest to the river. Smaller, lighter material is deposited further away. When the river floods again the process is repeated and in this way a levee builds up (Fig 117).

Fig 116 River Add, Argyleshire

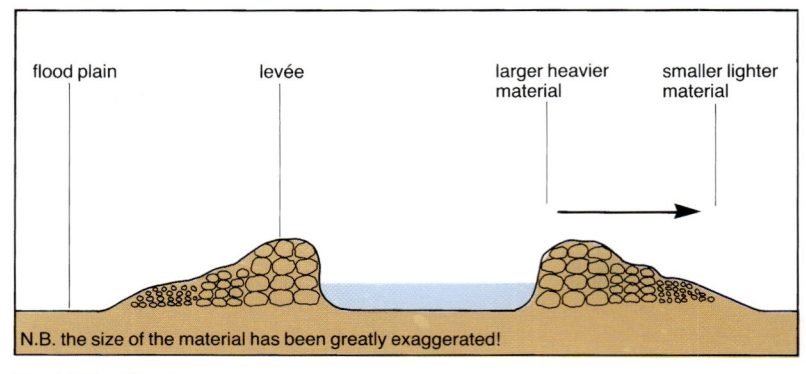

Fig 117 The formation of a levée

Deltas

A **delta** is a low-lying area of land at the mouth of a river where it enters the sea or a lake. A delta forms if the currents in the sea or lake are too weak to carry away the material being deposited by the river. As the delta builds up the river is forced to split into a number of smaller streams, known as distributaries.

There are two main types of delta — arcuate and bird's foot. Arcuate deltas, such as the Nile delta (Fig 118), are fan-shaped. They are made up of sand and gravel as well as finer sediments such as silt and alluvium.

If the sediments are very fine and the currents are very weak the river's distributaries are able to build out into the sea or lake without being disturbed at all. The result is a bird's foot delta, such as the Mississippi delta (Fig 119). Levées usually build up on either side of the distributary.

Changes in Base-level

Base-level means the lowest level a river can wear down to. This is usually the sea or an inland lake. If the base-level changes, the river has to adjust to this new condition. The Ice Age (see Section 3) produced many such changes. During glacial periods water was stored in ice sheets and glaciers, and the sea-level fell. During interglacials the ice melted, flowed back into the sea and caused the sea-level to rise. Other events, such as earthquakes, can also cause a change in base-level.

Terraces

A fall in base-level means that a river has to wear downwards in order to get back to the smooth curve of its ideal long profile. As it does so it cuts into its own flood plain. The remnants of the flood plain are left as flat strips of land on the side of the valley: these are known as terraces (Fig 120). The break of slope where the terraces meet is known as a knick-point and it is often the location of rapids or of a waterfall. As the knick-point wears backwards the terraces extend upstream, and as a result they can be found in any section of the river's long profile.

Fig 118 Satellite image of the Nile Delta

Fig 119 Satellite image of the Mississippi Delta

ENQUIRY

1 Explain, with the help of a diagram, how ox-bow lakes are formed.
2 Make a sketch of Fig 116. Label a meander, an ox-bow lake, a braided channel and the river's flood plain.
3 How many "floods" have formed the levee in Fig 117?
4 Study the satellite images, Figs 118 and 119. Sketch the outline of the two deltas, using a full page for each one. Use the information about deltas, the key, and an atlas to add as many labels as you can about the physical and human geography of these deltas. Include details about their formation.
5 Copy the diagrams in Fig 120 and add labels to explain how river terraces form.
6 Complete your copy of Fig 104, page 52 for the lower section of a river in the same way as you have already done for the upper and middle sections.

Fig 120 The formation of river terraces

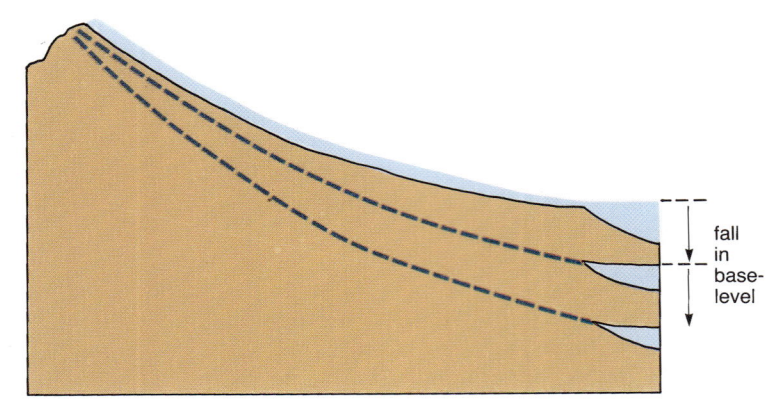

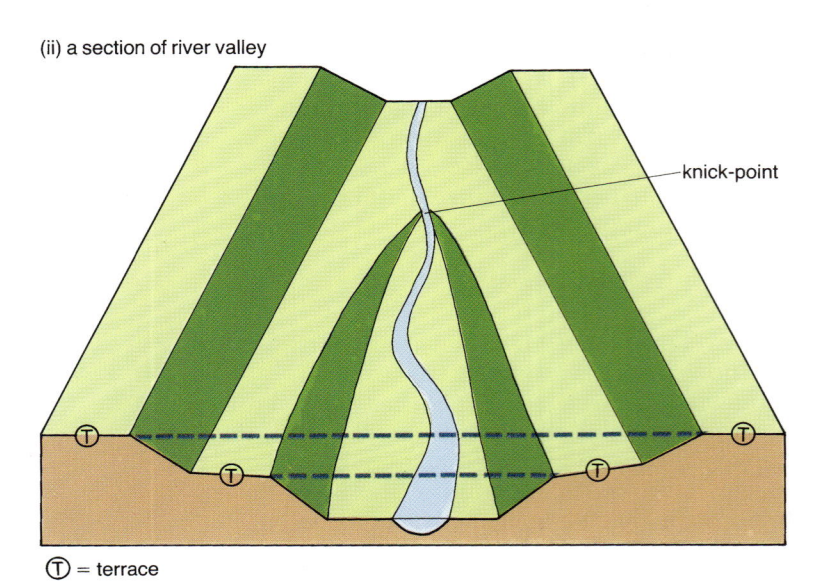

(i) cross section

fall in base-level

(ii) a section of river valley

knick-point

Ⓣ = terrace

2.7 Where does our water come from?

The water we use in our homes comes from three main places — underground, reservoirs and rivers (Fig 121).

Fig 121 (i) Wind pump drawing water, Australia

(ii) Grafham Water, Cambridgeshire

(iii) Extraction Works, Offord, River Great Ouse

Water from underground comes from rocks called **aquifers**. They are permeable rocks, which means that they let water in — think of them as being like a sponge. The level the water gets to inside an aquifer is called the water table. When it rains, the water table goes up. When it is dry, the water table goes down. If the water table reaches the surface it will seep out to make a spring.

Rocks which do not let water in are called **impermeable**. Reservoirs have to be built on this type of rock and rivers flow best across it.

ENQUIRY

1. Make a copy of Fig 122. Label the arrows using words from this list: water table, impermeable rock, spring, river, permeable rock, aquifer, well, reservoir, river.
2. Describe what happens to raindrop A.
3. Describe what happens to raindrop B.

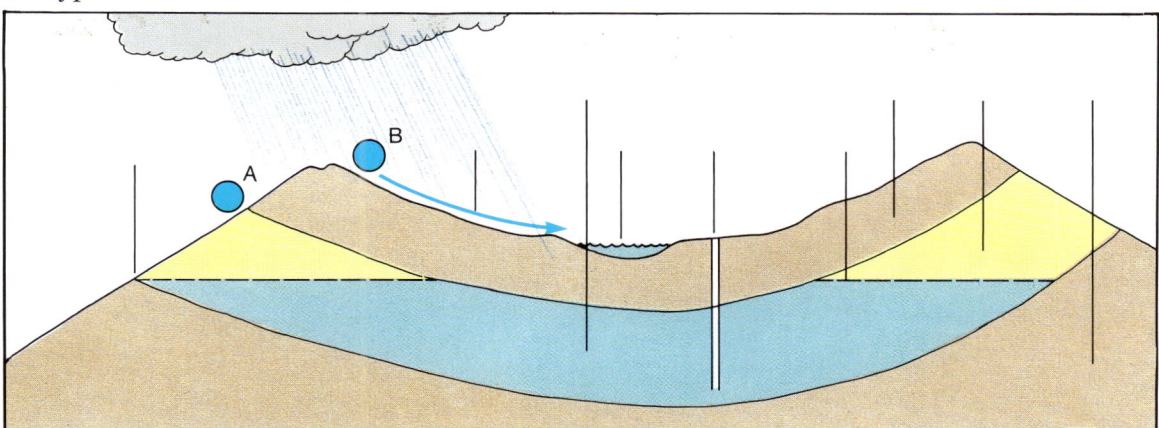

Fig 122 Where does our water come from?

WATER 2.7

What Do We Use Water For?

Fig 123 shows how much water is used in England and Wales every day; it adds up to an almost unbelievable 6.3 billion gallons. At home each one of us uses an average of 28·5 gallons every day. Fig 124 shows the amount we use for different things.

Use	Average amount (ml/d)
public water supplies	16 650
power stations	6 840
industry	3 950
fish farming	1 100
irrigation	100
farming	130

ml/d = megalitres per day
(1 ml = 220 000 gallons)

Fig 123 Water usage

Use	%
flushing the toilet	32
baths/showers	17
washing machines	12
outside use e.g. hoses	3
other uses, including cooking and drinking	36

Fig 124 Average household water use

ENQUIRY

1 Draw a bar chart to show the information in Fig 123. Do any of the figures surprise you?
2 Draw a pie chart to show the information in Fig 124. What is your reaction to these figures?

Getting Water To The People Who Want It — England and Wales

England and Wales get more than enough rain to meet the demand for water. However, there is a problem because the wettest parts of the country have few people living there but the driest parts of the country have a lot of people living there.

One way of solving this problem is to move water from the wettest to the driest parts of the country. This is not a new idea; for example, the Elan Valley Scheme (Fig 125) was built in 1892. A 150 km pipeline links it to Birmingham and it supplies 1.8 million gallons a day to the Severn Trent Water Authority (STWA). Water can also be pumped from one river to another.

Getting Water To The People Who Want It — Kabare in Kenya

Kabare is a small village 60 km south of Mount Kenya (Fig 126). It gets its water from streams above the village. First, the water is piped to a series of large brick storage tanks. From there it is taken by pipelines to big buildings like the secondary school. If a family lives near to one of these pipelines they can be connected to it. However, they have to pay for the extra piping and for the small concrete storage tank that the water is taken to (Fig 128).

WATER 2.7

Fig 125 Water transfer schemes

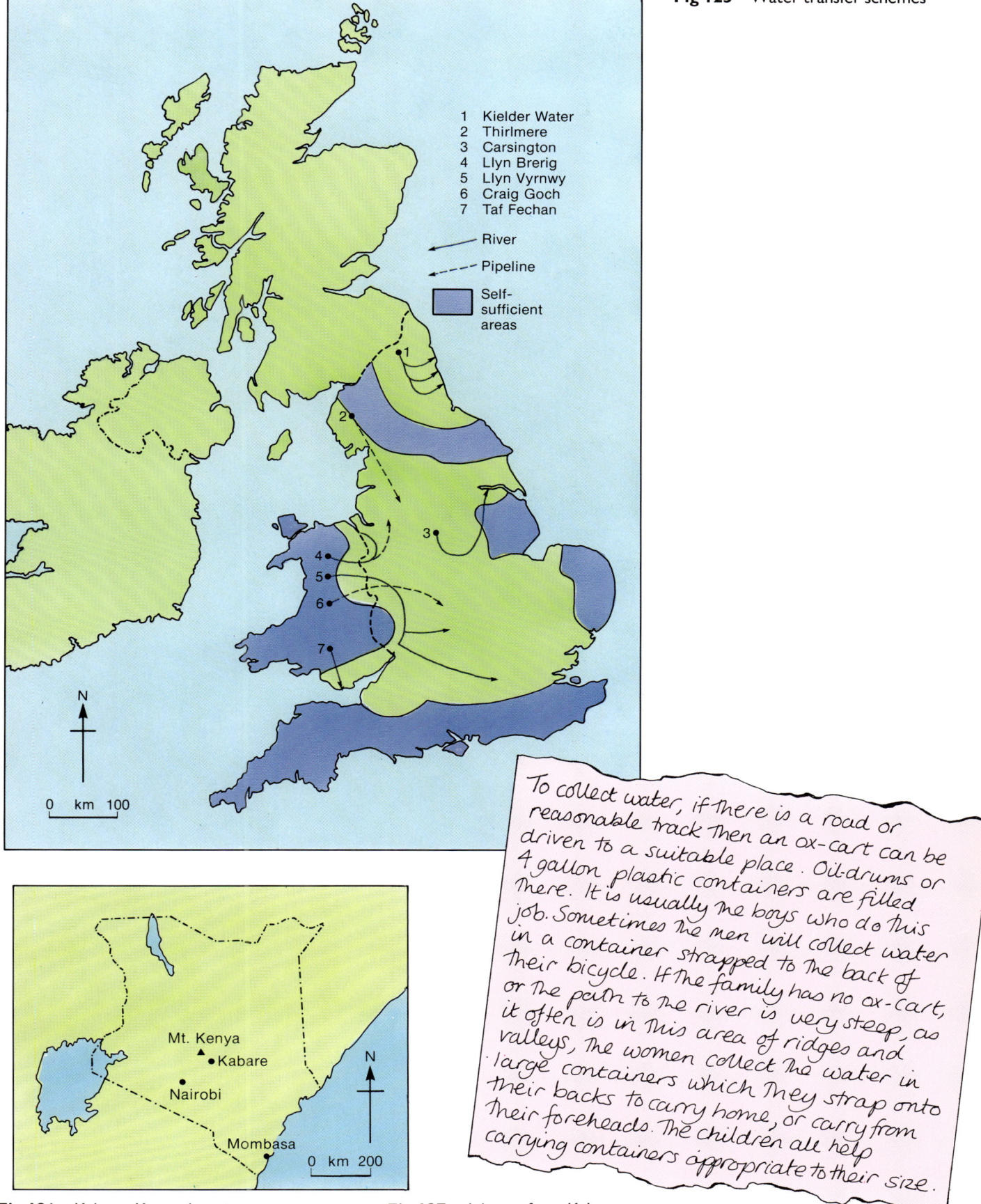

1 Kielder Water
2 Thirlmere
3 Carsington
4 Llyn Brerig
5 Llyn Vyrnwy
6 Craig Goch
7 Taf Fechan

→ River
⇢ Pipeline
▇ Self-sufficient areas

Fig 126 Kabare, Kenya: location map

Fig 127 A letter from Kabare

To collect water, if there is a road or reasonable track then an ox-cart can be driven to a suitable place. Oil-drums or 4 gallon plastic containers are filled there. It is usually the boys who do this job. Sometimes the men will collect water in a container strapped to the back of their bicycle. If the family has no ox-cart, or the path to the river is very steep, as it often is in this area of ridges and valleys, the women collect the water in large containers which they strap onto their backs to carry home, or carry from their foreheads. The children all help carrying containers appropriate to their size.

If a family is a long way from a main pipeline, or if it cannot afford to be connected, they have to collect their water straight from the river which is over an hour's walk away. Fig 127 is part of a letter from a visitor to Kabare describing how the water is collected.

Some families collect rainwater from the corrugated iron roofs of their homes, but this is not very common because guttering is expensive.

Fig 128   Storage tank, Kabare

Fig 129   Village scene, Kabare

ENQUIRY

1   Transfer the details from Fig 125 onto an outline map of England and Wales.
2   Label Newcastle-upon-Tyne, Liverpool, Manchester, Birmingham, Cardiff and London.
3   For each of the cities in question 2 writes down the name of the reservoir from which it gets most of its water.
4   How is getting water different in Kabare to getting it in England and Wales?
5   How do you think you would feel if you lived in Kabare and one of your jobs was to collect the water each day?

WATER 2.7

Building a Reservoir — Kielder Water in Northumberland

Fig 130 Kielder Water

In the early 1970s the Northumbrian Water Authority (NWA) predicted that the growing towns and cities of north-east England would need a more plentiful water supply. They decided to build a new reservoir at Kielder to meet this demand and began work in 1975. The dam was completed in 1982 and covers 1086 hectares.

The reservoir was made by drowning the North Tyne Valley between the villages of Kielder and Falstone. They chose Kielder because
- the valley had quite steep sides and was not too wide;
- the rocks were impermeable;
- few people lived there (58 families);
- most of the area was woodland;
- there were only a few farms.

The reservoir has brought a number of benefits. The whole of the North-East now has all the water it needs. Not only does the reservoir hold an enormous amount of water, but also, tunnels and aqueducts have been built to link the rivers Tyne, Wear and Tees.

The reservoir attracts visitors. Before it was built, about 6000 people visited the area each year to explore the countryside. While the dam was being built over 100 000 people a year went to the engineering works and Tower Knowe Information Centre, which explained how the dam was being constructed. The Forestry Commission has provided picnic sites, viewpoints, car parks, and nature trails.

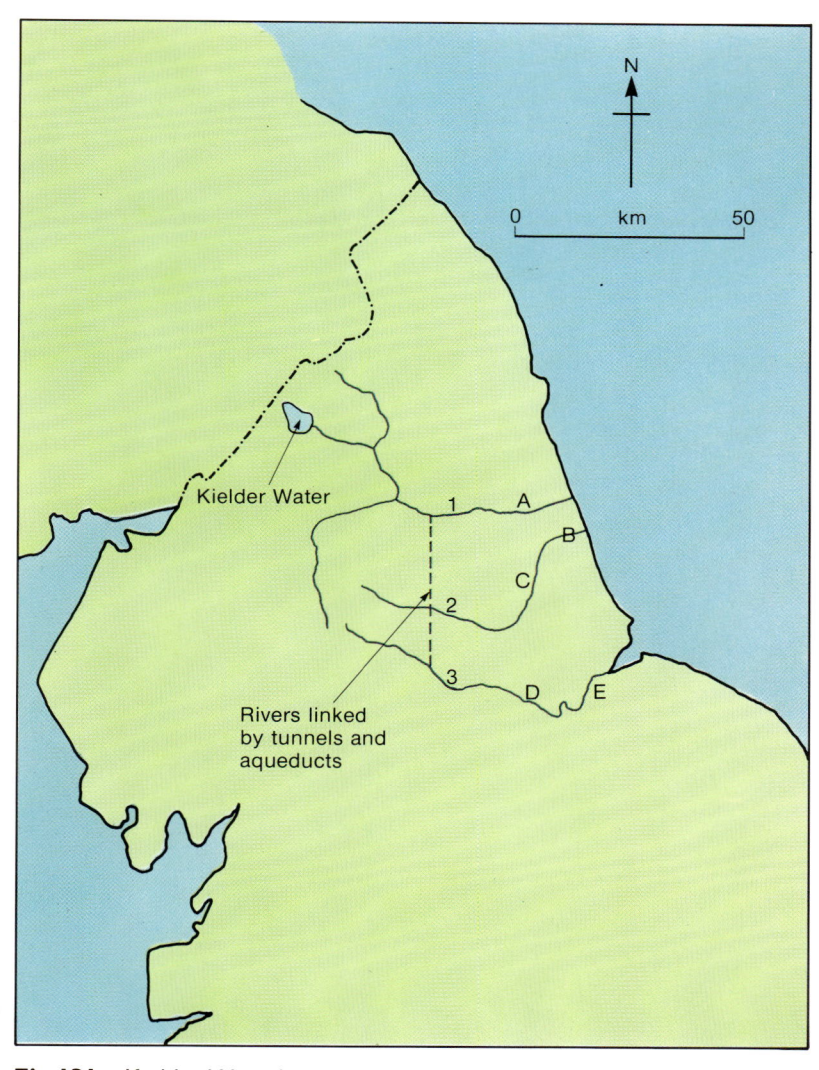

Fig 131 Kielder Water's supply reaction

In addition, the NWA has developed water sports like swimming, sailing, canoeing and fishing, and the area remains very popular.

However, there were also disadvantages. The NWA had to find the 58 families new homes. The woods and farms have been drowned forever. And it has emerged that the demand for water is actually much lower than predicted, so there was no need for such a big, expensive reservoir.

ENQUIRY

1 Make a copy of Fig 131. Finish it by using an atlas to help you name the towns (A) and (E) and the rivers (1) to (3).

2 Why did the Northumbrian Water Authority (NWA) decide to build Kielder Water?

3 Make a list of the reasons why Kielder was chosen as the site for the reservoir. For each of the reasons, explain why it was an advantage.

4 What might the following people have thought about the plan to build Kielder Water?
— the families who had to be moved;
— the owner of a factory in Newcastle-upon-Tyne;
— a local farmer;
— a keen windsurfer.

2.8 Assessment task: Rivers on OS maps

1 Give the four-figure grid references of:
a) Hardberry Hill; b) Hardberry Farm; and
c) Club Gill.

2 Work out the straight line distance in kilometres from the mile post (MP) in square 94 25 to the top of Hardberry Hill.

3 Draw a sketch map which shows the following detail:
   a) the 300, 400, 500 and 600 metre contour lines;
   b) all streams and rivers;
   c) all roads;
   d) all settlements.

4 Give the six-figure grid references of:
a) Woodside Farm; b) the telephone near Dent Bank; and c) the triangulation pillar WNW of Hudeshope Grains.

5 Compare the shape of the valley of Hudeshope Beck in 94 29 with the shape of the valley of the River Tees in 92 26.

6 Follow the route from the mile post (MP) at 946 253 north to Pikestone Brow (passing through Snaisgill, 955 270) and returning through Aukside, 942 268, to the Inn at 947 256. Describe the landscape and human features you would see.

7 Describe the site and situation of Middleton-in-Teesdale.

8 Use the sketch map you completed for question 3 for these tasks:
   a) Mark on the line of any watersheds that you can identify;
   b) Work out the stream order of Hudeshope Beck at 947 290;
   c) Label examples of any of the river features mentioned in Section 2.6 that you can identify.

9 Also on your sketch map, label one place where there is a clear relationship between human and physical features. Add a brief explanation.

10 Describe and explain the relationship between relief, settlements and roads on the map extract.

Scale 1 : 50 000   Ordnance Survey OS

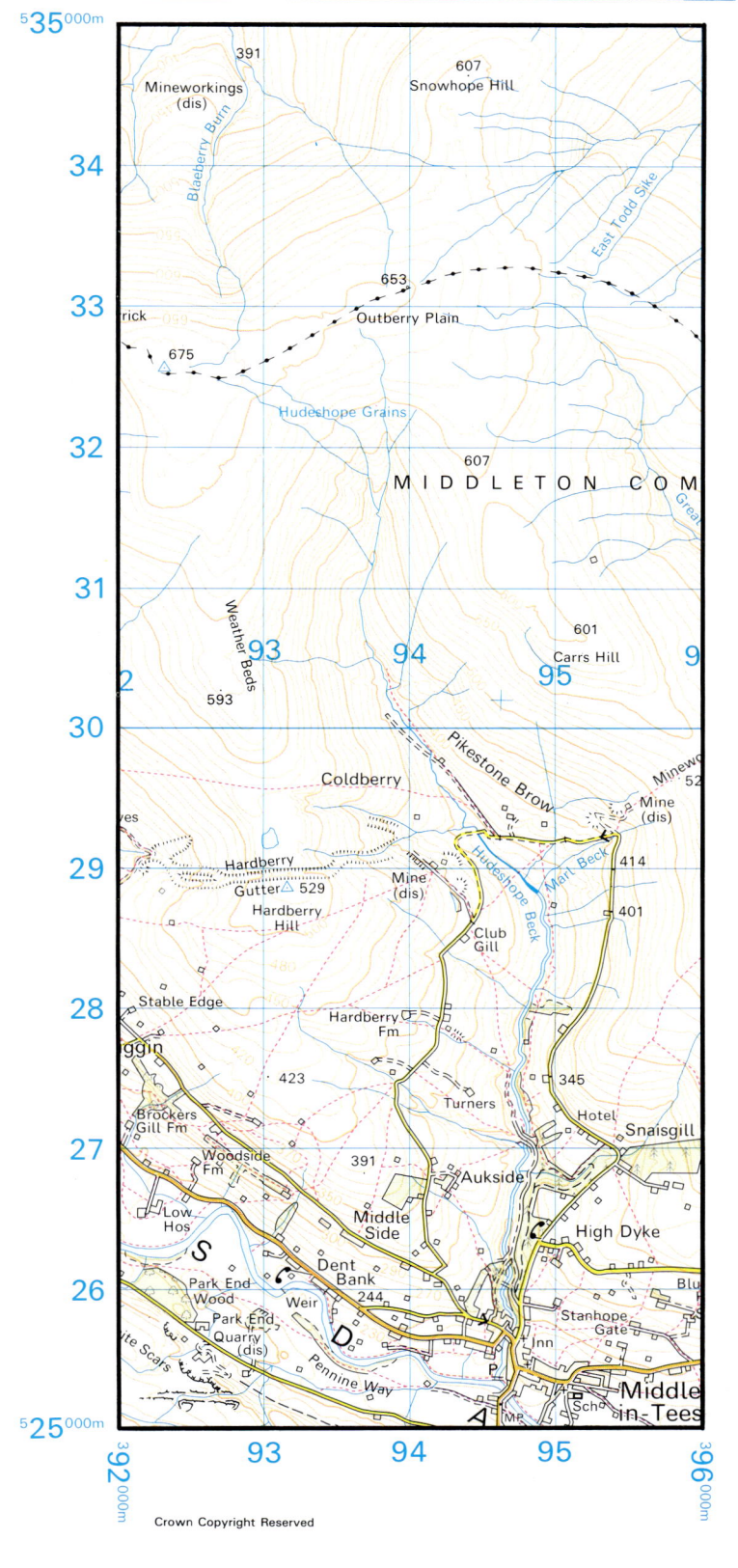

Fig 132 Ordnance Survey map, Middleton-in-Teesdale

ICE

3.1 What was the Ice Age?

Today, about 10 per cent of the earth is covered by ice. The main types of ice are: *ice sheets* and *ice caps* which are large areas of thick ice found in places like Antarctica, Greenland and Iceland (Fig 133); and *valley glaciers* which are slow moving rivers of ice (Fig 134).

However, in the Ice Age up to 30 per cent of the earth was covered by ice. It began about 2 million years ago and since then there have been at least four very cold periods — called glacials — when the ice has spread out from the North and South Poles and down from the mountains. In between the glacials there have been warmer periods — called interglacials — when the ice has melted. The last glacial began 70 000 years ago and ended 10 000 years ago.

The cause of these changes in the earth's climate is not known, but there are a number of ideas. Some scientists believe that changes in the power of the sun are the reason. Others think that the earth's orbit has changed so that sometimes we are further away from the sun than we used to be. Until we know its cause it will not be possible to say whether or not the Ice Age has ended.

During the cold periods the sea-level fell by up to 135 metres because so much of the earth's water was stored on the land as ice. One result of this fall in sea-level was that some countries which are now separated were joined by "land bridges". These land bridges made it easier for people to move from one region to another. The American Indians almost certainly walked across from Siberia when the Bering Straits was a land bridge. It is likely that the Aborigines reached Australia during the Ice Age when they could have travelled overland as far as Java or Kalimantan (Borneo) and then sailed across a much smaller stretch of water than there is today.

ENQUIRY

1   Name two countries in the northern hemisphere and one country and one continent in the southern hemisphere which have areas of permanent ice today.
2   What are the differences between an ice sheet and a valley glacier?
3   What do the following terms mean — Ice Age, glacial, interglacial, land bridge?
4   Why could we still be in the Ice Age?
5   How could the Ice Age have helped people from continental Europe get to the British Isles?
6   Mark onto an outline map of the British Isles:
— the limit of the last glaciation;
— the limit of the maximum (biggest) glaciation;
— the centres of ice dispersal – choose from Snowdonia, North West Highlands, Northern Ireland, Cumbrian Mountains, Southern Uplands, Pennines and Grampian Mountains;
— the place where you live.

Fig 133   Antarctica

ICE 3.1

Fig 136 The British Isles during the Ice Age

- – – limit of last glaciation
- —— limit of maximum glaciation
- A – G centres of ice dispersal
- → direction of ice flow

Fig 134 The Franz Josef Glacier, New Zealand

KEY
- main areas of permanent ice today
- extent of ice during the ice age
- land bridges

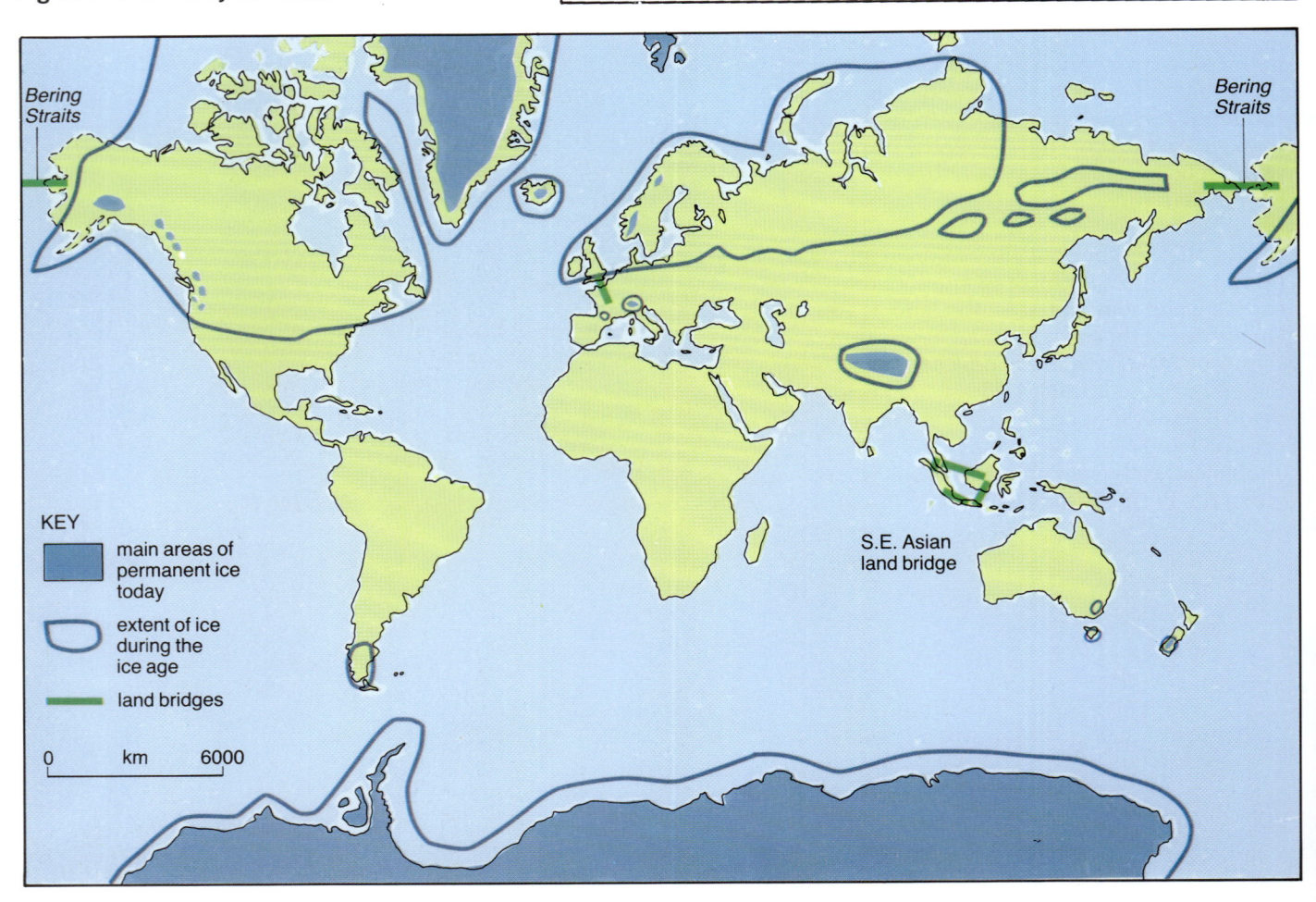

Bering Straits

S.E. Asian land bridge

Fig 135 Ice, past and present

The Glacier System

Experiments with markers have shown that glaciers move between 100 metres and 7 kilometres a year, and that the ice in the middle moves faster than the ice at the sides or base (Fig 137). As it moves deep cracks, known as "crevasses", open up in the ice because it is so brittle.

A fresh layer of snow has a lot of air trapped in between its ice crystals. In cold, glacial, conditions layers of snow pile up on top of each other and squeeze this air out. Last year's snow is called "névé" or "firn" and as it becomes more and more compressed by the layers above, it turns to ice. This build up of ice is known as "accumulation" and it is most likely to take place high in the mountains near the source of a glacier where temperatures are at their coldest. Very compressed ice looks blue (Fig 138).

When the surface of a glacier melts the process is known as "ablation". It is most likely to take place lower down the mountains where temperatures are warmer.

The balance between accumulation and ablation is very important. If accumulation is greater than ablation the glacier will move forward but if accumulation is less than ablation the glacier will retreat (Fig 139).

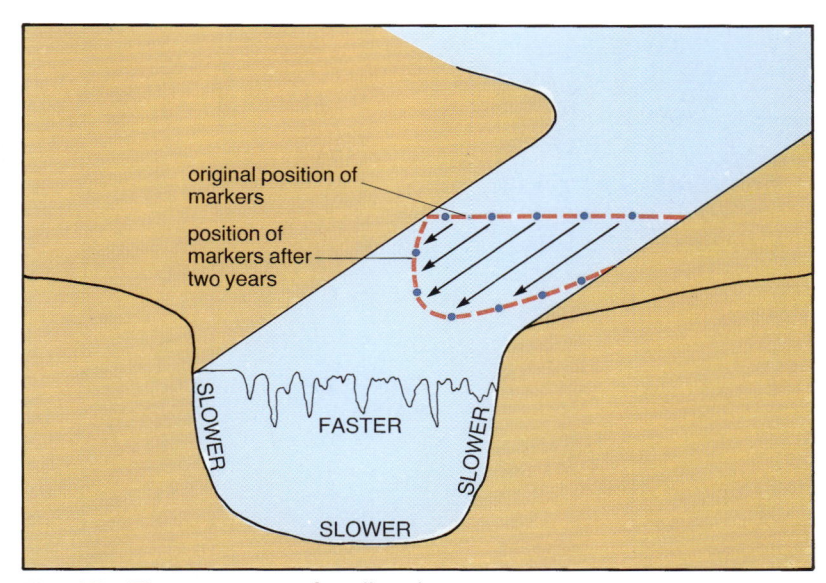

Fig 137 The movement of a valley glacier

Fig 138 Blue ice at the base of the Svartisan Glacier, Norway

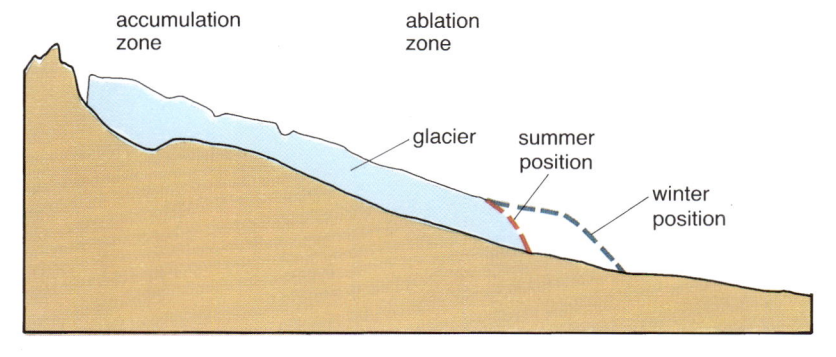

Fig 139 Accumulation and ablation zones

ENQUIRY

1 Describe an experiment to show how fast a glacier moves. What has been discovered?
2 Draw a column 10 cm tall and 1 cm wide. Mark off the top two centimetres and label them "this year's snow". Mark off the next ½ centimetres and label it "névé or firn – one year old". Mark off the next 3½ centimetres and label the bottom of this section "25 years old". Label the very bottom of the column "200 years old". Give your diagram the title "The accumulation of ice".
3 Explain why the balance between accumulation and ablation is very important. How does this balance change between summer and winter?

3.2 What do glaciers do to the land?

Features of Erosion

Corries

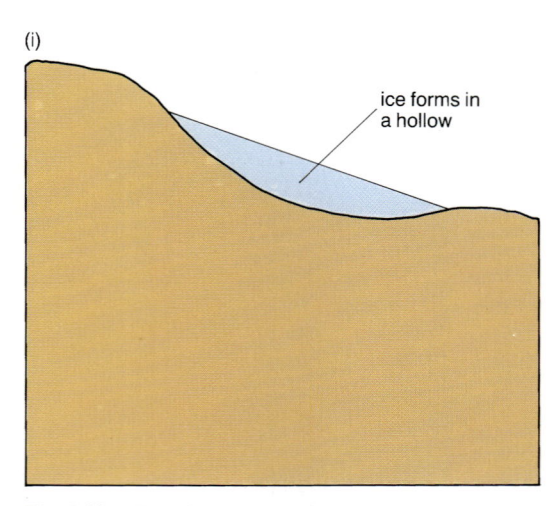

Fig 140 The formation of a corrie

Corries, which are also known as "cwms" or "cirques", are bowl-shaped hollows with a steep back wall and a shallow lip. They are found high in the mountains and are the place where a glacier begins. Small "corrie lakes" are often found in them.

Corries form when snow collects in a hollow and turns to ice. At first, the hollow is made bigger by freeze-thaw and by erosion as the ice slips. As the hollow becomes deeper, freeze-thaw and plucking become the main processes at work on the back wall while abrasion becomes the main process in the bowl of the corrie. The movement of the ice is rotational, and the lip forms because there is less erosion at the edge of the hollow than there is at the bottom of the hollow (Fig 140).

If two corries form back to back the land between them is worn away until only a knife-edge ridge is left, known as an "arête". If three or more corries form back to back the result is a pyramidal peak (Fig 141).

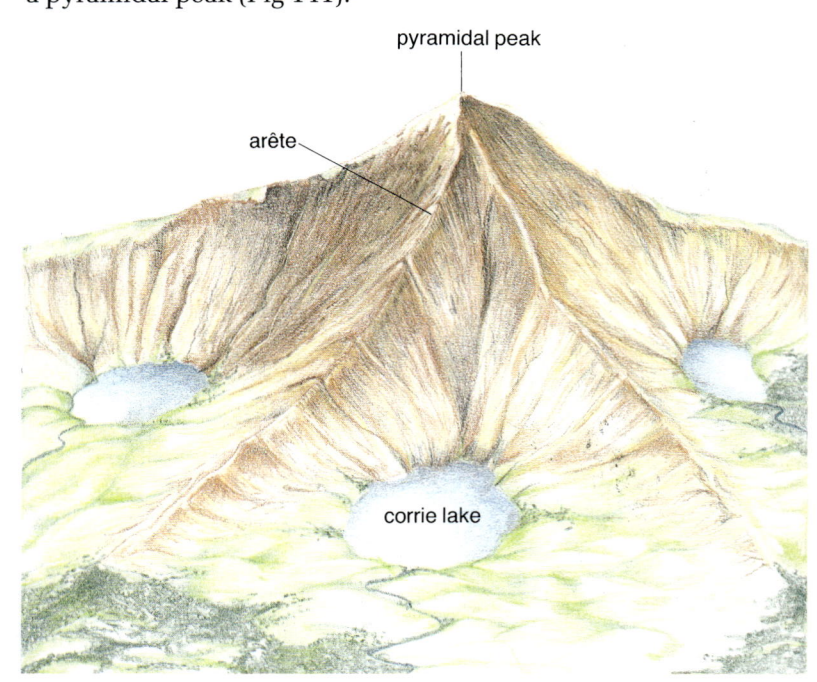

Fig 141 The formation of arêtes and pyramidal peaks

Fig 142 Corrie landscape, Cwmbychan, Snowdonia

U-shaped Valleys

River valleys in their upper sections are V-shaped or gorge-like (see page 52). However, glaciers change this shape into a U because they erode the sides as well as the bottom of the valley (Fig 143).

Truncated Spurs and Hanging Valleys

Ice is much less flexible than water. As a result, a valley glacier is unable to flow around **interlocking spurs** in the way that a river can. Instead, the erosive power of the glacier is concentrated on the spurs and eventually they are worn away leaving the valley with straight, smooth sides (Fig 144). The eroded spurs are known as **truncated spurs**.

Before glaciation a tributary valley would have joined a main valley at the same height (Fig 145 i). During glaciation the main valley would have been occupied by a large, powerful glacier which would have removed the interlocking spurs and eroded a deep valley (Fig 145 ii). The tributary valley would have been occupied by a small, less powerful glacier which would only have been able to erode a small valley. As a result, after glaciation the tributary valley finds itself hanging high above the main valley. If there is a stream in the **hanging valley** it plunges over the edge as a waterfall, depositing an alluvial fan on the main valley floor (Fig 145 iii).

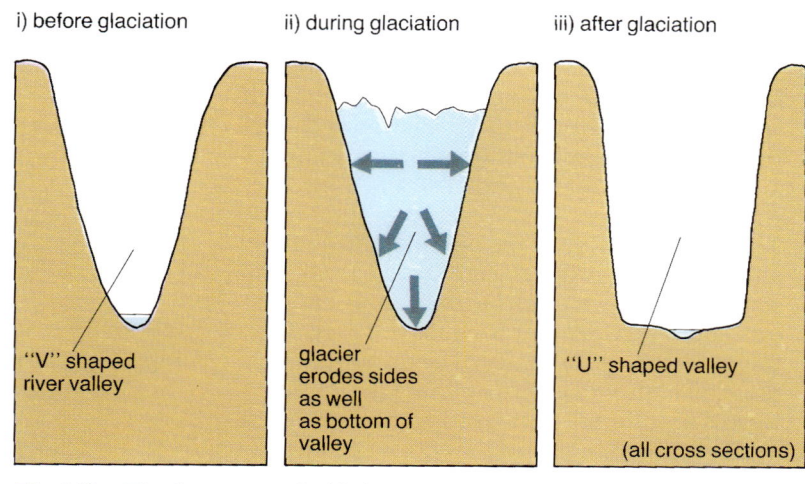

Fig 143 The formation of a U-shaped valley

i) before glaciation — "V" shaped river valley
ii) during glaciation — glacier erodes sides as well as bottom of valley
iii) after glaciation — "U" shaped valley
(all cross sections)

Fig 144 U-shaped valley, Newlands Beck, Lake District

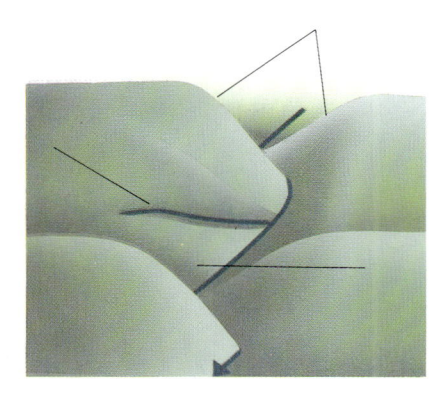

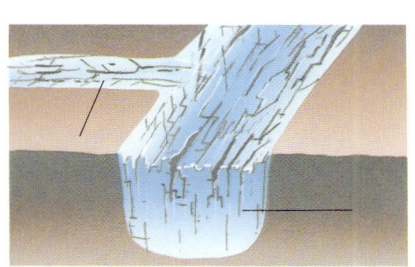

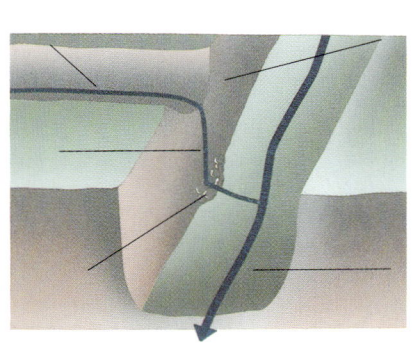

Fig 145 Truncated spurs and hanging valleys

Fig 146 Hanging valley, Yosemite National Park, California

Roches Moutonnées and Striations

When a glacier meets a hard outcrop of rock in the valley floor it may not be able to remove it completely. However, the glacier does change the outcrop's shape to form a feature known as a "roche moutonnée" (Figs 147 and 148).

The upstream side of the outcrop is smoothed and scratched as the glacier flows over it. The scratches, known as **striations**, are deeper at one end than the other because the rock fragments are ground down as they are dragged along. They are not only found on roches moutonnées but are a common feature of all glaciated rock surfaces (Figs 149 and 150).

The downstream side of the outcrop is plucked by the glacier as it moves over it. As a result, it remains steep and jagged.

Fig 147 The formation of a roche moutonnée

Fig 148 Roche moutonnée near Watendlath Tarn, Lake District

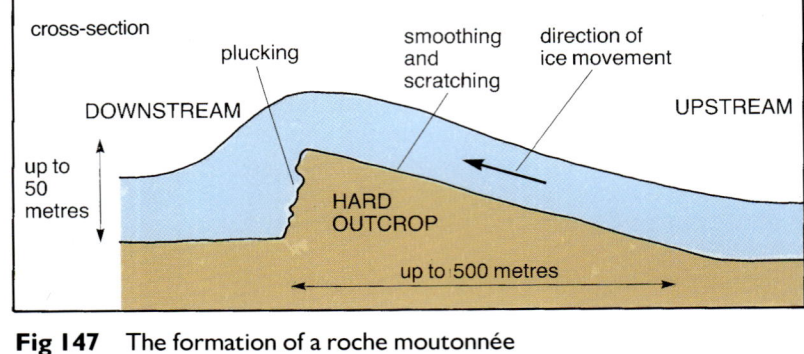

Fig 149 Cross-section of a striation

Fig 150 Striations on the shores of Wast Water, Lake District

Crag and Tail

If a hard outcrop of rock in the valley floor is in front of soft rock, a feature known as a **crag and tail** may form (Fig 151). The glacier is unable to erode the hard rock completely. Some of the ice flows over the top of the outcrop while the rest flows round the sides. The soft rock immediately behind the outcrop is therefore protected and it is not until the glacier joins up further downstream that it can start eroding its deep valley again.

Castle Rock in Edinburgh is a famous example of a crag and tail (Fig 152). The crag (the site of the castle) is a plug of hard volcanic rock. This has protected the tail of softer limestone and sandstone (the site of the Royal Mile).

Fig 151 The formation of a crag and tail

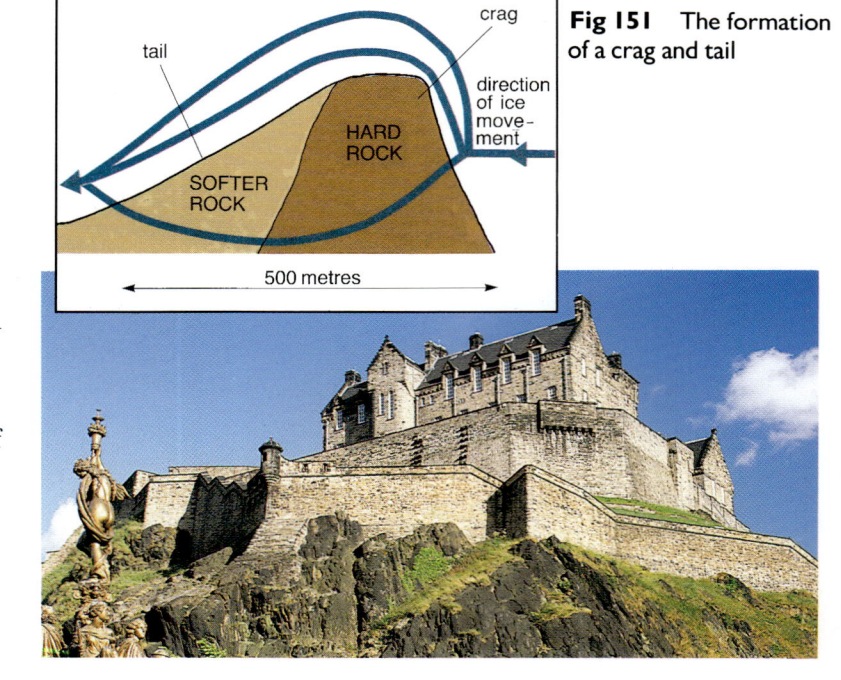

Fig 152 Crag and tail, Castle Rock, Edinburgh

Ribbon Lakes

The long, thin lakes found in many glaciated valleys are known as **ribbon lakes** (Fig 153). Streams flowing into these lakes deposit sediment which slowly builds up to form areas of flat land. This can be very important for farming in a region of otherwise steep slopes.

Fjords

Fjords are glaciated valleys which have worn down to the sea and which have been drowned by the rise in sea-level since the ice melted. They have steep sides and are very deep, although there is a shallow threshold at their mouth.

There are excellent examples of fjords on the west coast of Norway and the south-west coast of South Island, New Zealand (Figs 155 and 156). Both these places have high mountains very close to the sea. This helps to explain the steep slopes and the depth of the fjords because the glaciers would have been coming down from a great height and would therefore have been very powerful. Freeze-thaw is also thought to have been important because it would have shattered the rocks on the floor of the valley, leaving the glacier to bulldoze them away.

The shallow threshold is still something of a mystery. However, it probably marks the place at which the glacier ran out of energy, perhaps because it met the sea and began to melt.

Fig 153 Ribbon lake, Llyn Llydaw, Snowdonia

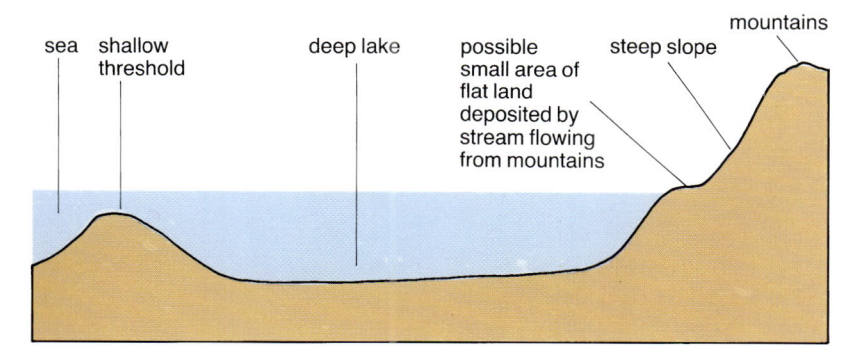

Fig 154 Cross-section of fjord

Fig 155 The Hardanger Fjord, Norway

Fig 156 Milford Sound, New Zealand

ICE 3.2

ENQUIRY

1. With the help of diagrams, describe a corrie and how it forms.
2. Draw and label the sketch of the corrie in Fig 141.
3. Explain why glaciated valleys are U-shaped and not V-shaped.
4. Copy the diagrams in Fig 145. Add your own labels to them to explain how truncated spurs and hanging valleys form.
5. Which process of glacial erosion is responsible for striations?
6. Why are striations useful for working out the direction of ice flow?
7. Describe and explain the formation of a roche moutonnée.
8. Describe and explain the formation of a crag and tail.
9. In what ways are a roche moutonnée and a crag and tail **a)** similar and **b)** different?
10. What is a ribbon lake? Why are most ribbon lakes becoming smaller?
11. Draw a large diagram of a fjord. Add labels to your diagram to explain what a fjord is and how it has formed.
12. Choose either the west coast of Norway or the south-west coast of South Island, New Zealand. Draw a sketch map of the fjord coastline of your chosen region and then copy and label the example shown in either Fig 155 or Fig 156.

Features of Glacial Deposition

Erratics

An **erratic** is a rock or boulder which has been moved by a glacier and deposited (dumped) in a place where it does not belong. The Norber Rocks (see page 22) are a famous example. Here, the sandstone boulders have been moved from Crummack Dale only a few kilometres away. Some erratics have been moved much longer distances, for example, rocks from Oslo in Norway can be found along the Yorkshire coast.

Fig 157 Terminal moraine, Franz Josef Glacier, New Zealand

Moraine

Moraine is a deposit of angular rock fragments. The different types of moraine are explained on page 27. When the ice melts the material is dumped and it forms low hills along the floor, sides, middle or at the front of the glacier. Fig 157 shows the terminal moraine at the snout of the Franz Josef Glacier in New Zealand, while Fig 158 shows terminal moraine left behind when the ice melted on the Isle of Skye in Scotland.

Fig 158 Terminal moraine, Glen Scaladal, Isle of Skye

Boulder Clay or Till

This is a mixture of angular rock fragments in a mass of clay (Fig 159). The clay is the result of rock fragments being ground down underneath the ice. Large areas of the British Isles have a covering of **boulder clay**. It is difficult to farm because it is heavy and sticky but in many parts of the country boulder clay soils have been successfully improved and have become areas of rich farmland e.g. the boulder clay soils of East Anglia.

In a number of places boulder clay forms a series of low hills known as **drumlins** (Figs 160 and 161). Exactly how they form is not fully understood but it is almost certain that they are deposited while the ice is still moving; this would help to account for their streamlined shape.

Fig 160 Drumlins

Fig 159 Boulder clay

Fig 161 Drumlins near Ribblesdale, North Yorkshire

Fluvioglacial Deposition

This means deposition by water, in particular streams and rivers; created by melting ice. Fluvioglacial deposits are mainly sand and gravel. The fragments are rounded by the process of attrition and because water is involved the deposits are often in layers.

Kames and Kame Terraces

A kame is a mixture of sand and gravel which has been deposited by meltwater in a crevasse. A kame terrace is a ridge of this material along the side of a valley which has been deposited by a meltwater lake at the edge of an ice sheet or glacier.

Eskers

When the ice begins to melt, streams often form within the ice itself. They deposit their load as long, winding ridges of sand and gravel known as eskers, as the ice retreats (Fig 162).

Fig 162 Esker, Hunstanton Park, Norfolk

Outwash Plains

The meltwater streams flowing away from the front of an ice sheet or the snout of a glacier deposit their load as a low flat plain. These can stretch for many kilometres and they are crossed by river channels which are constantly braiding (splitting) in order to regain energy. These deposits are naturally infertile.

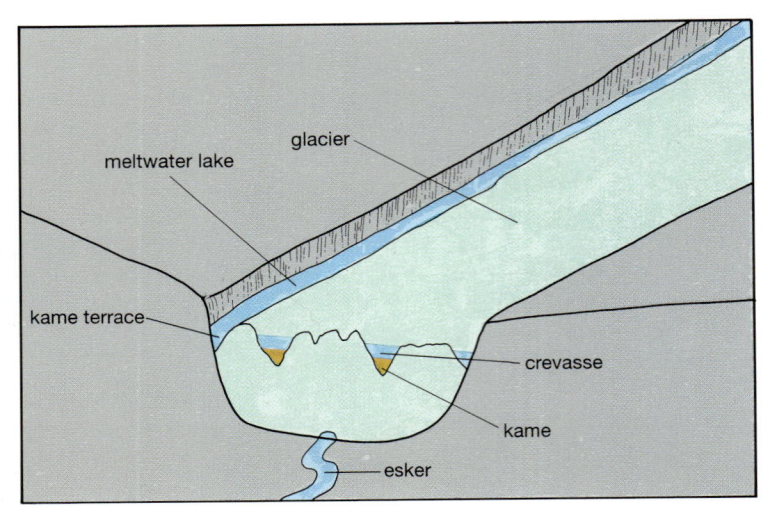

Fig 163 The formation of kames and eskers

Feature	Glacial or fluvioglacial?	Angular or rounded fragments?	Mixed or layered material?	Potential for farming – good or bad?
Erratic				
Moraine				
Boulder clay				
Kame or kame terrace				
Esker				
Outwash plain				

Fig 164 Glacial and fluvioglacial deposition: a summary table

ENQUIRY

1 With the aid of diagrams, describe and explain how drumlins form.
2 What is an esker and how do they form?
3 Copy and complete Fig 164. What does this tell us about the main differences between glacial and fluvioglacial deposits?
4 Make a sketch of Fig 165. Label as many features of glacial and fluvioglacial erosion and deposition as you can see.

Fig 165 Fox Glacier, New Zealand

3.3 How do we make use of glaciated uplands?

Snowdonia, North Wales

Glaciers have had a major effect on the landscape of North Wales. Snowdon, the highest mountain in England and Wales at 1085 metres, is an example of a pyramidal peak (Fig 166) and spectacular arêtes, corries and U-shaped valleys lead away from its summit (Fig 167). Glacial deposition has also left its mark; for example, many lakes have formed where valleys have been dammed or where the ground has been made uneven by moraine (Fig 168).

Snowdonia's harsh upland climate, steep slopes and poor soils mean that most of the land is only suitable for sheep farming (Fig 169). However, this type of farming is increasingly unprofitable and many hill farmers have been forced out of business in recent years. As the rural population has declined, services like shops and schools have closed down and this has made life even harder for the farmers who remain. Many disused farmhouses have been bought by outsiders as second homes, for use at the weekend and in the holidays, and this has also contributed to the break up of the community.

Fig 166   A pyramidal peak, Snowdon

Fig 167   Looking south east from the summit of Snowdon

Fig 168   Llyn y Gader

Fig 169   Hill sheep farm

In contrast, forestry has become increasingly important in the last 40 years. Conifers, such as the Sitka Spruce, can cope with the harsh conditions and now cover 20 per cent of the upland area. Many jobs have been created, both in the forests themselves and in wood-using industries. However, the long straight rows of identical trees have been criticised for spoiling the landscape (Fig 170); recently, attempts have been made to rectify this by introducing different species and by not planting all the way up to the top of a slope.

The region has a high rainfall but a low population: as a result, it has more water than it needs and for many years it has been supplying other parts of the country (see Section 2.7). Valleys have been dammed to create reservoirs and large areas of land have been lost. However, most of this land was of little value for farming and relatively few people have had to move their homes. The reservoirs have also created opportunities for leisure and recreation (Fig 171).

It has been possible to make use of the steep slopes and lakes to generate **hydroelectric power** (HEP). For example, Dinorwig (Fig 172) is the largest pumped storage scheme in the UK with a generating capacity of 1.5 gigawatts. During the day, when demand for electricity is high, water is allowed to drop from Marchlyn Mawr through tunnels inside the mountain to the power station on the shores of Llyn Peris. At night-time, when demand is low, it is pumped back up using electricity which would otherwise be wasted (see Fig 175, page 80).

Fig 170 Coniferous forest, Snowdonia

The most important economic activity in Snowdonia is tourism, with over 3 million visitors a year. Many of the attractions are related to the natural landscape, such as walking, rock climbing, and water sports, but

Fig 171 Watersports on Bala Lake

Fig 172 Dinorwig power station on the shores of Llyn Peris

there are also places of historical interest and many nearby beaches (Fig 173). Snowdon itself is climbed by over 2500 people a day in the summer while the Snowdon Mountain Railway takes a further 100 000 people to the summit every year (Fig 174).

Tourism brings employment and many millions of pounds to the region, but it also brings problems. Most of the jobs are seasonal. The roads can become very congested. Walkers stray off paths and damage fences, and as a result sheep can get out onto the roads. Footpaths became badly eroded; for example, there are six main footpaths to the summit of Snowdon and in the 1980s over £1.5 million was spent on reparing the damage caused by trampling.

A large part of the tourist area is within the Snowdonia National Park which was set up in 1949. The Park's task is to maintain the character of the area, while at the same time promoting its use and enjoyment by members of the public. With so many different types of land use, some of which conflict with each other, it faces difficult management decisions.

Fig 173 Dinas Beach, near Caernarfon

Fig 174 Snowdon Mountain Railway

ENQUIRY

1 With the help of an atlas, draw a sketch map of North Wales. Shade in the land above 200 metres. Mark on Porthmadog, Caernarfon, Bangor, Conwy, Lake Bala and Snowdon. Use the atlas to find out about the region's temperature and rainfall and add this information to your sketch map.

2 Draw a sketch of Fig 167. Label any features of glacial erosion which you can identify. Match it up with the OS map on page 80 and name the lake on the left hand side of the picture and the ridge in the foreground.

3 Use the OS map on page 80 to help you to draw and label a sketch map to explain how the Dinorwig power station works. What type of glacial feature is **a)** Marchlyn Mawr and **b)** Llyn Peris?

4 Draw and label a diagram to show how the different activities which take place in Snowdonia can come into conflict with each other, and with the environment.

5 Consider the following options open to the National Park Authority for managing Snowdon and the surrounding area. Decide on a rank order. Discuss the advantages and disadvantages of your "best" and "worst" options.
— to carry on with things as they are;
— to encourage visitors to be more careful by putting up warning signs and by clearly marking footpaths;
— to ask people at the start of the routes to the summit of Snowdon for a voluntary contribution towards the cost of maintaining the footpaths;
— to limit the number of people on the mountain e.g. by operating a permit system.

3.4 Assessment task: *Glacial features on OS Maps*

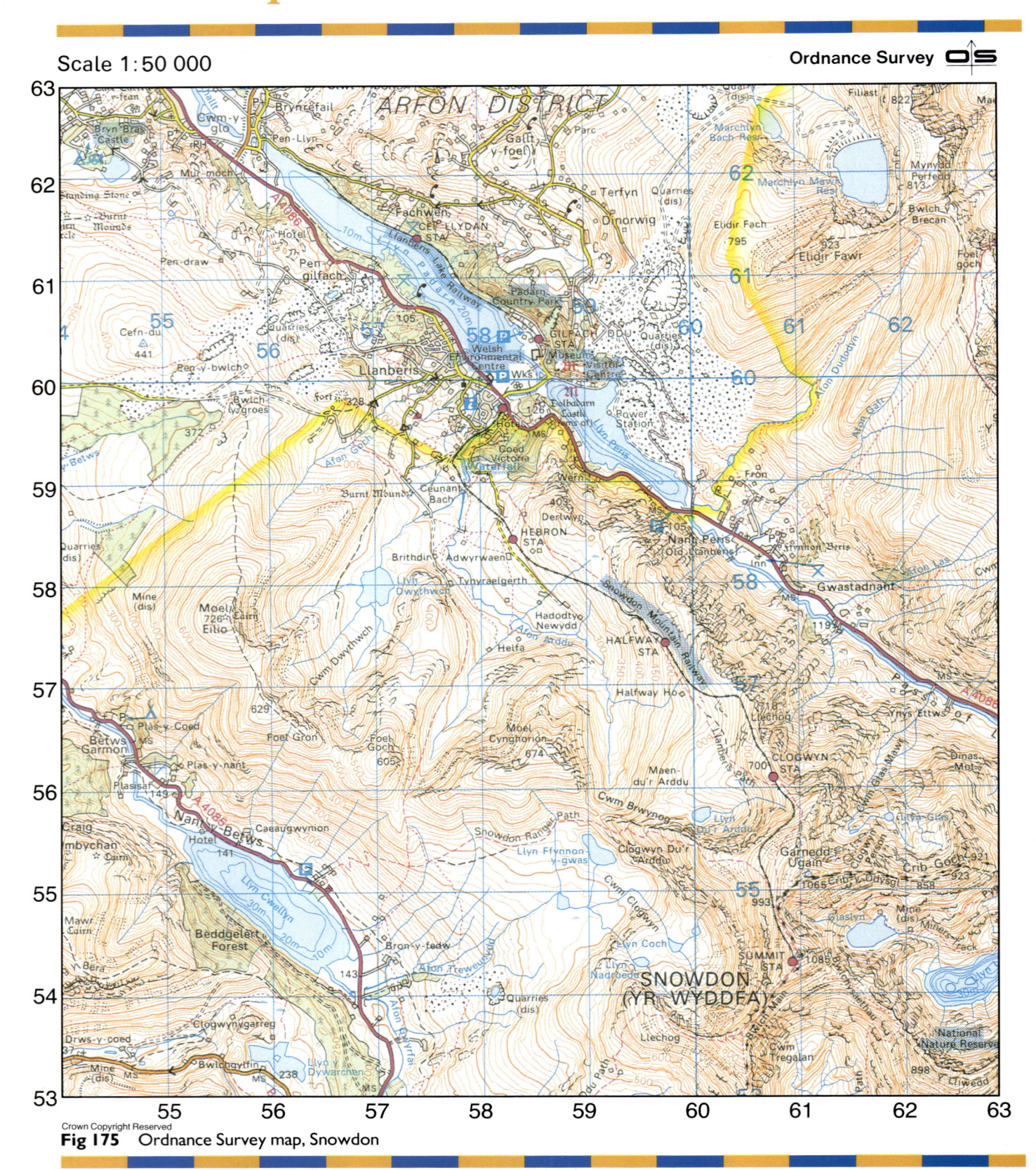

Scale 1:50 000

Ordnance Survey

Fig 175 Ordnance Survey map, Snowdon

Crown Copyright Reserved

ICE 3.4

ENQUIRY

1 Give the four-figure grid reference of :
a) Halfway Station (a station is a red dot); and **b)** Beddgelert Forest.

2 Work out the straight line distance in kilometres from the station at the summit of Snowdon to the station at the bottom of the mountain in square 58 59.

3 Draw a sketch map which shows the following detail:
   a) the 200, 400, 600, 800 and 1000 metre contour lines;
   b) all lakes, streams and rivers;
   c) all roads;
   d) all settlements.

4 Give the six-figure grid references of:
a) Hebron Station; and **b)** the Youth Hostel (red triangle) in the north of the map.

5 Follow the Snowdon Ranger Path from 564 551 to the summit of Snowdon: Describe how the steepness of the path changes.

6 Describe the landscape and human features you would see.

7 Describe the site and situation of the village of Nant Peris, 60 58.

8 Name and label onto the sketch map you completed for question 3 the glacial features found at the following grid references:
   a) Llyn Du'r Arddu 601 558;
   b) Crib-goch 620 551;
   c) Garnedd Ugain 611 551;
   d) Llyn Cwellyn 560 550;
   e) the valley at 547 547;
   f) the area of flat land between the main road and the lake in 56 54.
Explain how two of these features are formed.

9 Label onto your sketch map one place where there is a clear relationship between human and physical features. Add a brief explanation.

10 Describe and explain the relationship between relief, settlements and roads on the map extract.

CARBONIFEROUS LIMESTONE

4.1 Carboniferous Limestone — how should we manage a special landscape?

Carboniferous Limestone covers large areas of the British Isles (Fig 176). It is a hardy, grey shelly limestone and was deposited during the Lower Carboniferous period of geological time which lasted from 370 to 325 million years ago. It is made of the fossilised remains of crinoids, corals and brachiopods (Fig 177). It is pervious but not porous which means that water cannot soak into the rock but it can get through its regular pattern of joints (cracks) and bedding planes.

Carboniferous Limestone Scenery

Carboniferous Limestone forms a very special scenery known as **karst**. It is named after the limestone Karst district of the former Yugoslavia and is characterised by chemical weathering (see Section 1.4), its white/grey colour, its great hardness and its many joints and bedding planes.

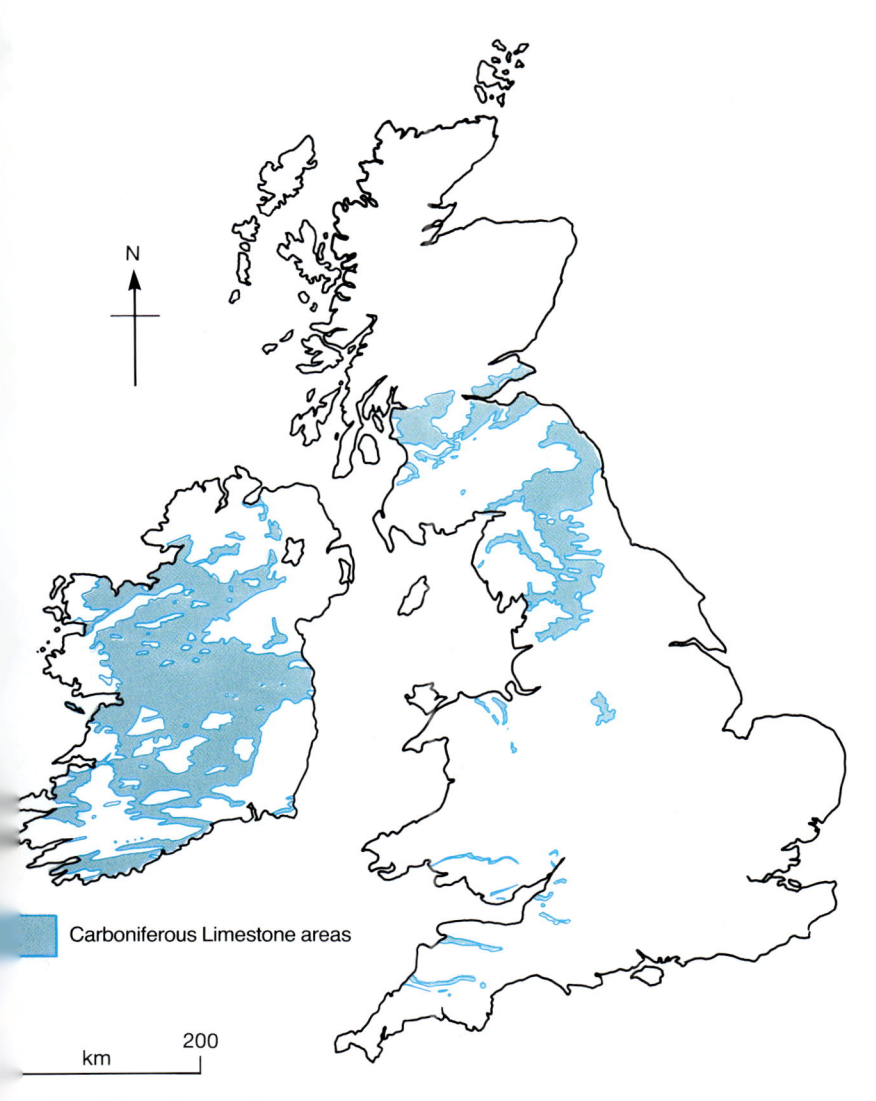

Fig 176 Carboniferous Limestone in the British Isles

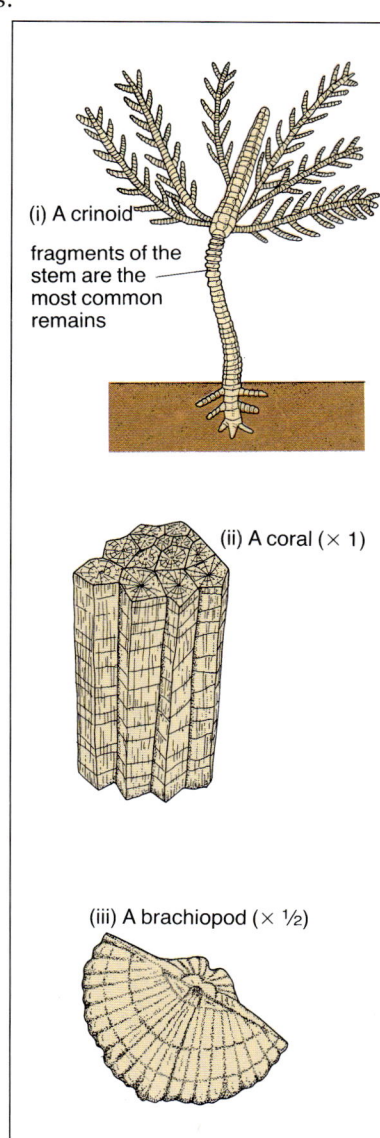

Fig 177 Fossils found in Carboniferous Limestone

(i) A crinoid — fragments of the stem are the most common remains

(ii) A coral (× 1)

(iii) A brachiopod (× ½)

CARBONIFEROUS LIMESTONE 4.1

The Yorkshire Dales National Park (Fig 178) has a large area of Carboniferous Limestone, and a walk of little more than 8 km takes you to examples of almost all the major features of this rock type (Fig 179).

Scars are steep, bare rock faces which are common in areas of Carboniferous Limestone because of its hardness and blocky structure. A good example is Gordale Scar; the rocks to the south of the scar are softer and more easily eroded and this helps to explain why it is such a prominent feature (Fig 180).

Surface water is unusual in areas of Carboniferous Limestone because it disappears down the joints and along the bedding planes. Chemical weathering makes the joints bigger and even streams go underground. The places where this happens are known as **swallow holes**, "sinks" or "pot-holes". The stream flowing southwards from Malham Tarn onto the limestone disappears down Water Sinks after only a few hundred metres (Fig 181).

The water carries on dissolving the limestone as it makes its way down through the system of joints and bedding planes. This can lead to the development of underground caverns. Stalagmites (which grow up from the floor), stalactites (which hang down from the roof) and pillars (which go from the floor to the roof) form when dripping water leaves behind tiny deposits of calcium carbonate (Fig 182).

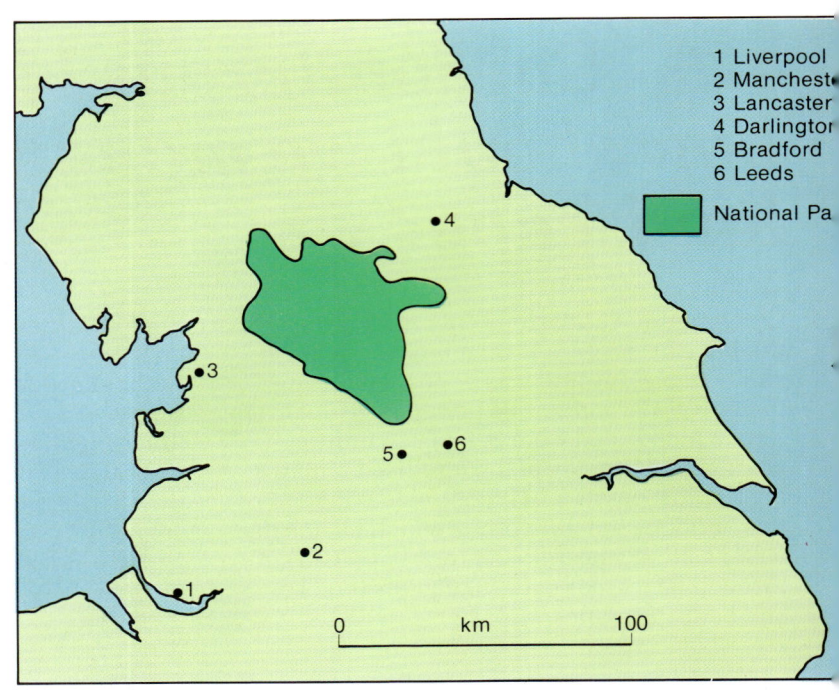

Fig 178 Yorkshire Dales National Park: location map

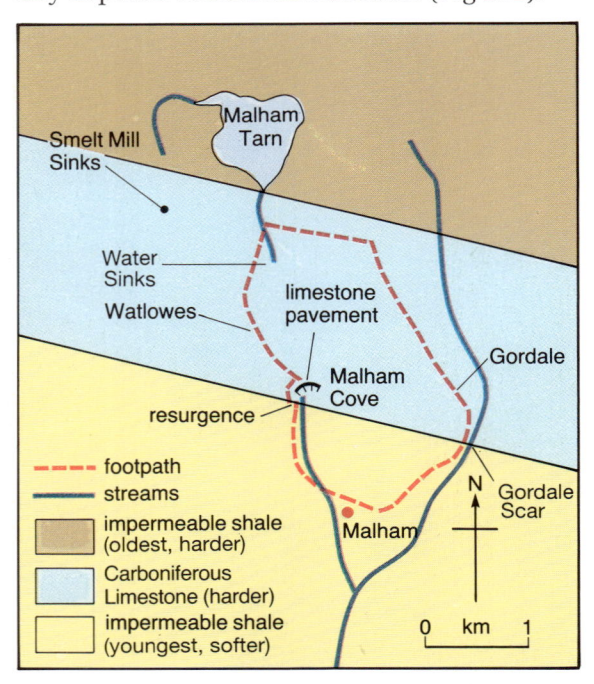

1 Liverpool
2 Manchester
3 Lancaster
4 Darlington
5 Bradford
6 Leeds

Fig 179 Malham: location map

Fig 180 Gordale Scar

CARBONIFEROUS LIMESTONE 4.1

Fig 181 Water sinks

Fig 182 Stalactites

Fig 183 Resurgence at Malham Cove

When the limestone meets an impermeable rock (one which water cannot get through) the water comes out as a spring, known as a **resurgence**. However, the water may have taken a long and complicated route underground. For example, the resurgence at the base of Malham Cove comes from Smelt Mill Sinks and not, as you might think, from Water Sinks (Fig 183).

With so little surface water **dry valleys** are a common feature of Carboniferous Limestone scenery. Watlowes (Fig 184) is an excellent example. It was probably eroded by a river when the climate was wetter or when the glaciers melted at the end of the Ice Age. It is an asymmetrical valley with the south facing (left hand) side of the valley being gentler than the north facing side. This is probably because freeze-thaw weathering at the end of the Ice Age was more severe on the south facing slope: it would have been warmed up by the sun during the day more than the north facing slope.

Fig 184 Watlowes

Gorges, like Gordale (Fig 185), are another impressive feature of this type of rock. The gorge might have formed when the roof of an underground cavern collapsed but it seems more likely that it formed, like Watlowes, when our climate was wetter, or when the glaciers melted.

There are many examples of **limestone pavements** in the Malham area but the most spectacular one is at the top of Malham Cove (Fig 186). The blocks are known as "clints" and the gaps are known as "grykes". The formation of limestone pavements is far from certain. Widening of the joints by chemical weathering is an important part of the process, but the bare rock surface is something of a mystery. One idea is that the soil was removed by a glacier. On the other hand, the soil may have been washed into the grykes by rain when the climate was wetter. A third idea is that deforestation by early settlers led to soil erosion which left the surface bare.

Soils on Carboniferous Limestone are naturally very thin: this is because so much of the rock is dissolved away, and because the water disappears so quickly, leaving the surface dry. The upland climate of the Malham area makes soil formation even more difficult.

In turn, the poor soils make life very difficult for vegetation. There are often large areas of almost bare rock and plants usually only grow if there are cracks or crevices where soil can collect and where they are sheltered. The grykes of limestone pavements are the home of species of lime-loving plants such as hart's tongue fern and wood sorrel. However, people are now placing such fragile environments at risk, not only by quarrying but also by careless discarding of litter (Fig 187).

The Malham area attracts an estimated one million visitors a year. Some come to enjoy the scenery while others come for more adventurous activities such as pot-holing and rock climbing. Most of these visitors are day trippers; some stay in one of the small guest houses or in the youth hostel; and school parties account for over 30 000 of the officially registered visitors. Malham itself is a small village with a population of 120, most of whom make their living from the tourist industry.

However, such a large number of people poses a threat to the environment. Traffic congestion, litter and damage to footpaths are

Fig 185 Gordale

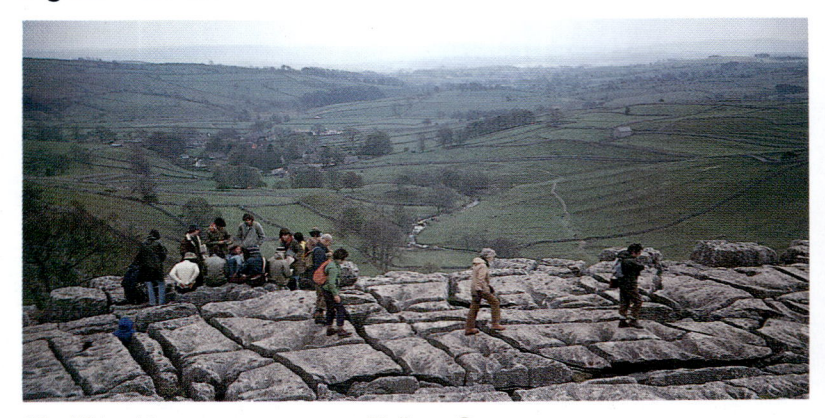

Fig 186 Limestone pavement, Malham Cove

Fig 187 Litter in a gryke

CARBONIFEROUS LIMESTONE 4.1

all a problem. Places of outstanding natural beauty, such as Malham Cove (Fig 188), are at risk, as well as sites of scientific interest, such as the wetland with the rare plant and animal communities which surrounds Malham Tarn (Fig 189).

It is an important area for hill farming (Fig 190), and the limestone is quarried for roads, buildings and rock gardens (Fig 191). These activities have an impact on the natural environment and they often come into conflict with leisure and recreation (Fig 192). It all adds up to a difficult management problem.

Fig 188 Malham Cove

Fig 189 Malham Tarn

Fig 190 Hill farming in the Yorkshire Dales

Fig 191 Quarrying

Fig 192 Countryside Commission notice near Malham Tarn

4.2 Assessment task: The Malham area of North Yorkshire

1 Look at the photographs in Section 4.1 and give one piece of evidence for erosion, one for transportation and one for deposition.

2 Draw a sketch of Watlowes (Fig 184). Add labels to identify the processes of weathering and the processes of erosion which have been important to its formation.

3 Describe and explain the formation of two other features of Carboniferous Limestone scenery.

4 Describe and explain the importance of **a)** chemical weathering and **b)** erosion by rivers to the formation of Carboniferous Limestome scenery.

5 Study Fig 194. Where do you think the following problems are most likely to occur in the Malham area and why: car parking; litter; and damage to footpaths (more than 200 people per hour indicates a serious problem)? Which two sites of special interest are most likely to be damaged and why?

6 Copy and complete Fig 193 by ticking the factors which help to explain each feature's formation and/or by writing in the appropriate information. Which factors are the most important in helping to account for the special scenery found in Carboniferous Limestone areas, and why?

7 The ice in this part of the British Isles melted 10 000 years ago. Is the natural rate of landscape change likely to be greater or lesser in the next 10 000 years? Explain your answer.

8 Draw and label a diagram to show how the different activities which take place in the Malham area can come into conflict with each other, and with the environment.

9 Why is the Carboniferous Limestone environment so fragile, and what do you think the consequences are for human activity?

10 Consider the following list of six options open to the National Park Authority for managing the Malham area. Decide on a rank order. Discuss the advantages and disadvantages of your "best" and "worst" option.
- to carry on with things as they are;
- to encourage visitors to be more careful in sensitive areas by putting up warning signs and by clearly marking footpaths;
- to restrict access to certain sites by operating a permit system;
- to increase the number of wardens looking after the area;
- to leave control and management to the local farmers;
- to increase the number of car parks and amenities for visitors in Malham village.

Feature \ Factor	Rock hardness	Rock structure	Chemical weathering	Glaciation/ Periglaciation	Other factors (please state)
Scars					
Swallow holes					
Caves, stalagmites etc.					
Resurgences					
Dry valleys/ gorges					
Limestone pavements					

Fig 193 Checklist for limestone scenery

CARBONIFEROUS LIMESTONE 4.2

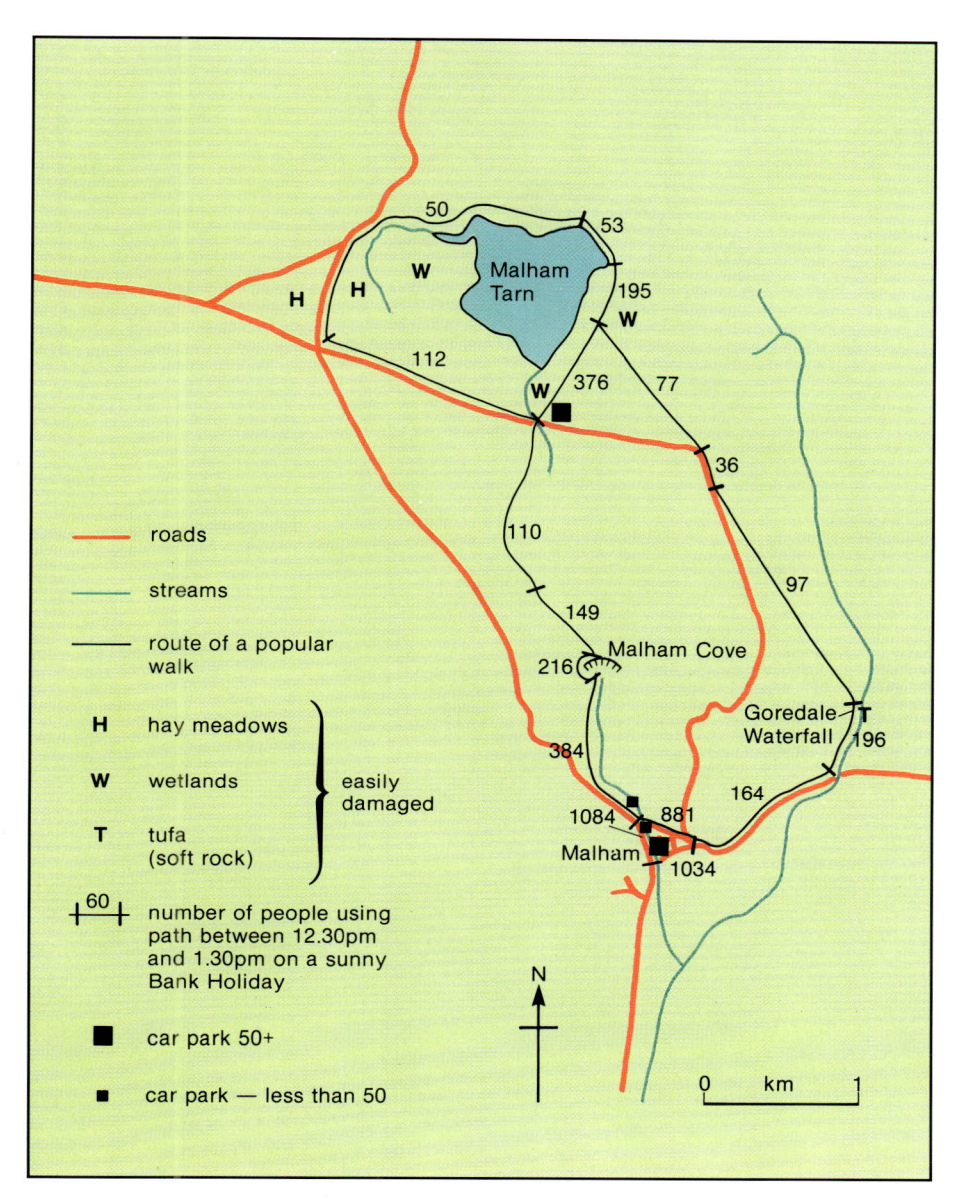

Fig 194 Malham impact map

SEA

5.1 What does the sea do to the land?

Features of Coastal Erosion

Cliffs and Wave-cut Platforms

Cliffs form where the sea meets the land. The power of the sea is concentrated between the high and low water marks. A notch develops and when the overhang becomes too heavy the land above collapses. In this way the cliff retreats. The area of rock in front of the cliff (which used to be underneath the cliff before it was eroded backwards) is known as the **wave-cut platform** (Fig 195).

The shape of a cliff depends on a number of things. Hard rock usually results in steep cliffs because it is less likely to collapse than soft rock. If the rocks are tilting towards the sea, the cliff will slope at the same angle. If the sea is eroding quickly, a steep cliff is likely but if it is eroding slowly the result is usually a gentle cliff because wind and rain have time to wear it down. Some different cliff shapes — profiles — are shown in Fig 196.

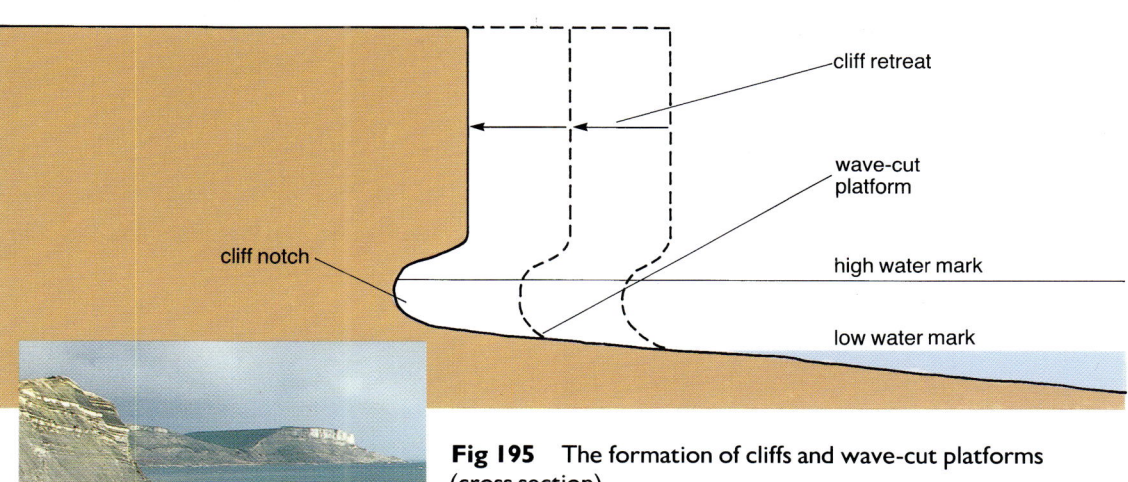

Fig 195 The formation of cliffs and wave-cut platforms (cross section)

Fig 196 Cliff profiles

(i) steep cliffs with wave-cut platforms: the Kimmeridge Ledges, Dorset

(ii) gentle profile in soft rocks being slowly eroded

(iii) profile controlled by dip and strata

Bays and Headlands

A **bay** is an opening in the coastline. A **headland** is a stretch of high land jutting out into the sea. They form because the sea erodes some parts of a coastline more quickly than others, usually because some of the rocks are softer than others (Fig 197 and 198).

Although headlands are areas of hard rock, they are very exposed to wave attack and eventually they are eroded away. This happens in stages (Fig 199). Firstly, the sea picks on an area of weakness, such as a band of soft rock or a crack, and erodes a cave. Holes in the roof of the cave are known as "blowholes" or "gloups" and the sea shoots out of these at high tide. If the cave wears right through the headland, the result is a natural arch. The roof of the arch is then attacked — from below by the sea and from above by weathering — until it becomes so thin that it collapses. This leaves a pillar of rock known as a "stack". The stack itself is then undercut by the sea. It eventually collapses leaving a stump which can only be seen at low tide.

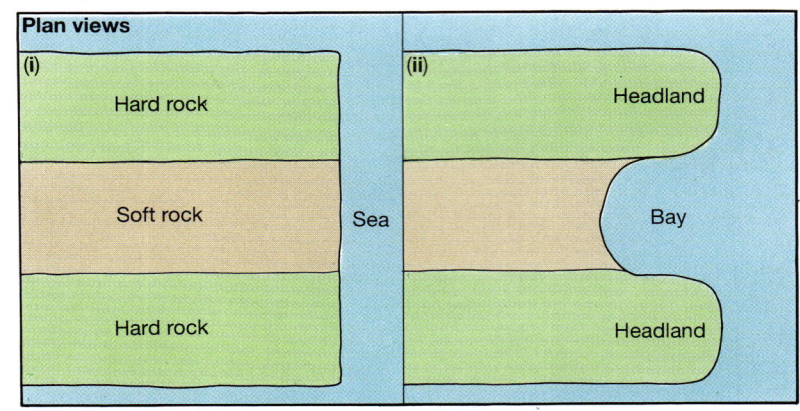

Fig 197   The formation of bays and headlands

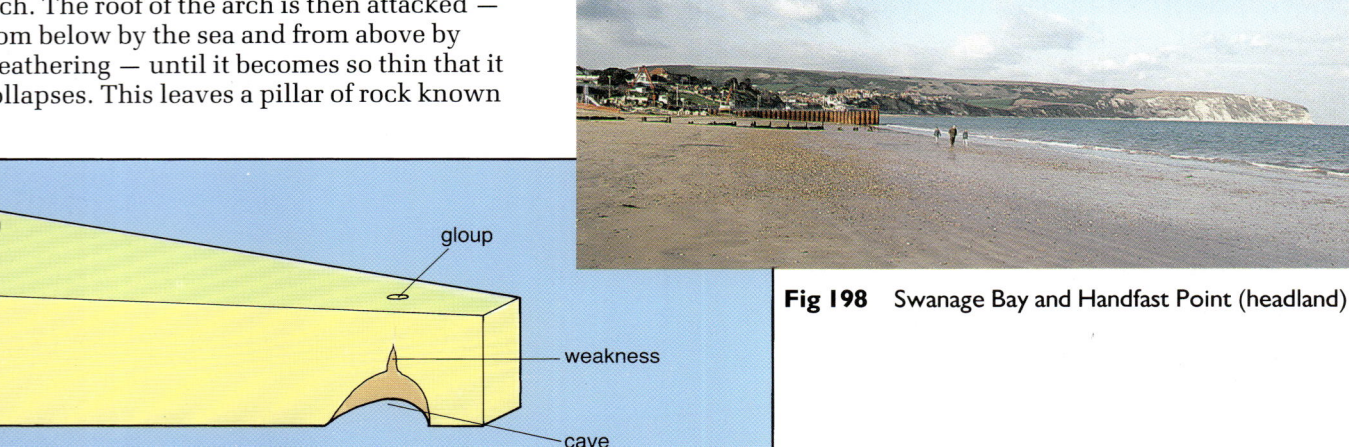

Fig 198   Swanage Bay and Handfast Point (headland)

Fig 199   The erosion of a headland

SEA 5.1

ENQUIRY

1. Draw and label a diagram to explain the formation of cliffs and wave-cut platforms.
2. Sketch the cliffs shown in Fig 196. For each cliff, add a label to explain its shape.
3. Add labels to Fig 197 to explain the formation of bays and headlands.
4. Make a sketch of Fig 200. Identify the following features: cliff, wave-cut platform, cave, natural arch and stack. Label these features and add brief definitions/explanations.

Fig 200 Old Harry Rocks, near Swanage

Features of Coastal Deposition

Beaches

The character of a beach depends on a number of things. The rocks which make up the coastline are important. For example, soft sandstone cliffs are likely to produce a sandy beach, whereas hard, granite cliffs are likely to produce a pebble beach. Tides, currents and processes such as longshore drift are also significant.

The larger the material, the steeper the slope of the beach. As a result pebble beaches are usually steeper than sandy beaches.

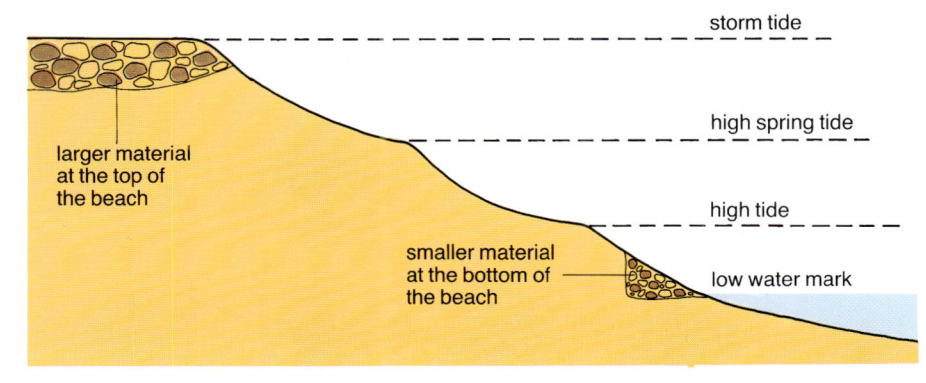

Fig 201 Cross-section of a typical beach

Also, material at the top of a beach tends to be larger than material at the bottom. This is because the more powerful swash is able to throw all material up the beach but the less powerful backwash can only carry the smaller material down the beach.

Beaches often have different levels because of the different heights of the tide (Fig 200). The shape of a beach is constantly being changed by the sea and the level may vary during the course of a year.

Fig 202   Measuring beach levels

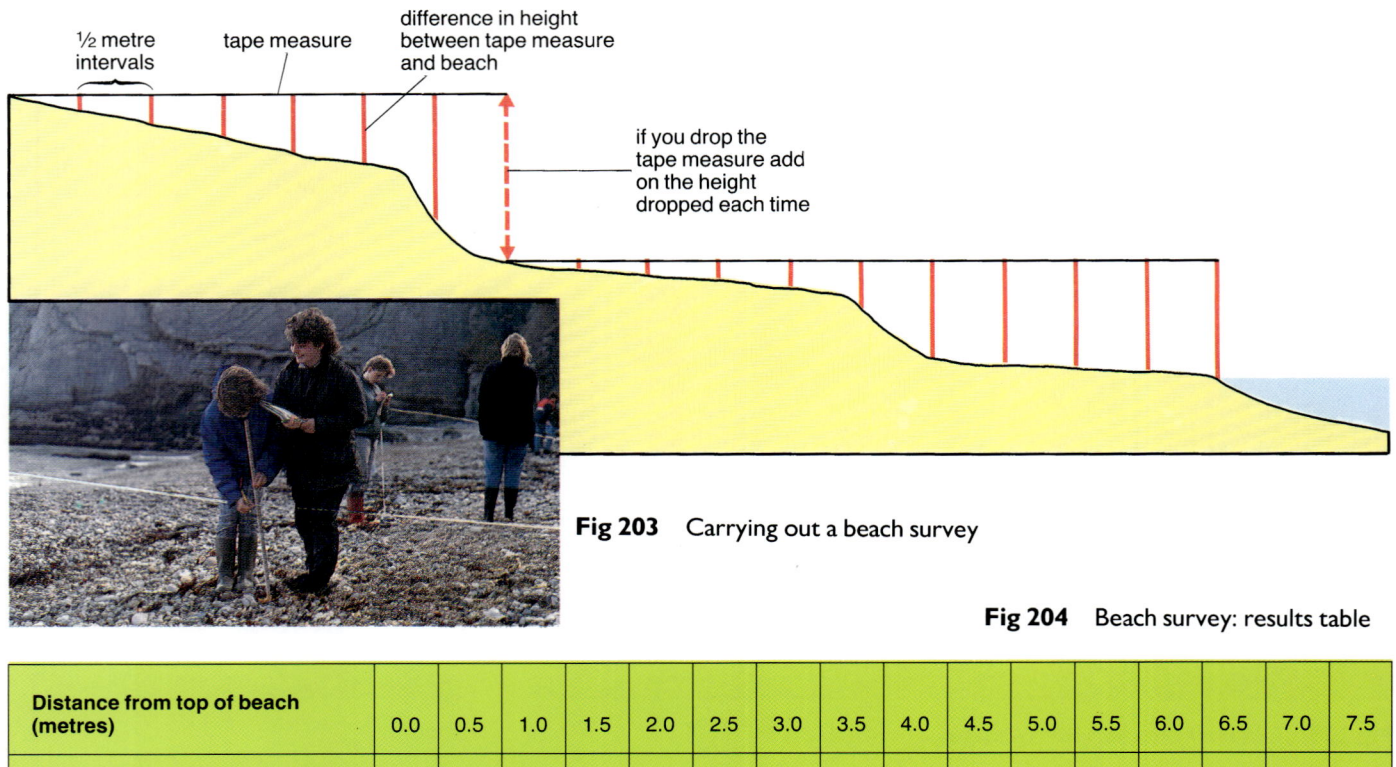

Fig 203   Carrying out a beach survey

Fig 204   Beach survey: results table

Distance from top of beach (metres)	0.0	0.5	1.0	1.5	2.0	2.5	3.0	3.5	4.0	4.5	5.0	5.5	6.0	6.5	7.0	7.5
Height from measure to beach (metres)																
Long axis of pebble (centimetres)																

Beach surveys
Beaches offer many opportunities for simple geographical projects. The following survey tests two ideas at the same time.

Aim
To test the ideas that:
1 Beaches have different levels.
2 Material at the top of a beach is larger than the material at the bottom.

Equipment
Tape measure. Metre rule. Clinometer or spirit level.

Method

1 Stretch the tape measure across the beach. Use the clinometer or spirit level to keep the tape measure horizontal. Measure the difference in height between the tape measure and the surface of the beach at ½ metre intervals. If the beach falls away steeply it will be necessary to drop the tape measure and to add on the height dropped each time (Fig 202).
2 Measure the long axis of the pebble directly underneath the tape measure at each ½ metre interval.
3 Record your results in a table like the one in Fig 204.

Presentation of Results

1 Plot the beach levels as a line graph (Fig 205). Choose a suitable scale for the horizontal line which represents the width of the beach. The vertical scale allows you to show the difference in height between the tape measure and the surface of the beach. When you join up the points, the beach levels should stand out.

2 Plot pebble size as a scatter graph (Fig 206). The horizontal axis represents the width of the beach and the vertical axis represents the diameter of the pebbles. If there is a trend, it should stand out.

Interpretation and Explanation

- Were there different beach levels? If yes, how many and why? If no, why not?
- Was material at the top of the beach larger than material at the bottom? If yes, why? If no, why not?

Conclusions

Briefly return to the ideas at the start of the survey. Have they been proved or disproved for the beach you have been studying?

Limitations

Did you have any problems when you carried out the survey? Were there any local factors which might limit the value of your results e.g. disturbance of the beach by tourists?

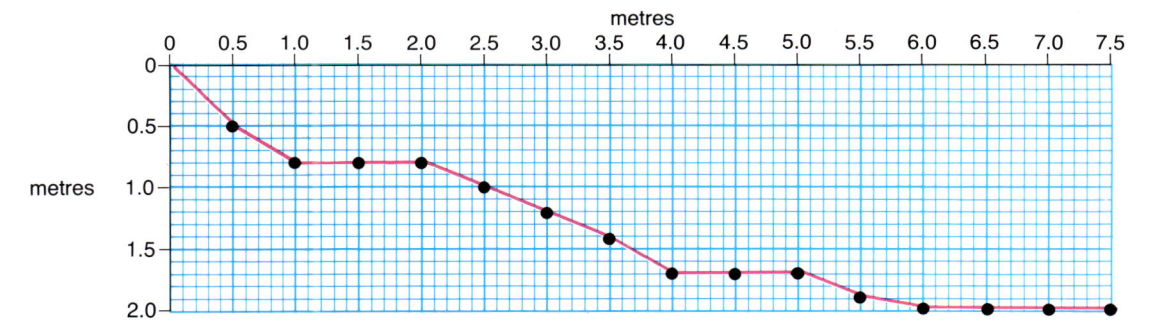

Fig 205 Plotting beach levels

Fig 206 Plotting pebble size

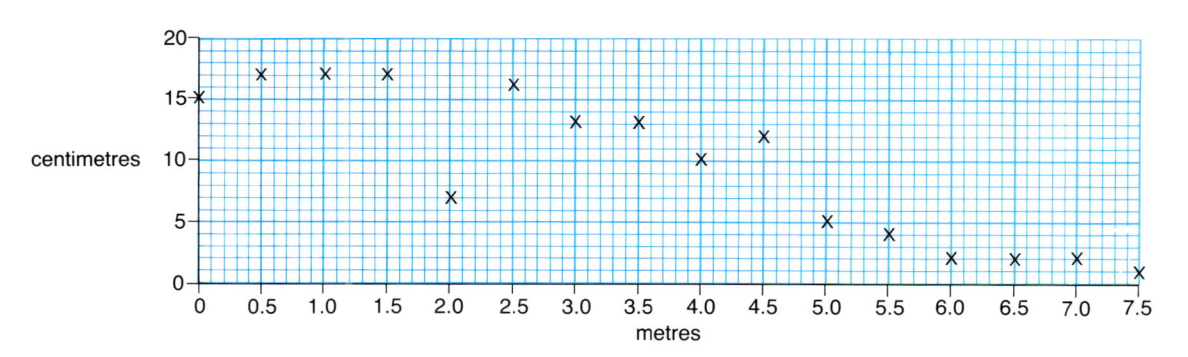

Spits

A **spit** is a beach which has grown out into the sea (Fig 207). Spits form only in certain conditions: if longshore drift is taking place; if there is a sudden change in the direction of the coastline; if the sea is shallow; and if currents are gentle.

Many spits are curved at one end by the action of the waves. These are known as "hooked spits", and Dawlish Warren in Devon is an example (Fig 208).

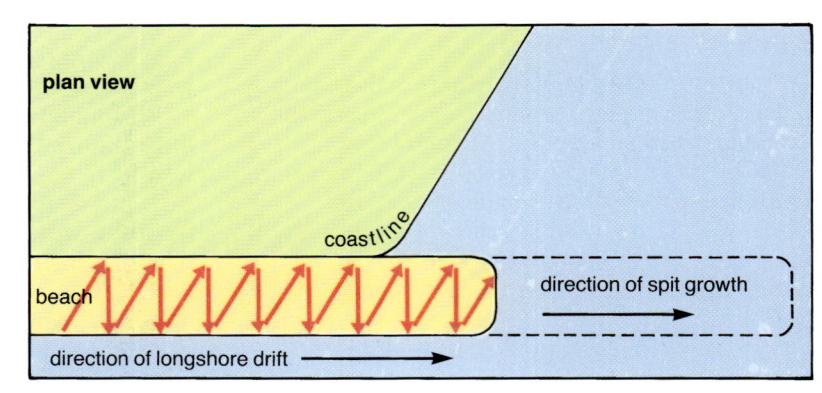

Fig 207 The formation of a spit

Fig 208 A hooked spit, Dawlish Warren, Devon

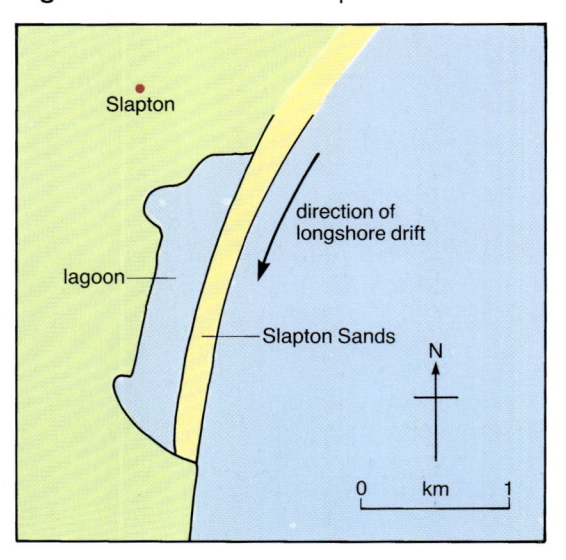

Fig 209 A bay bar or barrier beach, Slapton Sands, Devon

Sometimes, a spit may grow right across the mouth of a bay. These spits are known as "bay bars" or barrier beaches, and Slapton Sands in Devon is an example (Fig 209).

Occasionally, a spit may link the mainland to an island. Such a spit is known as a tombolo and a famous example is Chesil Beach which links the Dorset mainland to the Isle of Portland (Fig 210).

Fig 210 A tombolo, Chesil Beach, Dorset

ENQUIRY

1. Four things are necessary for spits to form — what are they and why are they important?
2. Draw and label a sketch or sketch map of each of the different types of spit mentioned in this section.

5.2 How do changes in sea-level affect the coastline?

The world's sea-level has changed a great deal in the last two million years, mainly because of the Ice Age (see pages 67-68). This had a big effect on the coastline.

A Rise in Sea-level

A **fjord** is a glaciated valley which has been drowned by a rise in sea-level (see page 73). A **ria** is a V-shaped river valley which has been drowned by a rise in sea-level. Rias are therefore found in places where hills and river valleys which have not been glaciated meet the sea. There are many examples of rias in Devon and Cornwall, such as Salcombe (Fig 211).

If hills and valleys running parallel to the coastline are drowned by a rise in sea-level the result is a series of long, thin islands separated from the shore by narrow strips of water (Fig 212). This is known as a **Dalmatian coastline** and is named after a region in former Yugoslavia.

If the mouth of a lowland river valley is drowned by a rise in sea-level an estuary is formed. Estuaries are tidal and the deposition of silt can lead to the build up of mud flats (Fig 213).

Fig 211 A ria, Salcombe, Devon

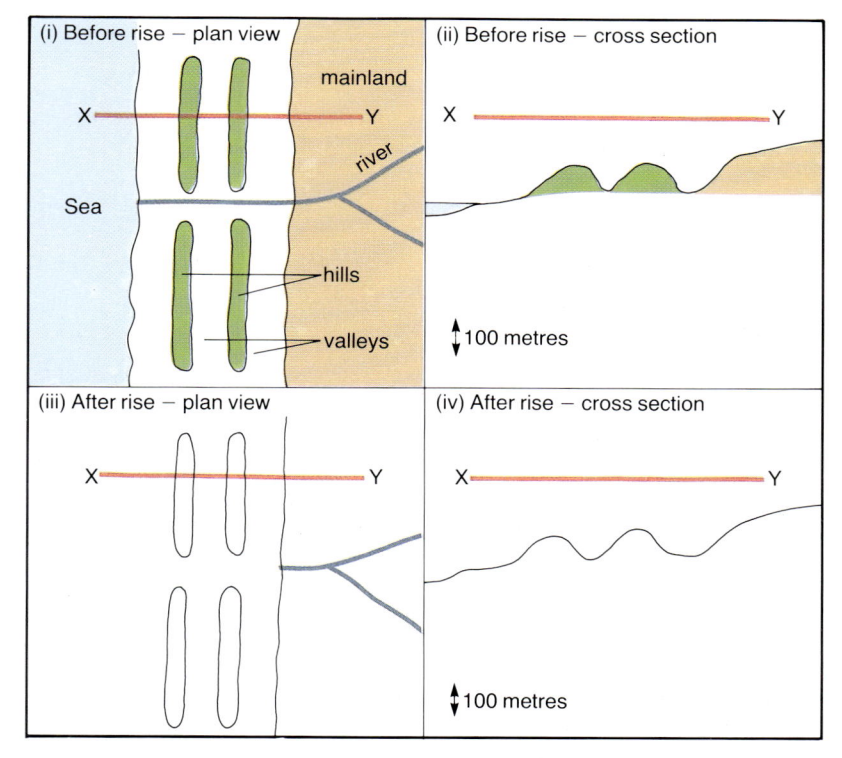

Fig 212 The formation of a Dalmatian coastline

Fig 213 The Thames Estuary

A Fall in Sea-level

There are some parts of the British Isles where the coastline shows evidence of a fall, rather than a rise, in sea-level. This is because of a process called isostatic readjustment. During glacial periods the ice sheets were thickest in the north of the country. The tremendous weight of these ice sheets caused the land to sink slightly into the earth's crust. When the ice sheets melted this enormous weight was removed and the land was able to recover, rising at the rate of a few millimetres a year. This recovery is still happening (Fig 214) and as a result there are places where the coastline is at a higher level than it was immediately after the Ice Age.

Isostatic readjustment has made the north and the south of the country behave very much like the two ends of a see-saw. When the north sank, the south rose. Now that the north is rising the south is sinking and this is adding to the flood risk which has made schemes such as the Thames Barrage necessary (Fig 215).

A relative fall in sea-level can leave cliffs, beaches, wave-cut platforms and even stacks and stumps stranded above the present high water mark. Raised beaches and old cliff lines are a common feature on the west coast of Scotland (Fig 216).

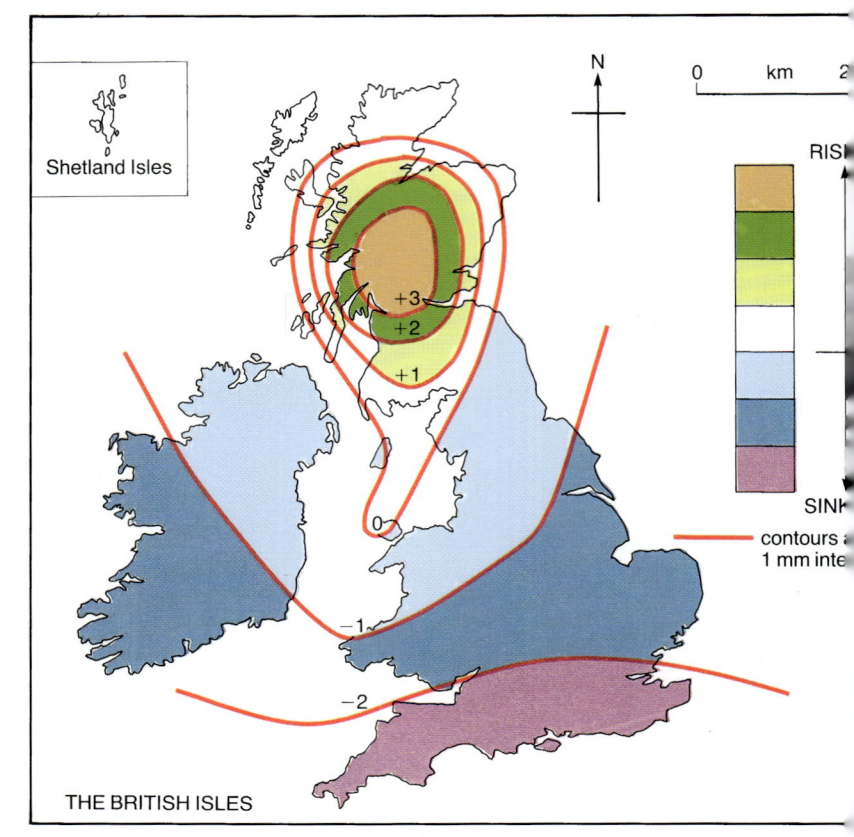

Fig 214 Present-day changes in sea-level

Fig 215 The Thames Barrage

Fig 216 Raised beach with old cliff line

ENQUIRY

1. In what ways do you think the cross section of a ria will be different to that of a fjord, and why?
2. Compare a ria with an estuary under the following headings — appearance; formation; other features.
3. Re-draw Fig 212 to show what this section of coastline would look like after a 100 metre rise in sea-level.
4. Draw a sketch map of the former Yugoslavian coastline from Rijeka in the north to Dubrovnik in the south. Add a suitable title and a brief explanation.
5. Make a sketch of Fig 216. Identify and label the raised beach and the old cliff line.
6. Explain what is meant by the process of isostatic readjustment. How has this affected the coastline of the British Isles?

5.3 How do we cope with the threat from the sea?

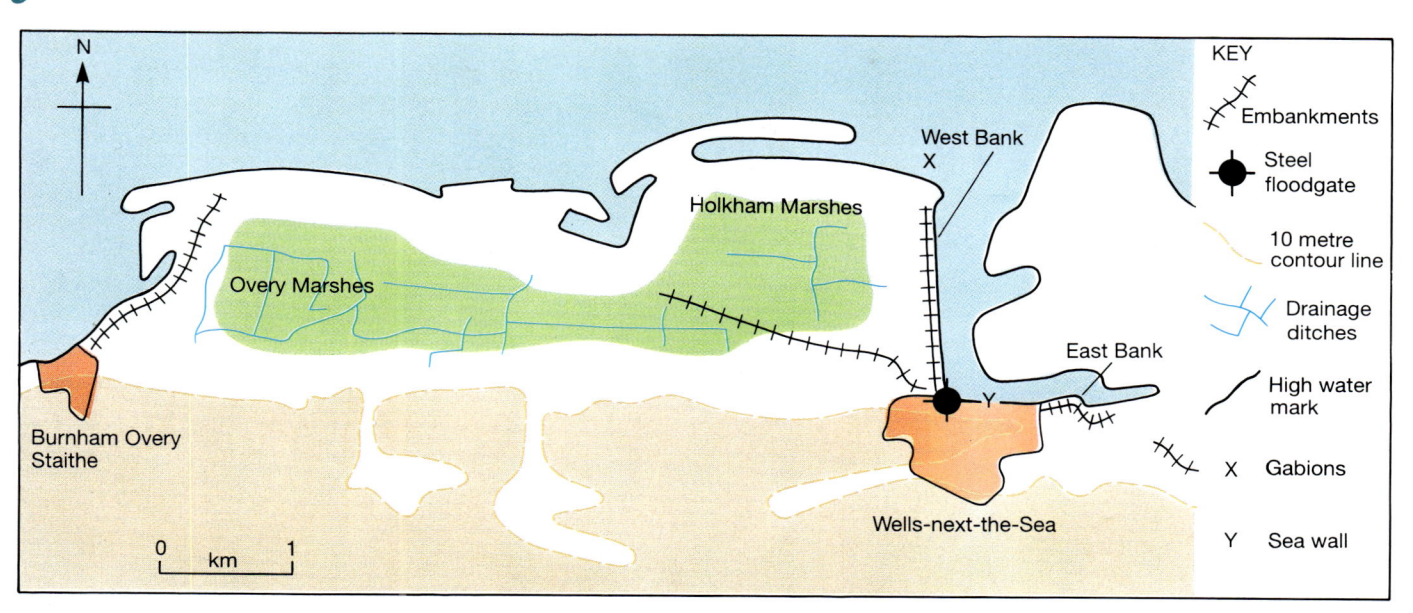

Fig 217 Wells-next-the-Sea: sketch map

Fig 218 Holkham Marshes

The people of Wells-next-the-Sea on the north Norfolk coast have had a long battle with the sea. They began to reclaim land in the early eighteenth century by building embankments and digging drainage ditches. In this way the Holkham and Overy Marshes were brought into use (Figs 217 and 218).

However, on a number of occasions the sea has overwhelmed the coastal defences. On 31 January 1953 gale force winds and a very high tide resulted in a surge of water which broke through the West Bank and flooded the reclaimed land.

On 12 January 1978 similar conditions resulted in the West Bank being washed away in two places. The marshes were flooded, together with shops, offices and houses in Wells itself.

This time, it was decided not just to repair the defences but to improve them, and a scheme costing more than £1.5 million was carried out. The West Bank was re-built to a height of 6.5 metres and the seaward side was strengthened with concrete facing blocks (Fig 219). The East Bank and the flood wall in Wells were improved. Gabions (steel cages filled with rocks) were put in place to protect the sand dunes at the northern end of the West Bank (Fig 220). Most ingeniously of all, a steel floodgate which can be rolled across the road (Fig 221) was built to protect the low-lying part of the town.

These new defences have been put to the test on a number of occasions and so far they have worked. However, gale force winds and excessively high tides could produce conditions which would destroy them.

ENQUIRY

1 On a copy of Fig 217 shade in the land to the north of the 10 metre contour line (the land most likely to flood if the defences fail).
2 Look at Fig 218 (i) and (ii). What different types of land use are shown at Holkham Marshes?
3 Make a sketch of the Wells West Bank, Fig 219, and label the following in their correct place: Holkham Marshes; mud flats; footpath; road; concrete facing blocks.
4 As well as gabions, how else is the coastline being protected in Fig 220?
5 The steel floodgate is designed to protect the eastern side of Wells. In which compass direction was the camera pointing when the photograph in Fig 221 (ii) was taken?
6 Make a summary list of all the ways in which Wells tries to protect itself against the sea.

Fig 219 Wells West Bank

Fig 220 Gabions protecting sand dunes, Wells West Bank

Fig 221 Steel floodgates, Wells

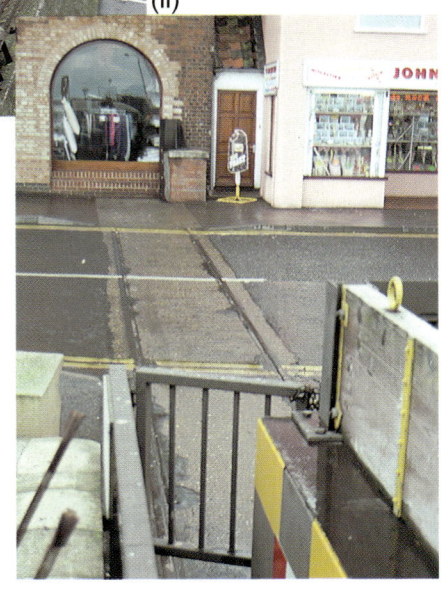

5.4 How do we sometimes make things worse?

There are many ways in which we make use of the coastline; for example, we build ports, we create tourist resorts, and we reclaim land for farming. We also spend millions of pounds protecting the coastline from the sea. However, sometimes we make things worse, quite unintentionally.

An example of this relates to the movement of material along a coastline. It has been discovered that longshore drift and currents do not usually move sediment for hundreds of kilometres. Instead, movement takes place in a number of **sediment cells** (Fig 222). Each cell has a source region which provides the material (e.g. a cliff or a sand bank); a transfer zone (the stretch of coastline along which the material moves); and a sink region where the material is deposited (e.g. a spit or a sand bank).

The movement of material along the East Anglian coastline consists of a whole series of these sediment cells (Fig 223) and it has been discovered that there are at least two ways in which we have unintentionally upset this natural system.

Firstly, various sections of the coast suffer from erosion because the cliffs are made of soft rock and the region is exposed to the full force of north-easterly winds blowing across the North sea. Where buildings and farmland are threatened, these cliffs have been protected — at Sidestrand the cliffs are shielded by a sea wall, gabions, revetments and groynes (Figs 224 and 225). However, cliffs are often the source region for a sediment cell and when we protect them from erosion we cut off the supply of material to beaches in the transfer zone. As a result these beaches become smaller or disappear completely and this leaves the coastline exposed to wave attack.

Secondly, dredging is necessary to keep open the port of Harwich. However, this part of the coastline is a tranfer zone, so removing material from it means that the coast to the south loses out. The beaches near Clacton have already become steeper and narrower and this is increasing the risk of coastal erosion and threatening the tourist industry.

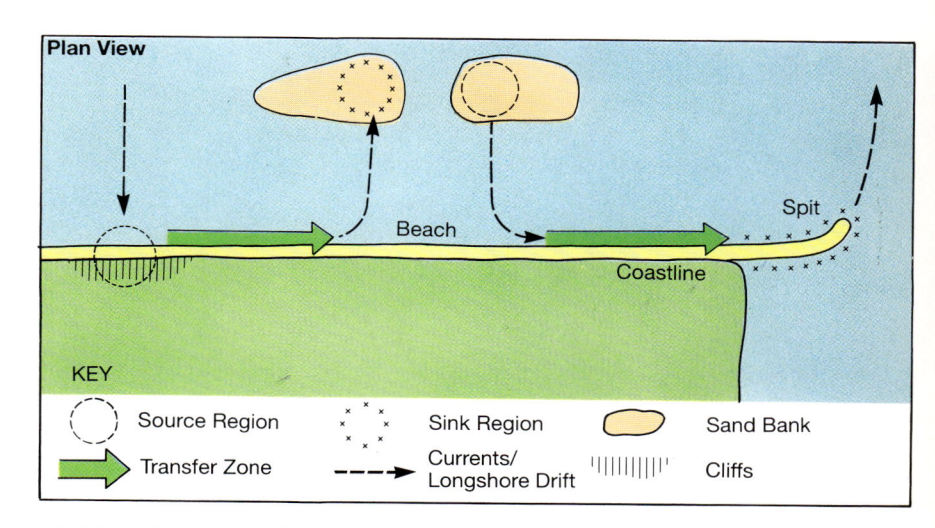

Fig 222 Sediment cells

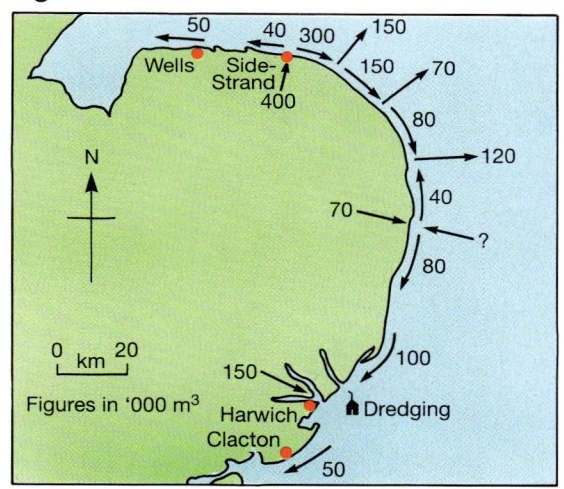

Fig 223 Sediment cells on the East Anglian coastline

Fig 224 Cliff protection, sea wall and gabions, Sidestrand

Fig 225 Cliff protection, revetments and groynes, Sidestrand

These examples teach us important lessons about how we should manage the coastline. If protecting cliffs in one place threatens beaches and land in another, it is necessary to decide what is best for the whole coastline and not just for a part of it. If dredging takes place in a transfer zone the material should be dumped further along the coastline so that the rest of the sediment cell is kept supplied with material. Similarly, if sand is dredged for the building industry it should come from a sink region, rather than a source region or a transfer zone.

ENQUIRY

1 Copy Figure 226 (i) and complete it by adding labels to explain what is meant by the terms source region, transfer zone and sink region.
2 Copy Figure 226 (ii) and complete it by adding labels to explain what has happened.
3 Copy Figure (iii) and complete it by adding labels to explain what has happened.
4 How much material do the dredgers remove each year to keep the port of Harwich open? Can you think of possible reasons why this material is not dumped further along the coastline?
5 Look at Fig 227. Would you protect the cliffs at A? Would you dredge for building sand at B or C? Would you dredge at D to keep the port open? In each case explain your answer.
6 Briefly explain how we have upset natural processes on the East Anglian coastline.

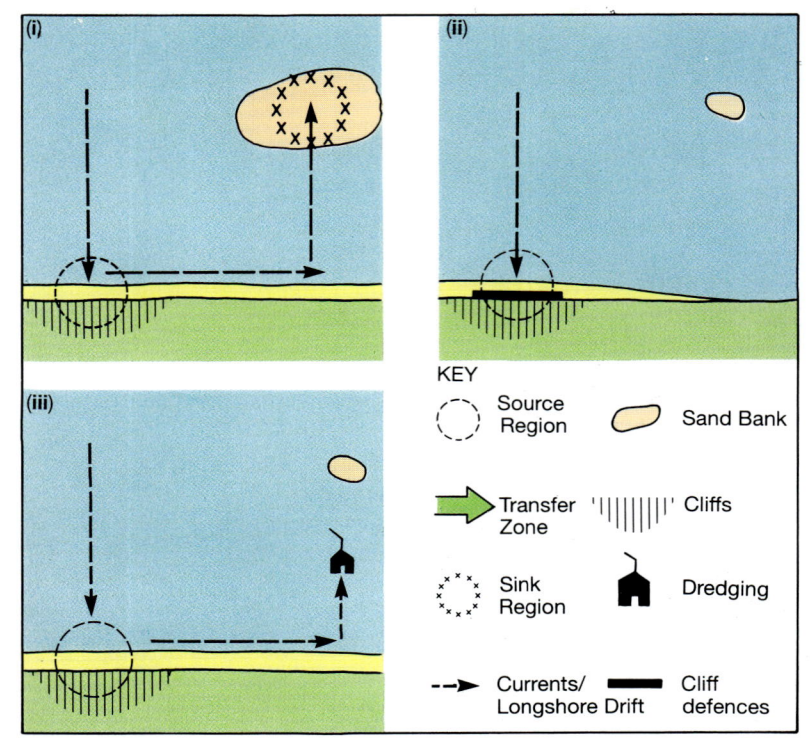

Fig 226 Examples of sediment cells

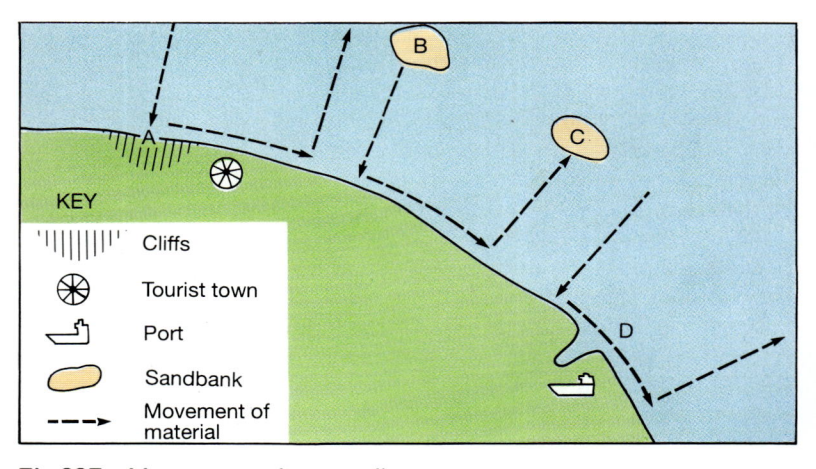

Fig 227 Managing a sediment cell

5.5 How can we explain a physical landscape?

The Isle of Purbeck, Dorset

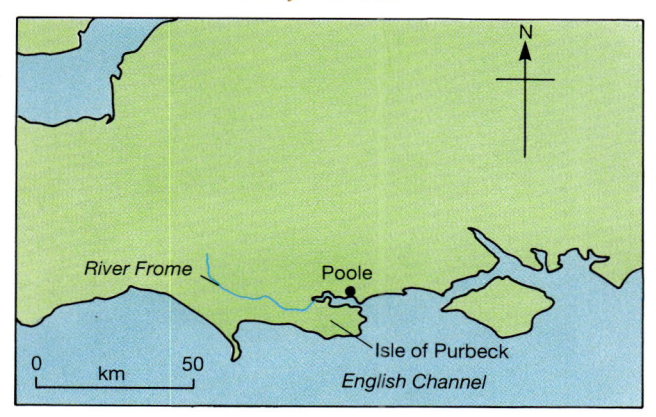

Fig 228 Isle of Purbeck: location map

Fig 229 Looking north from Purbeck across Poole Harbour

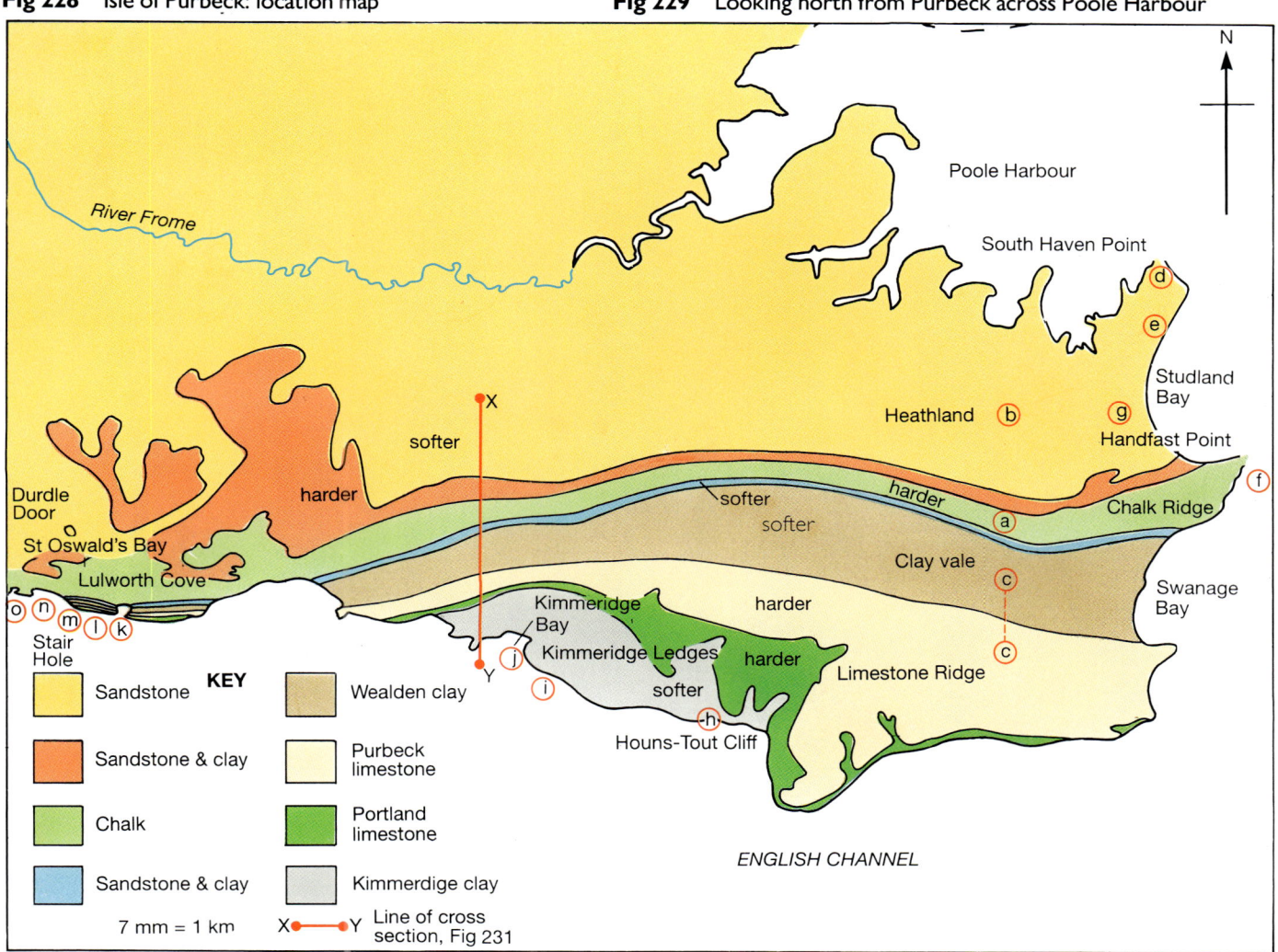

KEY
- Sandstone
- Sandstone & clay
- Chalk
- Sandstone & clay
- Wealden clay
- Purbeck limestone
- Portland limestone
- Kimmerdige clay

7 mm = 1 km

X——Y Line of cross section, Fig 231

Fig 230 Geology and physical features

SEA 5.5

a) Chalk ridge

b) Heathland

c) Clay vale and limestone ridge

d) Spit, South Haven Point

e) Sand dunes, Studland Bay

f) Natural arch and stacks, Old Harry Rocks (see Fig 200, page 93)

g) Beach, Studland Bay

k) Bay, Lulworth Cove

i) Cliff and wave-cut platform, Kimmeridge Ledges (see Fig 196, page 91)

h) Landslide, Houns-tout Cliff

j) Kimmeridge Bay (fault guided)

The location of each of these photographs (a to o) is shown on Fig 230 on page 103.

The Isle of Purbeck in South Dorset is an area of about 250 square kilometres, bounded in the north by the River Frome and in the south by the English Channel (Fig 228). It gets its name because the northern part of the area used to be marshland which was difficult to cross, although it has never been an island completely surrounded by the sea (Fig 229).

It is made up of sedimentary rocks (see page 6), the oldest of which is Kimmeridge Clay, laid down in a muddy sea in the Jurassic period of geological time some 155 million years ago. The youngest rocks are the Tertiary sandstones which are about 45 million years old.

These rocks differ in hardness (Fig 230). This helps to explain much of the area's scenery because the softer rocks are worn away more quickly than the harder rocks, a process known as **differential erosion**. They were all deposited in horizontal layers but since then they have been tilted, folded and faulted (cracked) in earth movements (Figs 230 l and 231).

Running east-west across the centre of the Isle of Purbeck is a steep-sided chalk ridge (Fig 230 a). It stands out because it has been tilted up on end by earth movements and because it is relatively harder than the sandstones to the north and the clays to the south.

To the north of this ridge is fairly soft, infertile sandstone which has resulted in a large area of low-lying heathland (Fig 230 b). To the south is the clay vale and then another ridge of more resistant limestone (Fig 230 c).

The importance of alternating bands of hard and soft rock is also reflected in the coastal scenery. In the east the coastline is described as being **discordant** because the bands of rock are at or near right angles to the sea. Such an

l) Folding at Stair Hole

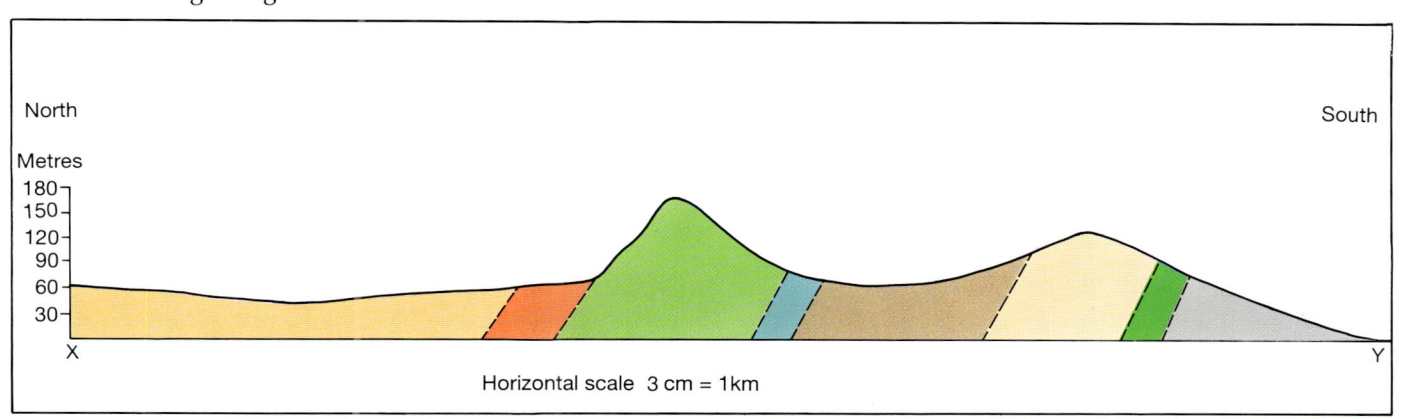

m) Bay, Stair Hole

n) St Oswald's Bay

o) Natural Arch, Durdle Door

Fig 231 Geological cross section of the Isle of Purbeck

arrangement makes it very easy for a series of bays and headlands to develop because there is nothing to stop the sea differentially eroding the softer bands of rock. This explains the formation of Studland Bay and Swanage Bay (Fig 232).

However, on the south coast the rocks are parallel to the sea, an arrangement described as being **concordant**. This makes it much more difficult for the sea to form bays and headlands because a hard band of rock can protect a soft band of rock.

These features can still form, though, as the area west of Lulworth Cove clearly shows (Fig 233). Stair Hole (Fig 230 m) represents Stage 1 where the sea has managed to break through the hard limestones, perhaps by eroding along the line of a fault. It is then able to wear away the soft clays. The result is Stage 2, a bay lined up against the next hard band of rock, which is represented by Lulworth Cove (Fig 230 k). Stage 3 in the development of a concordant coastline is represented by the 'double bay' formed by the erosion of the headland which used to separate Man o' War Cove and St Oswald's Bay (Fig 230 n).

Some of Purbeck's most spectacular scenery is the result of the sea eroding headlands. Eventually, it will remove these on both discordant and concordant coastlines — the sequence of events is described on page 92.

Not all bays and headlands are caused by the differential erosion of bands of hard and soft rock. Kimmeridge Bay (Fig 230 j), for example, is the result of the sea eroding rocks which have been weakened by faulting. This helps to explain its rectangular shape.

Purbeck also has some fine examples of cliffs and wave-cut platforms and the processes which produce these are discussed in Section 5.1.

Coastal deposition has produced a range of features as well. Many of the bays along the south coast have pebble beaches, while the softer rocks in Swanage Bay and Studland Bay have produced wide, sandy beaches (Fig 230 g). At the northern end of Studland Bay winds have blown this sand inland to form a series of dunes. Longshore drift has produced a small spit at South Haven Point (Fig 230 d).

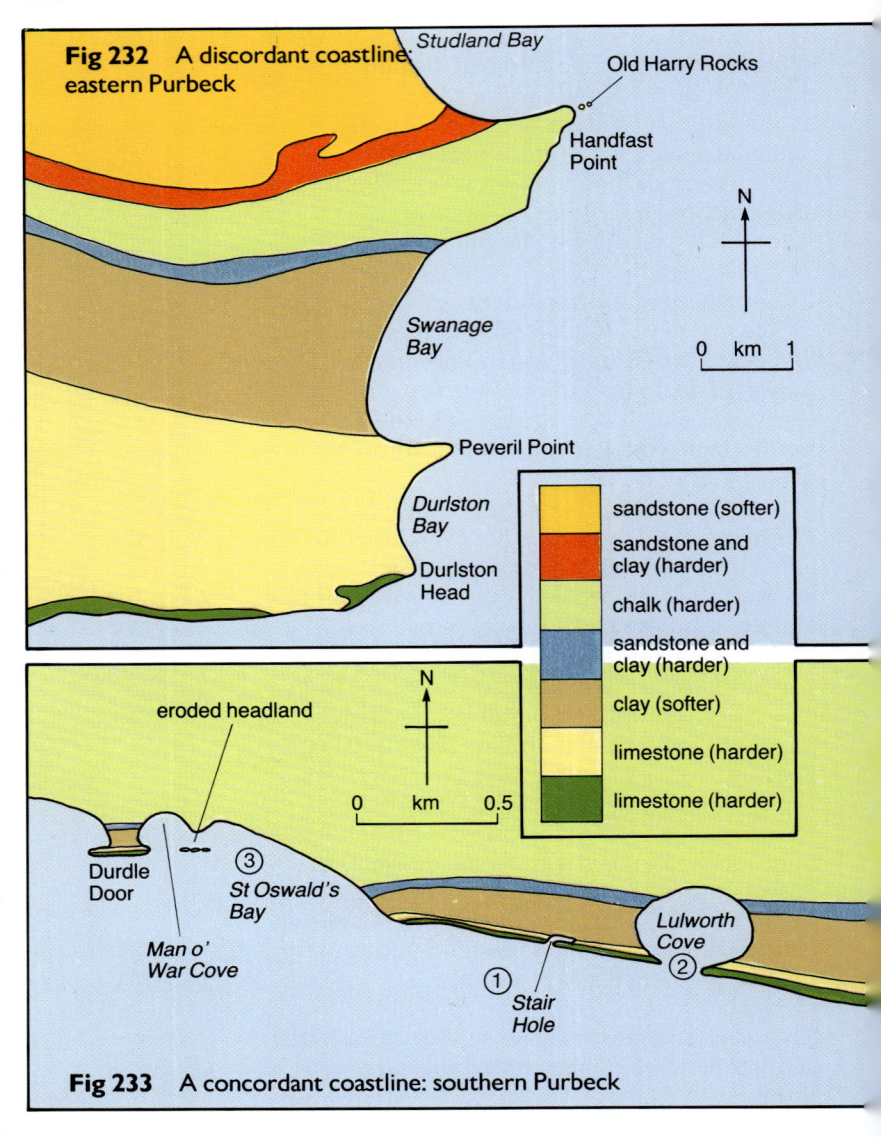

There are many other processes which affect the physical landscape of the area, but a major one is mass movement (the movement of weathered material downhill under the influence of gravity), particularly landslides. Fig 234 explains how these happen while Fig 230 h shows their effect on Houns-tout Cliff. Here, the rocks are tilted gently towards the sea and light coloured blocks of permeable limestone have slipped over dark coloured blocks of permeable clay.

Fig 232 A discordant coastline: eastern Purbeck

Fig 233 A concordant coastline: southern Purbeck

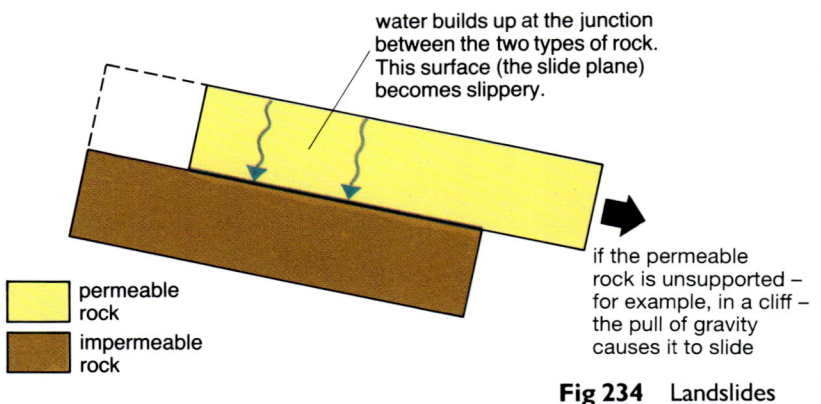

Fig 234 Landslides

5.6 Assessment task: The landforms of the Isle of Purbeck

1 Draw a sketch map of the Isle of Purbeck. Mark on the places labelled a-o. Use symbols to show the type of feature found at each of these places and the main process(es) involved in its formation.

2 Make a copy of Fig 231. Label onto it: each of the rock types; the heathland; the chalk ridge; the clay vale; and the limestone ridge.

3 Fig 235 shows the results of a survey of the beach in St Oswald's Bay by Year 10 pupils. They used the method described on page 95.
 a) Draw a line graph to show the beach profile. Describe and explain its shape.
 b) Draw a scatter graph to show the relationship between pebble size and its position on the beach. Describe and explain the relationship.

4 What evidence in the photographs in Figs 230 (page 104) and 198 (page 92) is there of human interference in the development of this coastline?

5 a) Describe and explain the shape of the cross section you labelled for question 2.
 b) Describe and explain the development of bays and headlands on the Isle of Purbeck. In your answer identify the main factors and processes involved and mention the similarities and differences between the east coast and the south coast.
 c) What factors and processes help to explain the features of coastal deposition found on the Isle of Purbeck?

6 How might the coastline of the Isle of Purbeck develop in the future? Explain why, and under what conditions, things might happen.

Distance from top of beach (metres)	0.0	0.5	1.0	1.5	2.0	2.5	3.0	3.5	4.0	4.5	5.0	5.5	6.0	6.5	7.0	7.5
Height from measure to beach (metres)	0.0	0.2	0.4	0.5	0.5	0.6	0.6	1.0	1.1	1.2	1.2	1.6	1.7	1.8	1.8	1.8
Long axis of pebble (centimetres)	18	15	20	14	13	14	11	10	2	9	7	10	5	1	1	2

Fig 235   Beach survey results

WEATHER, CLIMATE AND VEGETATION

WEATHER, CLIMATE AND VEGETATION 6.1

6.1 What makes up weather and climate?

Weather, Climate and Microclimate

Weather refers to what temperature, rain and wind are like from day to day. For example, weather in the British Isles is very changeable — one day it can be warm and sunny while the next day it can be cold and rainy (Fig 236).

Climate refers to what temperature, rain and wind are like over a longer period of time. For example, the climate of the British Isles is described as "temperate" which means that it is neither very hot nor very cold and that it is neither very wet nor very dry.

If a small area has its own special climate it is called a **microclimate**; for example on a hot, sunny day it is cooler in the shade of a tree while on a cold, windy day you might want to shelter behind a wall while you are waiting for the bus.

Fig 236 What makes up the weather?

Measuring Temperature

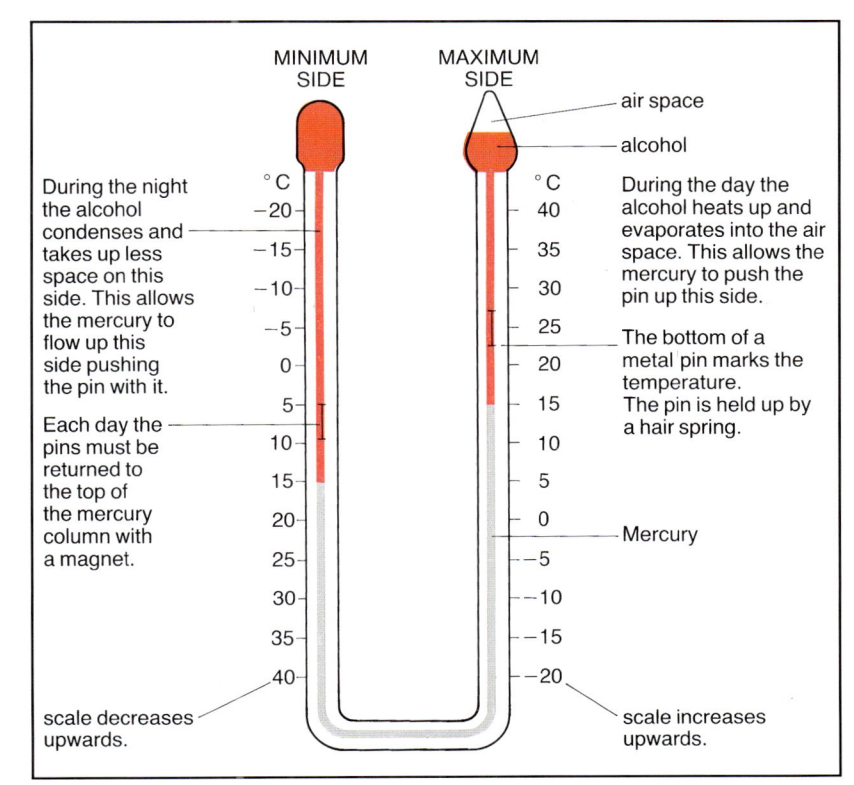

MINIMUM SIDE

During the night the alcohol condenses and takes up less space on this side. This allows the mercury to flow up this side pushing the pin with it.

Each day the pins must be returned to the top of the mercury column with a magnet.

scale decreases upwards.

MAXIMUM SIDE

air space
alcohol

During the day the alcohol heats up and evaporates into the air space. This allows the mercury to push the pin up this side.

The bottom of a metal pin marks the temperature. The pin is held up by a hair spring.

Mercury

scale increases upwards.

Fig 237 Maximum and minimum thermometer

WEATHER, CLIMATE AND VEGETATION 6.1

The two most important temperatures of the day — the highest and lowest — can be measured with a maximum and minimum thermometer (Fig 237). It is best to keep thermometers in a Stevenson's Screen (Fig 238) because it protects them from direct sunlight or wind.

Measuring Rain

Rainfall can be measured accurately with a rain gauge (Fig 239). This is a metal cylinder which contains a funnel and a collecting jar. Any rain which is collected is poured into a glass jar and measured in millimetres.

It is important to place a rain gauge in an open space away from trees and buildings and the top of the cylinder must be at least 30 cm above the ground in case of splashing.

Fig 238 Stevenson's Screen

Fig 239 Rain gauge

Cloud Type

Clouds form when air is cooled and water vapour condenses out to form water droplets or ice particles. Clouds are put into groups mainly according to their shape and height. Some useful words to know are — cirrus (wispy clouds); cumulus (lumpy clouds); stratus (a layer cloud); nimbus (rain bearing); and alto (medium height). Some common cloud types are shown in Fig 240.

Cloud Cover

The amount of cloud covering the whole sky is estimated to the nearest eighth and shown with one of the symbols in Fig 241. An eighth of cloud cover is known as an okta and therefore 3/8 cloud cover is 3 oktas, for example.

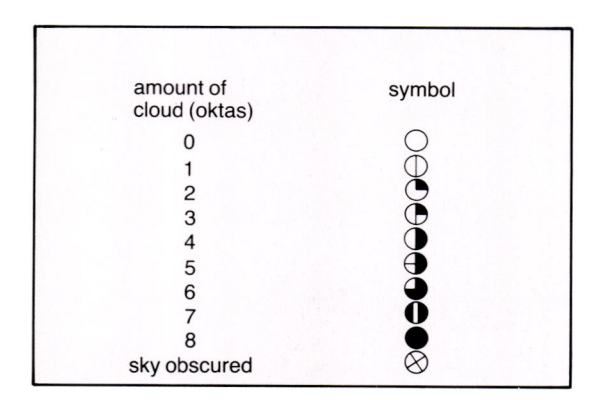

amount of cloud (oktas)	symbol
0	○
1	◐
2	◔
3	◕
4	◑
5	◕
6	◕
7	◕
8	●
sky obscured	⊗

Fig 241 Cloud cover

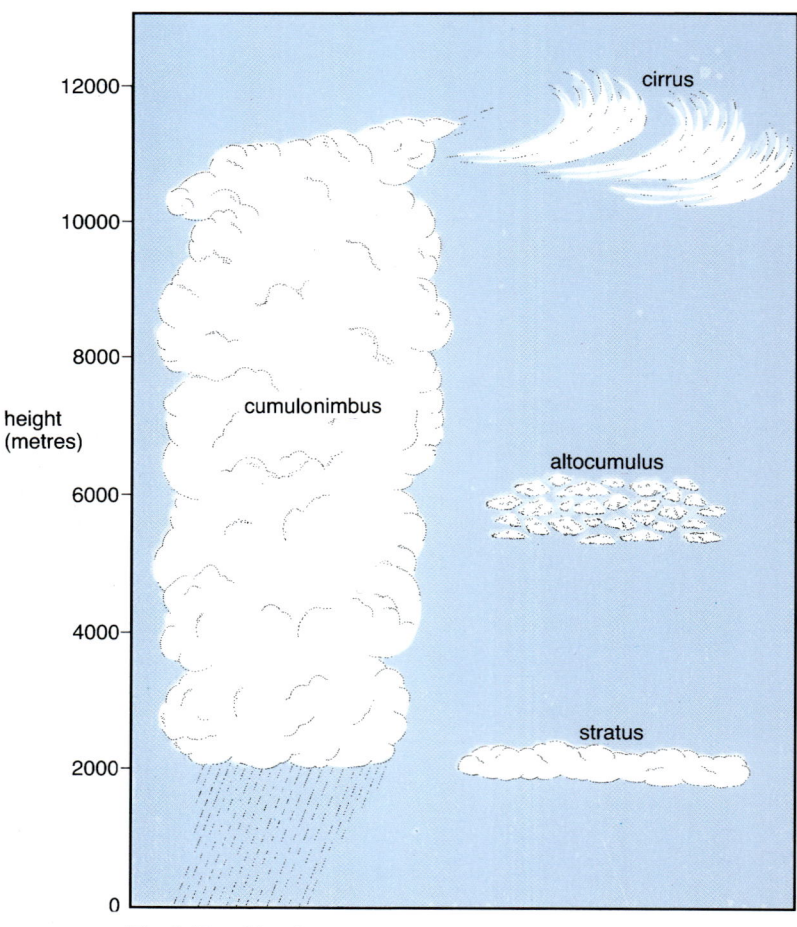

Fig 240 Cloud types

WEATHER, CLIMATE AND VEGETATION 6.1

Measuring Sunshine

An instrument like the one in Fig 242 can be used to measure the amount of sunshine per day. The glass sphere focuses and concentrates the sun's rays onto a piece of card which is marked off in hours. When the sun shines the card is burnt and at the end of the day the time represented by the burnt sections can be added together to give the total amount of sunshine.

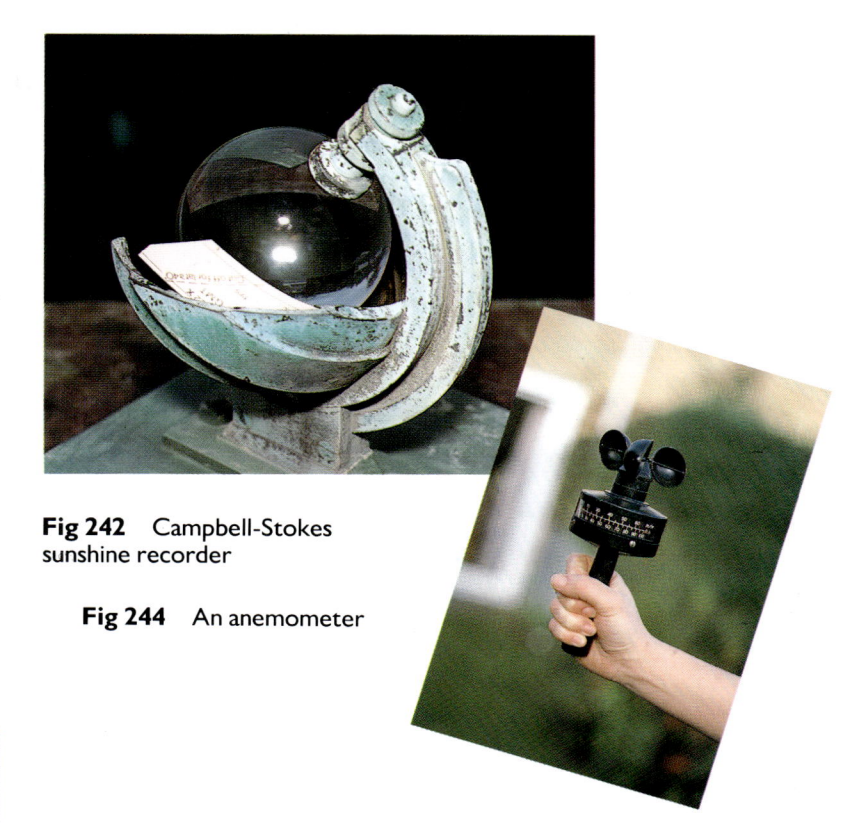

Measuring Wind Speed and Direction

Wind speed can be estimated using the Beaufort wind scale (Fig 243). Alternatively, it can be measured with an anemometer which can be fixed to a post above the ground, or held in the hand (Fig 244). The wind blows the cups round and the speed is read off a dial in miles, kilometres or knots per hour (a knot is a nautical mile, which is 1.85 km).

Fig 242 Campbell-Stokes sunshine recorder

Fig 244 An anemometer

Wind direction is measured by a wind vane (Fig 245). The arrow always points in the direction from which the wind is coming, and this is the direction which gives the wind its name.

Number	Wind	Characteristics
0	calm	you cannot feel any wind at all
1	light air	you can just feel the wind on your face
2	light breeze	leaves rustle
3	gentle breeze	leaves, twigs, flags all moving
4	moderate breeze	small branches move, paper blown about
5	fresh breeze	small trees begin to sway
6	strong breeze	large branches move
7	moderate gale	trees sway
8	fresh gale	twigs break off trees
9	strong gale	tiles blown off roofs
10	whole gale	trees blown over
11	storm	a lot of damage
12	hurricane	really bad, widespread damage

Fig 243 Beaufort wind scale

Fig 245 Wind vane

Measuring Atmospheric Pressure

Atmospheric pressure is the weight of air pressing down on the earth's surface. The easiest way to understand this is to think of a column of air above each of us extending upwards to the limit of the atmosphere. This column of air weighs a little over 1 kilogram per square centimetre. Fortunately, we have adapted to this weight so we do not notice it!

Atmospheric pressure is measured in millibars (mb). It can be recorded with a barometer (Fig 246), or a barograph (Fig 247). The barograph is made up of a metal cylinder, the top of which goes up and down with changes in air pressure. The cylinder is connected by levers to a pen. This rests on a piece of card attached to a drum which rotates once every 24 hours. A continuous record of pressure is marked onto the card as it moves under the pen.

Fig 246 Aneroid barometer

Fig 247 Barograph and barogram

Measuring Humidity

Humidity is the amount of water vapour in the air. Warm air can hold more water vapour than cold air so it is more important to know the relative humidity of the air than the absolute humidity. When relative humidity reaches 100 per cent the air is completely saturated and the water vapour condenses out to form clouds or rain.

Relative humidity can be measured with a hygrometer (Fig 248). This consists of a wet bulb and a dry bulb thermometer. The wet bulb is an ordinary thermometer with a piece of muslin tied round it which stays wet because it is dipped into a container of water. The dry bulb is just an ordinary thermometer.

Water evaporates until air reaches its saturation point, and evaporation produces cooling. Therefore, water evaporates from the wet bulb until the air reaches its saturation point and the cooling means that the wet bulb shows a lower temperature than the dry bulb. When saturation point is reached there is no evaporation and no cooling so the thermometers record the same temperature. Thus, the difference in temperature between the two thermometers can be used to work out the relative humidity of the air.

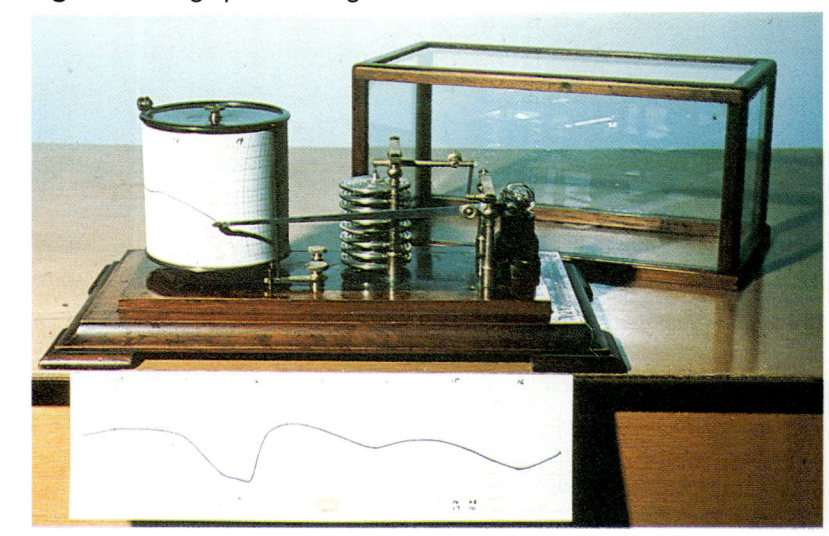

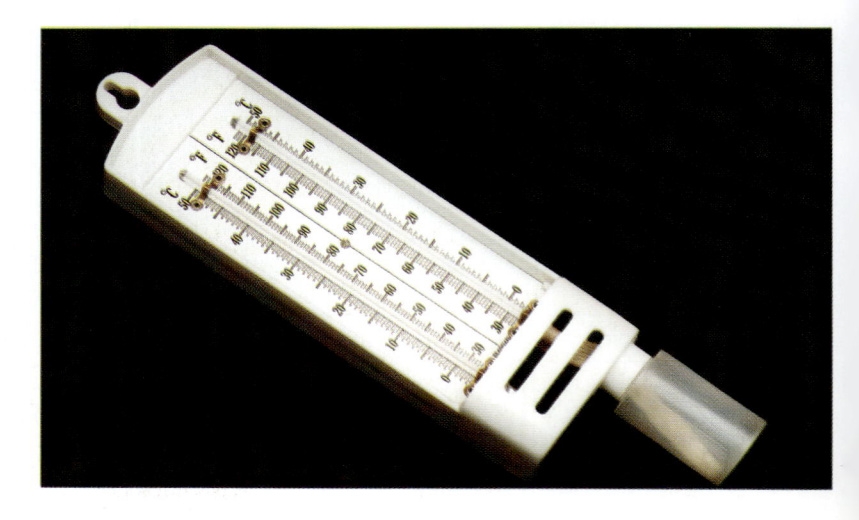

Fig 248 Hygrometer

WEATHER, CLIMATE AND VEGETATION 6.2

6.2 Assessment task: *Weather survey*

Aims
- to test the idea that weather conditions vary a great deal even in a small area;
- to compare weather and climate in the Home Region.

Method
Choose a small area for your survey and decide on a number of different sites to investigate; your home and garden (Fig 249) or the school grounds would be ideal.

Decide which aspects of weather you are going to record. Cloud type, cloud cover, wind speed and wind direction can all be estimated without special equipment. For temperature a maximum-minimum thermometer is best but an ordinary garden thermometer will do. For rainfall you can use containers or jars as long as they are all the same size. Pressure and humidity will require borrowing special equipment. Draw up a data collection sheet like the one in Fig 250.

Draw a sketch map and field sketch of your survey area. Measure and record the weather for a least five days. Make sure that you take your readings at the same time each day.

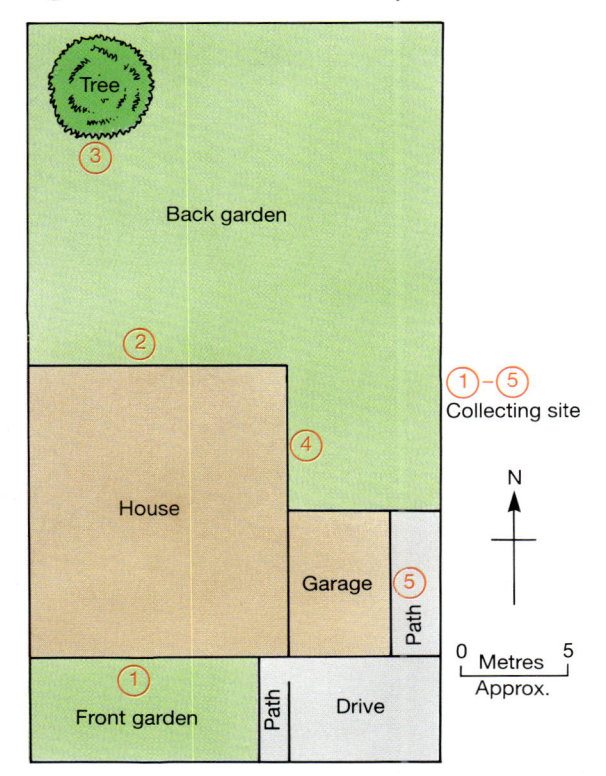

Writing up your Results

Aim and Method
- State the aims of the survey.
- Describe the differences between weather, climate and microclimate.
- Explain how you carried out the survey.

Presentation of Results
- Make best copies of your sketch map, field sketch and results table.
- Present your results on a large base map. For example, you could show temperature as "thermometer pictures"; rainfall as bar graphs; and wind speed and direction using columns like in Fig 250.

Fig 249 Sites for a weather survey

Fig 250 Weather survey: data collection sheet

SITE	WEATHER FEATURE	DAY	MAXIMUM Temp°C	MINIMUM Temp°C	RAIN mm	CLOUD	CLOUD COVER oktas	WIND SPEED Beaufort	WIND DIRECTION	PRESSURE mb	HUMIDITY %
①	Description front garden of house Aspect south facing	1 2 3 4 5	16	8	4	cumulus	8	4	S W	996	96
②	Description _____ Aspect _____	1 2 3 4 5									
③	Description _____ Aspect _____	1 2 3 4 5									
④	Description _____ Aspect _____	1 2 3 4 5									
⑤	Description _____ Aspect _____	1 2 3 4 5									

Fig 251 Presenting wind speed and direction

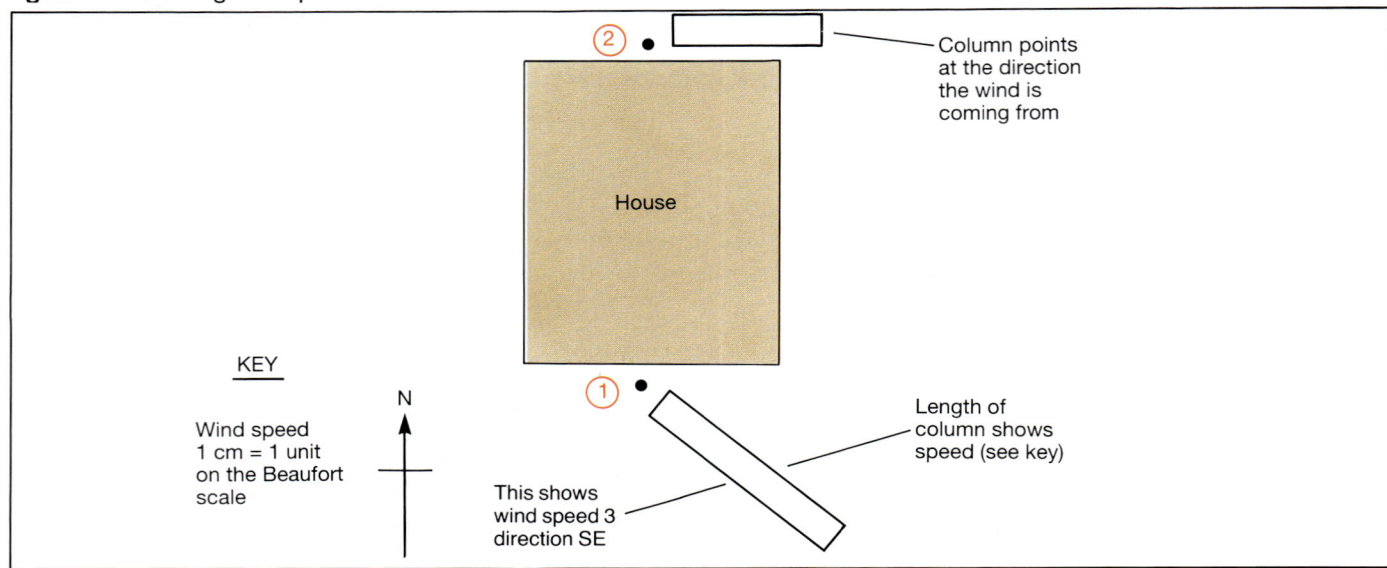

Interpretation and Explanation

- Look at your results for just one of the days. Were there any differences between sites? If "yes", describe and try to explain them.
- Look at the results for all of the days. Can you identify any relationships between the weather you recorded and the general factors you noted down e.g. rainfall and site, temperature and aspect?

Conclusion and Limitations

- Summarise your main findings.
- Find out about the climate of your home area. Was the weather you recorded usual for the time of year? Try to explain any differences.
- Did you have any problems carrying out this investigation? If you were to repeat this study are there any ways in which you would try to improve it?

6.3 What is the climate of the British Isles like?

A climate graph shows average monthly temperatures and average monthly rainfall (Fig 252). Three more climate graphs are shown in Fig 253 and the Enquiry on this page asks you to draw two more.

Climate graphs can be used to work out two figures which are very useful when we want to compare the climate of different places:
- *range of temperature* This is simply the difference between the highest temperature on the climate graph and the lowest temperature on the climate graph. For example, for Penzance (Fig 252) the highest temperature is 17°C and the lowest temperature is 7°C so the range of temperature is 17 − 7 = 10°C.
- *total rainfall* To work this out you add up the rainfall for each of the 12 months. For example, for Penzance (Fig 252) this is 130 + 80 + 75 + 70 + 60 + 50 + 75 + 75 + 80 + 120 + 130 + 130 = 1075 mm.

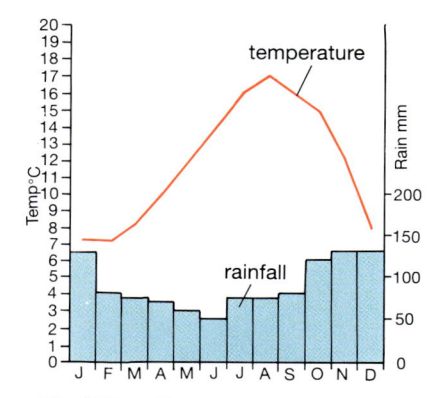

Fig 252 Climate graph – Penzance

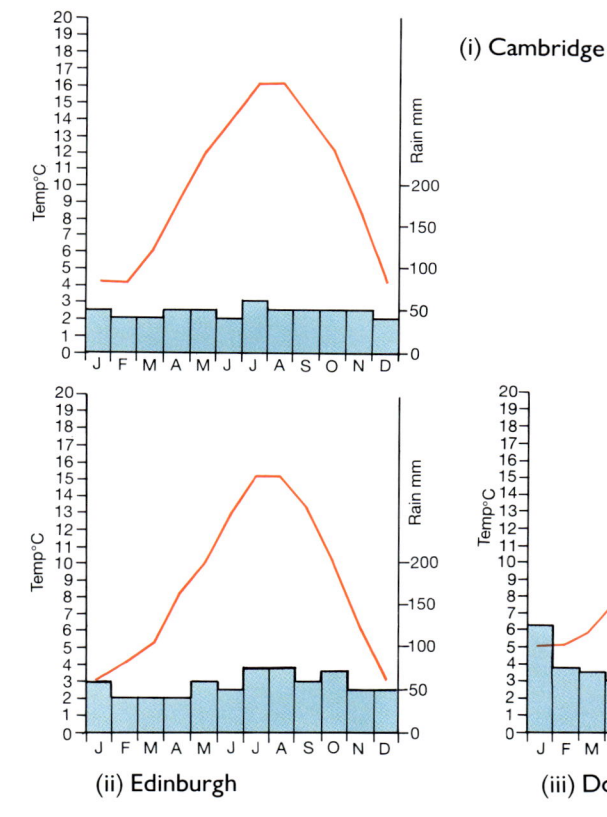

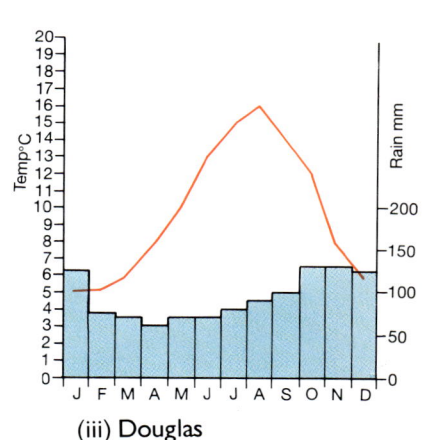

Fig 253 Climate graphs
(i) Cambridge
(ii) Edinburgh
(iii) Douglas

ENQUIRY

1. Onto a map of the British Isles mark on and label the places mentioned in Figs 252 and 253.
2. On graph paper, draw climate graphs for Stornoway and Margate (Fig 254). Use the same scale as for Figs 252 and 253.
3. Work out the range of temperature and the total rainfall for the places in Figs 253 and 254.
4. Use the information on your graphs and the figures you have worked out to match the letters A, B, C, D, E and F on Fig 255 with the following descriptions: cooler summers; colder winters; wetter; milder winters; warmer summers; drier.
5. Look at maps in an atlas with information about temperature and rainfall. Do these maps agree with your answer to question 3?
6. Write a paragraph to describe the climate of the British Isles.

Stornoway

Month	J	F	M	A	M	J	J	A	S	O	N	D
Temp °C	5	5	6	7	8	11	13	13	12	10	7	6
Rain mm	140	120	110	80	70	60	80	100	100	140	150	160

Margate

Month	J	F	M	A	M	J	J	A	S	O	N	D
Temp °C	5	5	6	8	11	15	17	18	17	13	8	6
Rain mm	50	40	45	40	45	50	55	50	55	75	60	60

Fig 254 Climate statistics for Stornoway and Margate

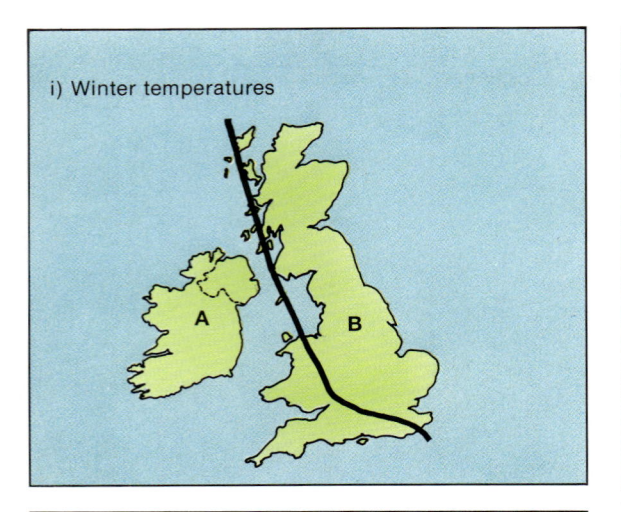

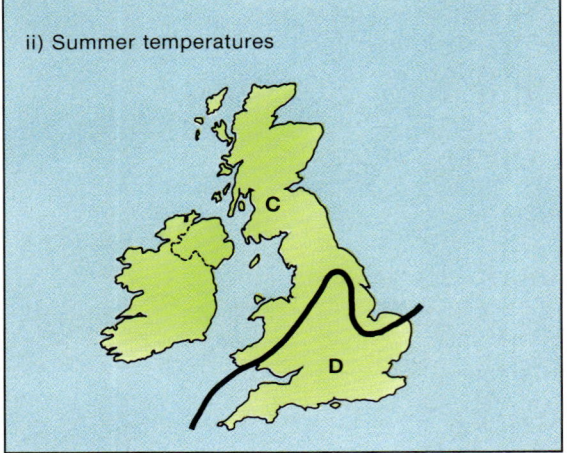

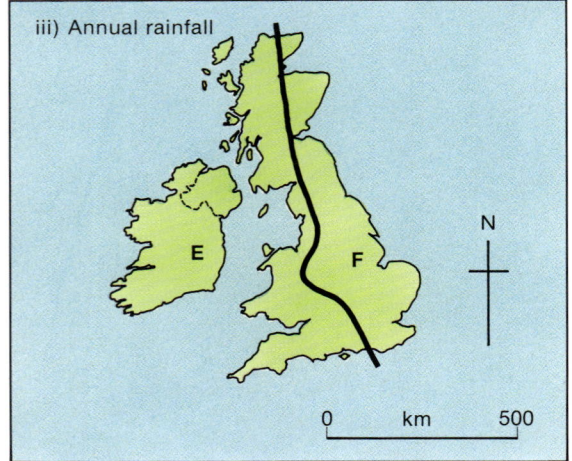

Fig 255 Climate in the British Isles: a summary

6.4 Why does it rain?

Rain is caused by air rising and cooling. If temperatures fall below the condensation point, the water vapour in the air turns into water droplets which build up to form clouds. Of course, not all clouds produce rain. This is because the droplets have to become heavy enough to fall out of the cloud. There are three main reasons why air is forced to rise and therefore there are three main types of rainfall.

1 Depression or Frontal rain This happens because warm air is forced to rise at the fronts of a depression (Fig 256). Rain at the cold front is heavier than rain at the warm front because the air is forced to rise more quickly; the result is towering cumulonimbus clouds (see Fig 240, page 110).

2 Convection rain This happens when air at the earth's surface is heated and therefore rises. As it rises it cools down, clouds form, and rain follows (Fig 257). Temperatures and relative humidity have to be high for this to happen.

The currents of rising air are strong. As a result, water droplets have to reach a large size before they fall out of the cloud. This explains why convection rain tends to fall as heavy showers.

3 Relief or Orographic rain The third reason why air can be forced to rise is if it meets a chain of mountains (Fig 258). As it rises it cools down and the rain making process goes into operation. On the other side of the mountains the air falls. As it does so it warms up and the rain stops; this area is known as the rain shadow.

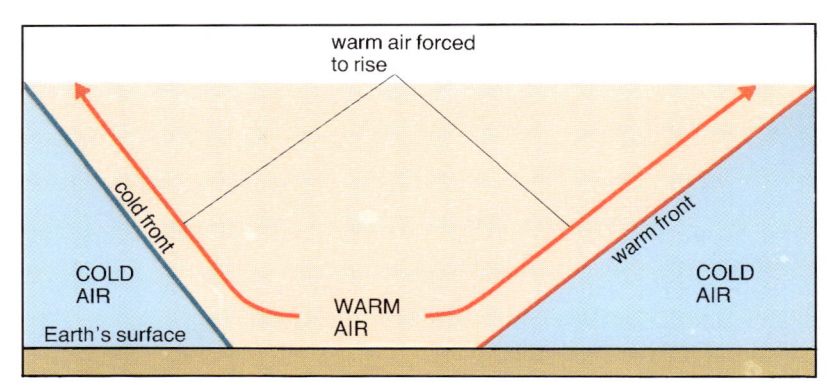

Fig 256 Depression rain

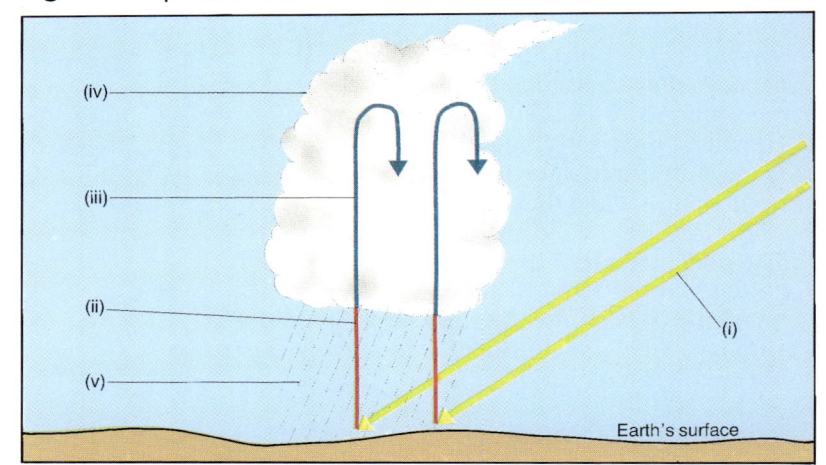

Fig 257 Convection rain

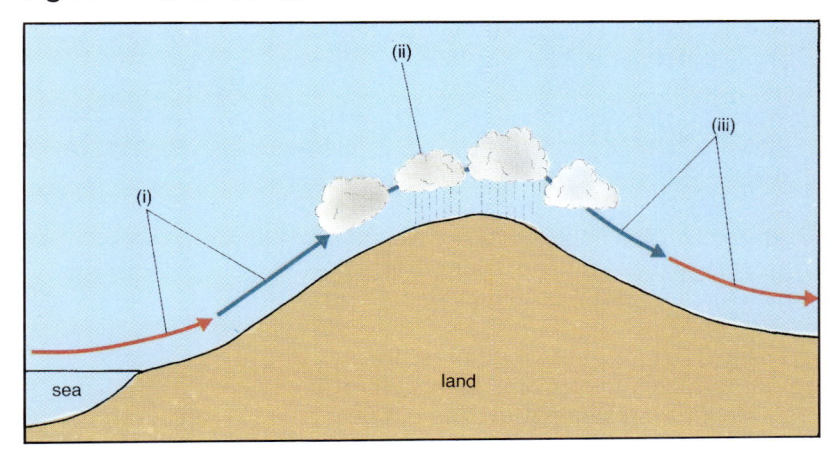

Fig 258 Relief rain

ENQUIRY

1. Explain why depressions bring rain.
2. Add labels to a copy of Fig 257 to explain how convection rain forms.
3. Add labels to a copy of Fig 258 to explain how relief rain forms.
4. Most depressions blow across the British Isles from the south west to the north east. How does this help to explain the pattern of rainfall in the British Isles?
5. Why do you think places in the south east of the British Isles have more rain in the summer than in the winter?
6. Why do you think the west of the British Isles is wetter than the east?

6.5 Where does Britain's weather come from, and why?

Air Masses

Weather in the British Isles is very changeable because it can be affected by one of five main **air masses** (Fig 259). An air mass is a large body of air which has more or less the same characteristics throughout, i.e. temperatures will be similar in all places covered by it.

The maritime air masses pick up moisture from the sea and as a result they bring wet weather. The continental air masses are dry because they cross only land and consequently pick up very little moisture. However, polar continental winds can bring snow showers in the winter because they pick up moisture when they cross the North Sea.

The polar and arctic air masses are generally colder than the tropical air masses. However, when the continental interiors warm up in the summer, the polar continental air mass brings hot weather with it.

Winds and Pressure

Air masses are brought to us by the wind which, in turn, is the result of differences in atmospheric pressure (Fig 260).

Warm air rises and expands. This means that the weight of air pressing down on the earth's surface is lighter. The result is an area of low pressure. In comparison, cool air sinks and contracts. This means that the weight of air pressing down on the earth's surface is heavier. The result is an area of high pressure.

The heavier air in the high pressure area is squeezed out towards the low pressure area — think of the air being squeezed out of a football. Wind is this movement of air from high to low pressure.

Of course, the system has to complete itself or we would run out of air. This happens at high altitude where rising air spills out to take the place of sinking air. As a result, high altitude winds blow in a different direction to low altitude winds. You can sometimes see this happening when there is cloud at two different levels.

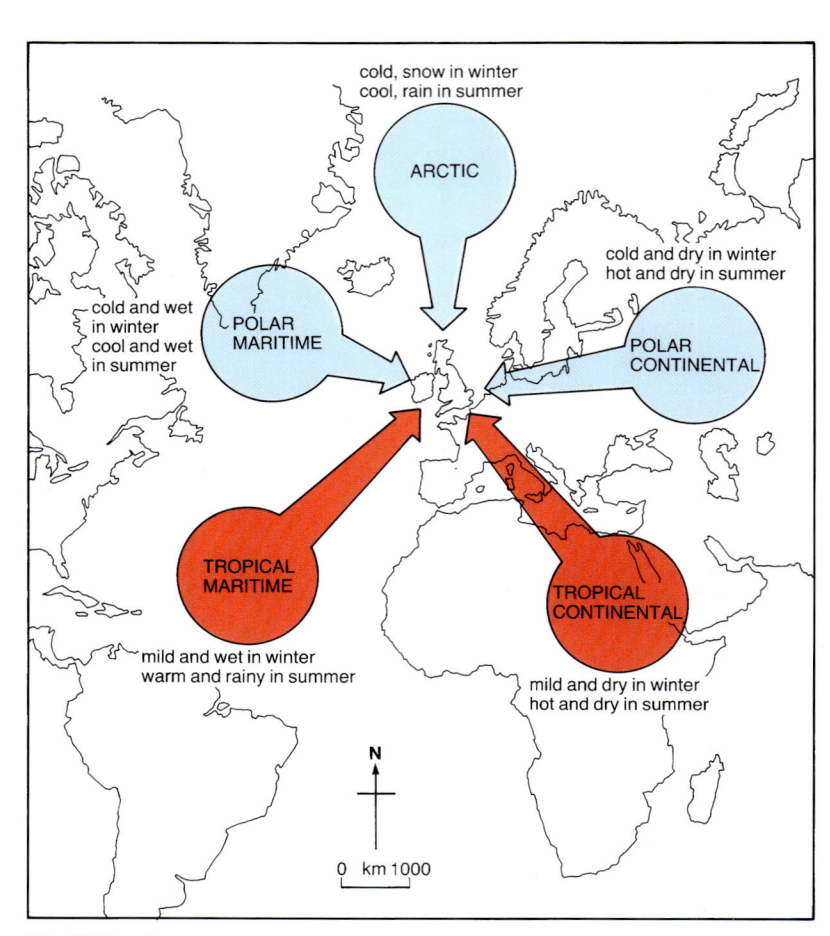

Fig 259 Air masses

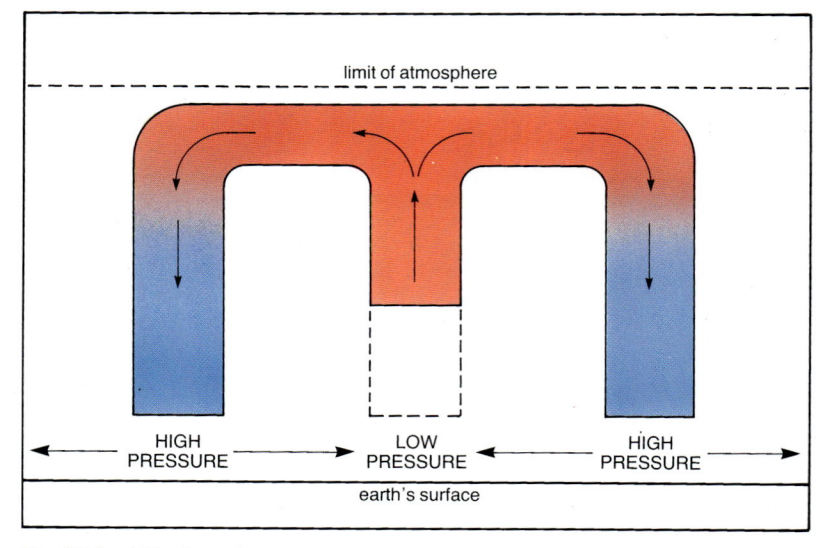

Fig 260 Winds and pressure

WEATHER, CLIMATE AND VEGETATION 6.5

Isobars

Isobars are lines drawn on weather maps which join places of equal pressure. Winds blow from higher to lower numbers i.e. from higher to lower pressure. The closer together are the isobars, the stronger is the wind.

However, the wind does not blow in a straight line from high to low pressure because of the west-east rotation of the earth. Winds in the northern hemisphere are swung to their right while winds in the southern hemisphere are swung to their left.

In the northern hemisphere this means that winds will always blow out from a high pressure system in a clockwise direction and into a low pressure system in an anticlockwise direction (Fig 261). In the southern hemisphere this relationship is the other way round.

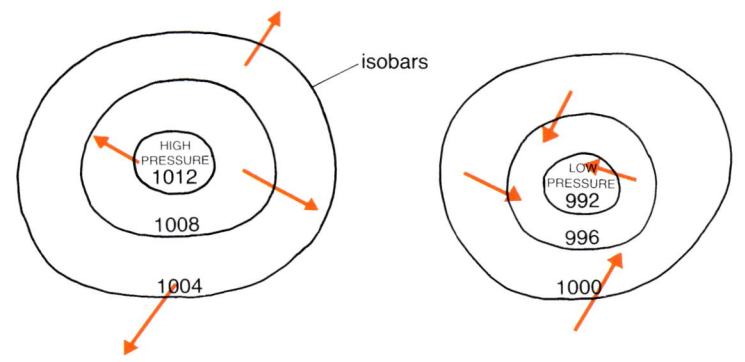

Fig 261 Winds and pressure systems

Air Mass	Wind Direction	Winter Weather	Summer Weather
	North		
Polar Maritime			
		cold and dry; possible snow showers	
			warm and rainy
	South East		

Fig 262 Air masses — a check list

ENQUIRY

1 Copy and complete the table in Fig 262.
2 Copy Fig 261 and add labels to explain the causes of high pressure, low pressure and wind.
3 Label onto a copy of Fig 263 the centres of high and low pressure; the approximate wind directions at places X and Y; an area of relatively strong winds; an area of relatively light winds; and the name of the air mass affecting the British Isles. What type of weather is this air mass probably bringing?

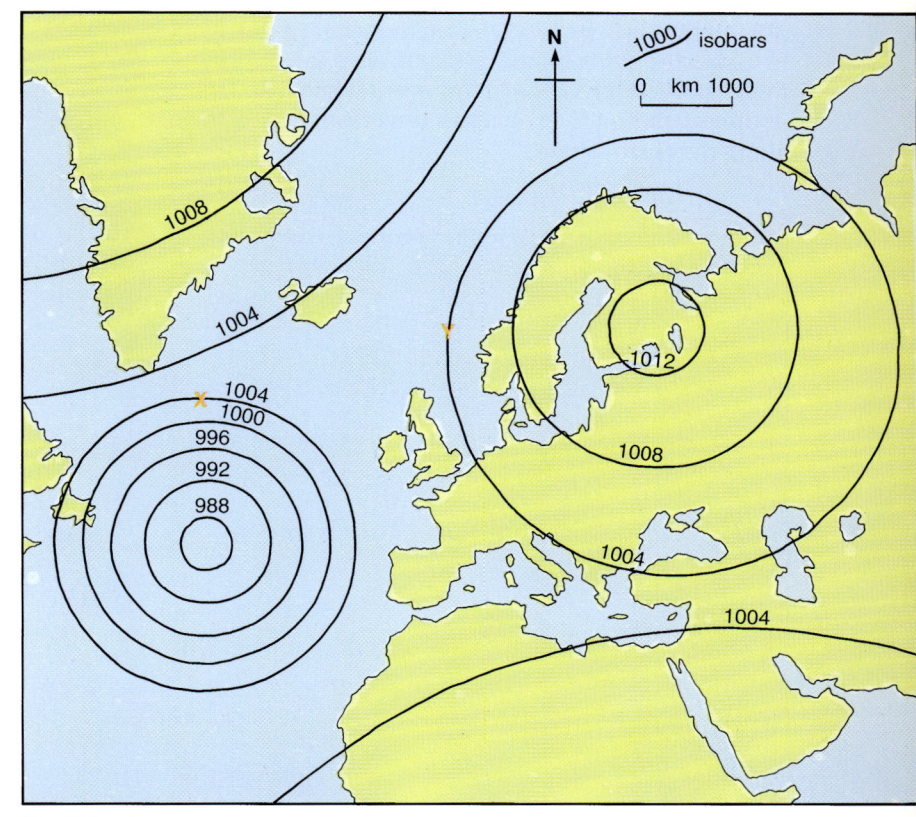

Fronts and Depressions

A **front** is the boundary between two air masses. Fronts are a common feature of the weather of the British Isles because it is often the meeting place for polar and tropical air masses.

The warm tropical air rises when it meets the cold polar air. This causes a bulge to develop in the front. The warm and cold fronts are the two sides of this bulge: the warm front marks the arrival of the tropical air and the cold front marks the arrival of the polar air. An occluded

Fig 263 Pressure systems map

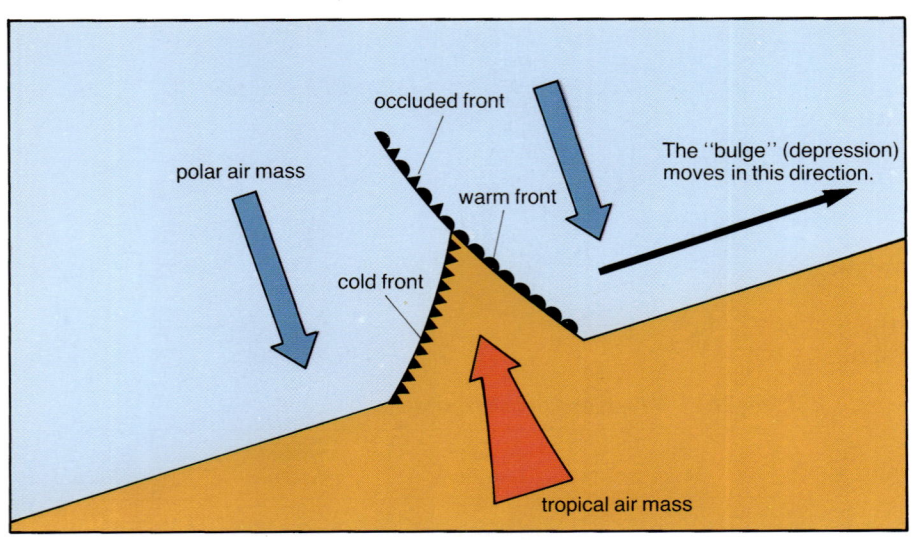

Fig 264 Fronts

front is where the warm and cold fronts meet at the apex of the bulge (Fig 264).

Two other things happen as the warm air rises. Firstly, a low pressure system develops, and this is what is known as a **depression**. Secondly, the air cools down and water vapour condenses out to form clouds which eventually produce rain (see page 117).

Depressions move eastwards under the influence of the prevailing westerly winds. As they blow across the country each sector brings with it its own particular conditions (Fig 265): this explains why the weather of the British Isles is so changeable. It is easy to forecast the approach of a depression because of the regular pattern of cloud types found along the warm front.

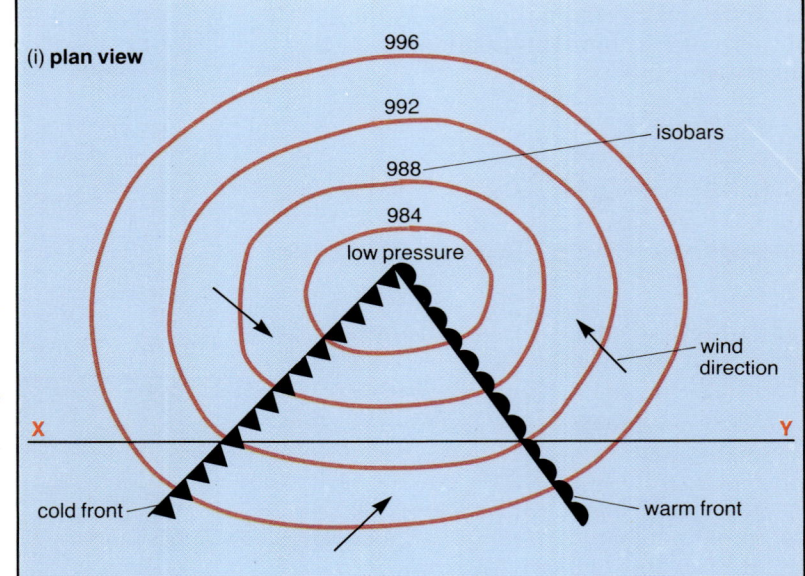

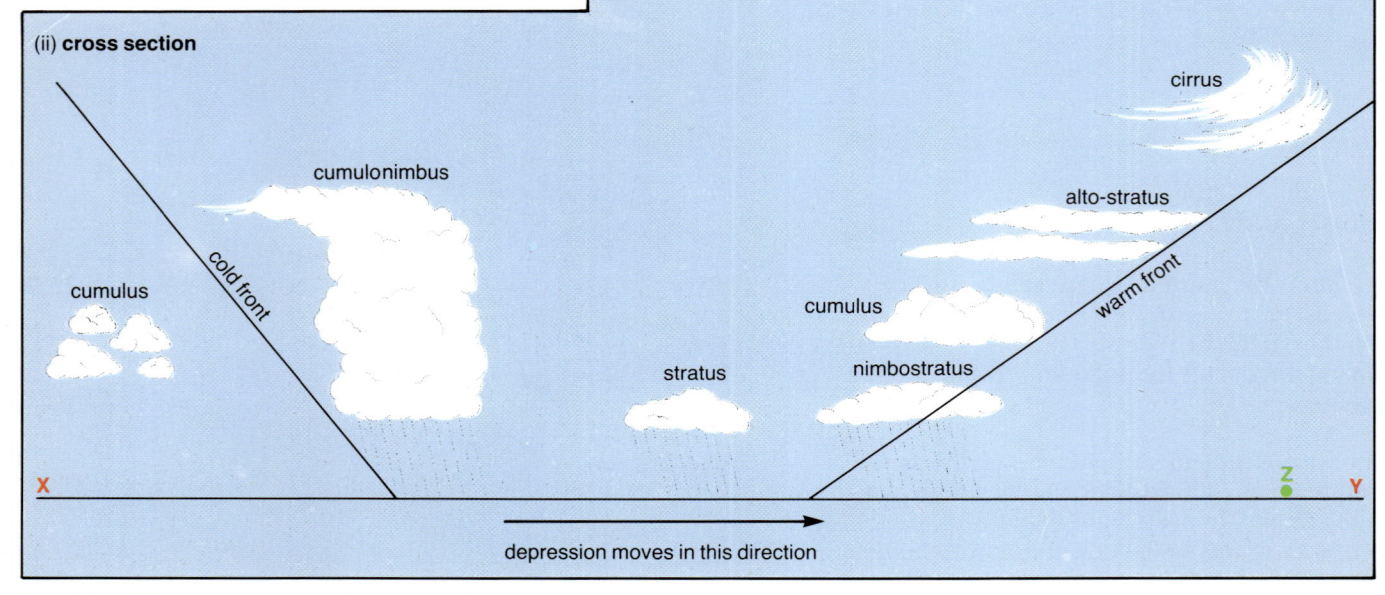

Fig 265 The characteristics of a depression

WEATHER, CLIMATE AND VEGETATION 6.5

Anticyclones

Anticyclones are high pressure systems. Unlike depressions, they move slowly so they usually produce settled weather for several days. Isobars tend to be widely spaced so wind speeds are usually light.

High pressure systems are, of course, associated with sinking air. This means that clouds are unlikely to develop which makes fine, dry weather a feature of anticyclonic conditions. However, there are important differences depending on the season.

In the summer, anticyclones tend to bring sunny, dry, hot weather. However, the cloudless skies mean that heat can escape rapidly at night-time. As a result, nights can be quite cool.

Later on in the year, this night-time cooling can produce quite cold temperatures near the ground. When this happens water vapour condenses out to form mist or fog. The mist or fog persists until the heat of the sun the next day clears it.

In the winter, the weak sun means that day-time temperatures tend to be low and the clear skies mean that night-time temperatures are even lower. Typical days are therefore cold and bright and typical nights are dry but very cold and icy. If fog forms during the winter the sun is very often too weak to clear it. If it is very cold, freezing fog and frost can form.

ENQUIRY

1 What is a front, and why are they a common feature of the weather of the British Isles?
2 What is a depression, and why do depressions form where the polar and tropical air masses meet?
3 Make a copy of Fig 265 (ii). Label the warm and cold sectors and the wind direction in each of these sectors (see Fig 265 (i)). Describe how the weather would change at place Z as the depression passes over.
4 What is an anticyclone?
5 Why are depressions, but not anticyclones, associated with rain?
6 Copy and complete Fig 267 which compares anticyclonic conditions in summer and winter.
7 Explain why anticyclones are often associated with mist and fog.

	Summer	Winter
Temperatures		
Cloud cover		
Wind speed		
Rain		
Other features		

Fig 267 The characteristics of an anticyclone

Fig 266 An autumn fog

WEATHER, CLIMATE AND VEGETATION 6.5

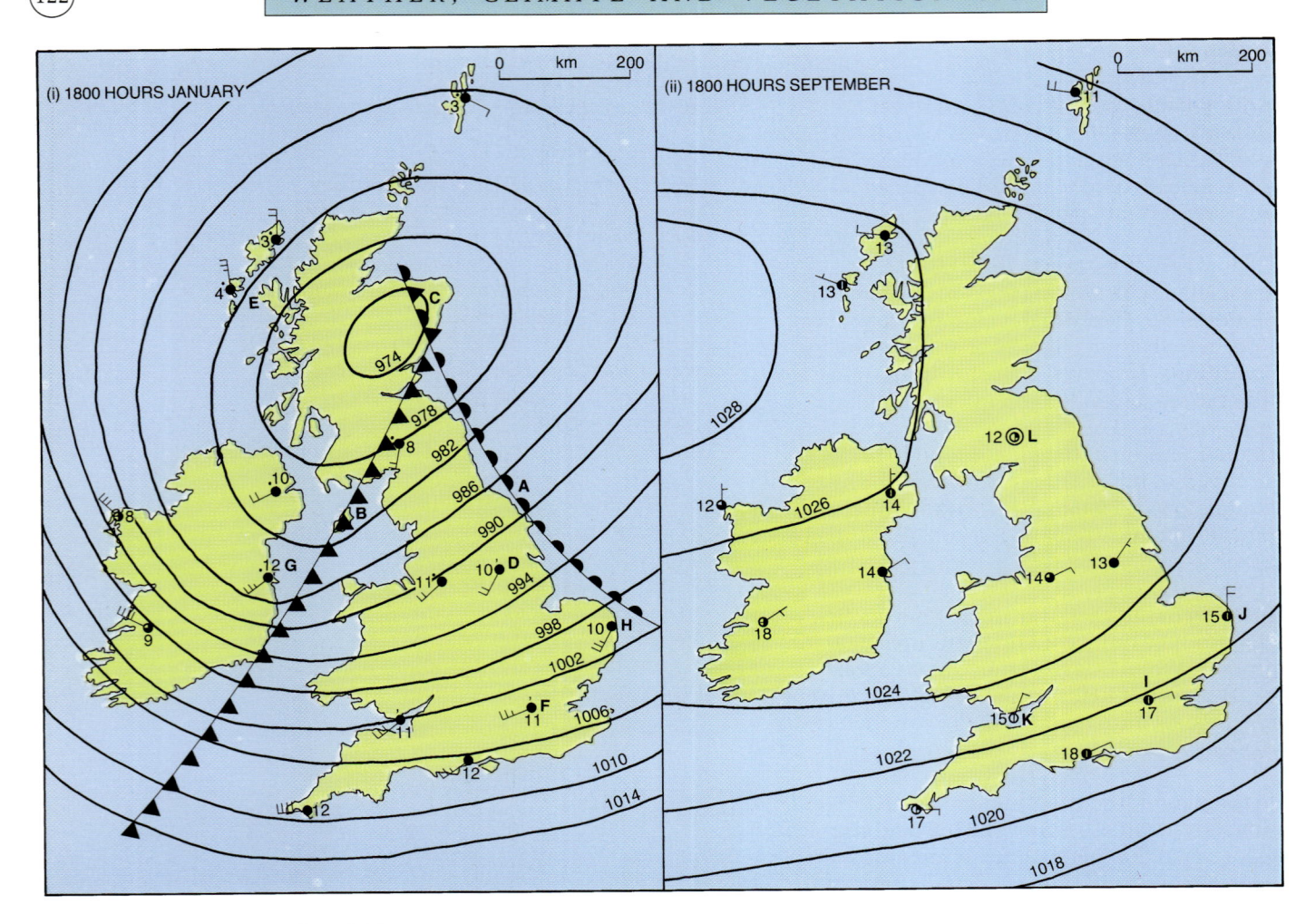

Fig 268 Synoptic charts (i) and (ii)

Synoptic Charts

The weather maps drawn by the Meteorological Office are called synoptic charts because they give a synopsis (summary) of the weather at a particular time. The symbols used on these maps are shown in Fig 269. A set of symbols is drawn for each weather station; an example is given in Fig 270.

These synoptic charts make it possible to identify fronts, depressions and anticyclones. We have seen the type of weather these systems bring, and how they move and develop. By studying the charts and applying this knowledge it is possible to forecast the weather.

WEATHER, CLIMATE AND VEGETATION 6.5

ENQUIRY

For Fig 268 (i)

1. What type of pressure system is shown? Name the fronts A, B and C.
2. Why is it warmer at D than E?
3. What type of cloud is most likely to be found at F, and G?
4. How would you describe wind speeds in southern England?
5. What are weather conditions at H likely to be by the morning?

For Fig 268 (ii)

6. What type of pressure system is shown?
7. Why is it warmer at I than J?
8. What type of cloud is most likely to be found at K?
9. How would you describe wind speeds in southern Britain?
10. What are weather conditions at L likely to be by the morning?

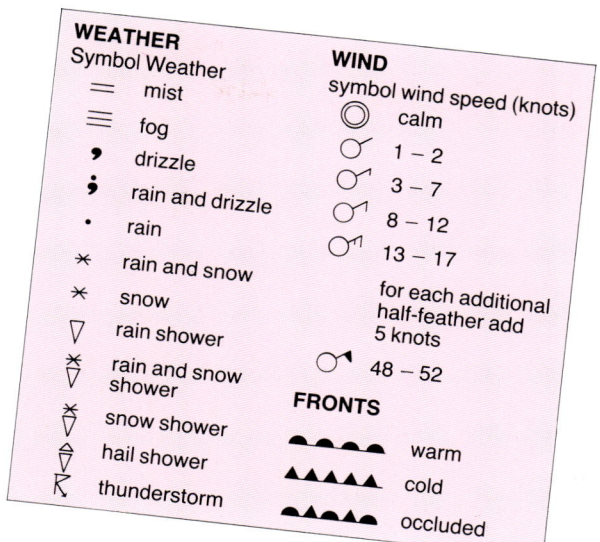

WEATHER
Symbol Weather
= mist
≡ fog
, drizzle
; rain and drizzle
• rain
* rain and snow
✶ snow
▽ rain shower
rain and snow shower
snow shower
hail shower
thunderstorm

WIND
symbol wind speed (knots)
○ calm
1 – 2
3 – 7
8 – 12
13 – 17
for each additional half-feather add 5 knots
48 – 52

FRONTS
warm
cold
occluded

Fig 269 Weather symbols

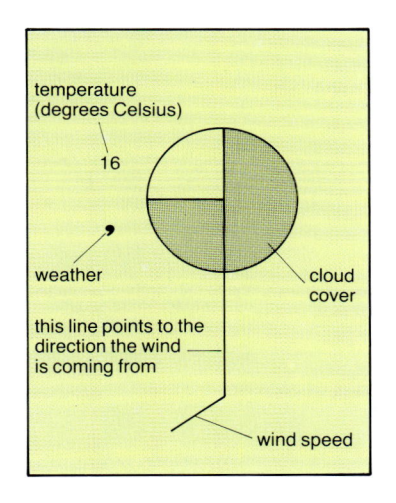

Fig 270 Weather station

temperature (degrees Celsius)
16
weather
cloud cover
this line points to the direction the wind is coming from
wind speed

6.6 How does climate and vegetation vary from place to place?

Fig 271 shows the distribution of three types of climate: the temperate climate, the continental climate and the equatorial climate. Fig 272 shows the distribution of three types of vegetation. The similarities between the two distributions can be clearly seen.

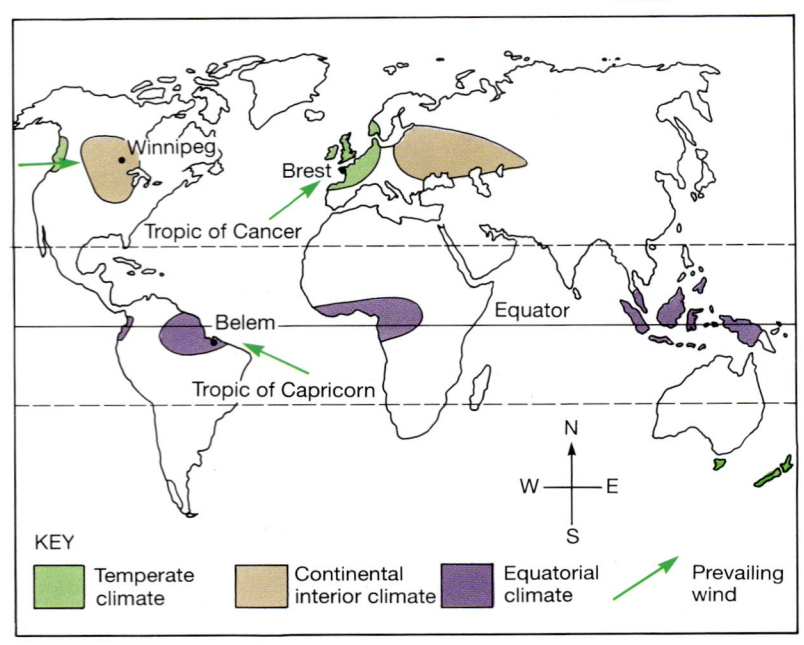

Fig 271 World distribution of three types of climate

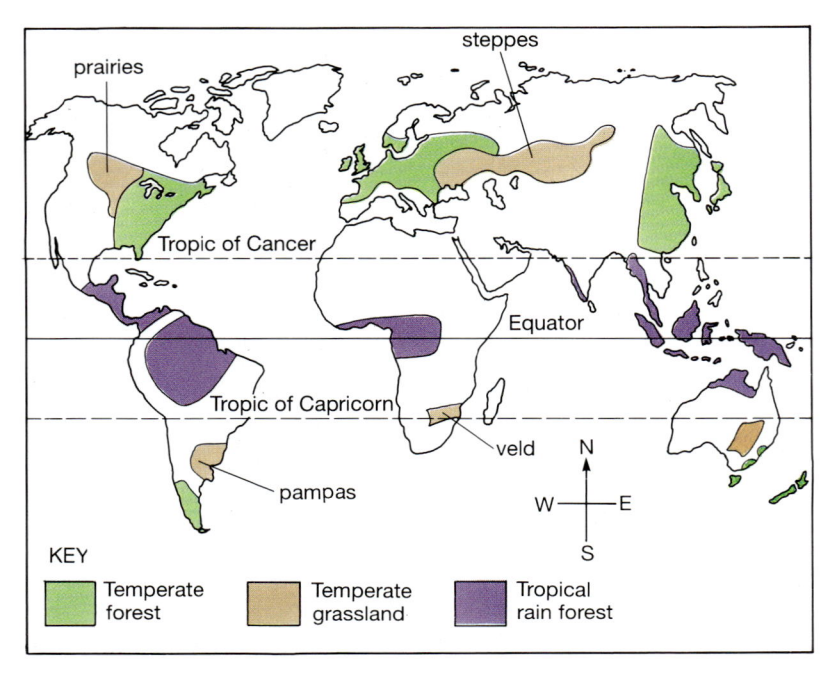

Fig 272 World distribution of three types of vegetation

The Equatorial Climate and the Tropical Rain Forest

The hot, wet conditions of the equatorial region mean that trees and plants grow very quickly. This means that there is great competition for light and space and it explains why the trees have tall, straight trunks with few branches until the roof (**canopy**) of the forest. It also explains why other plants, such as lianas (creepers), grow up to the canopy to flower.

The climate is much the same throughout the year which means that the trees lose their leaves gradually rather than all at once. When a tree dies and falls to the forest floor new trees quickly grow up to take its place; this explains why the canopy can be at different levels within the forest. Many of the trees have buttress roots to support their huge size.

The canopy makes the floor of the forest very dark so very little can grow there. Its most important feature is a thick layer of litter — rotting vegetation. This decomposes very rapidly, mainly because of the fungi which thrive in the hot, wet, dark conditions. As it decomposes the nutrients needed by the trees and plants are released. When the forest soils are thin, e.g. in Brazil, these nutrients are quickly taken up by the trees and stored in their roots and trunks. Where soils are thicker, e.g. in Malaysia, more of these nutrients are stored in the soil itself.

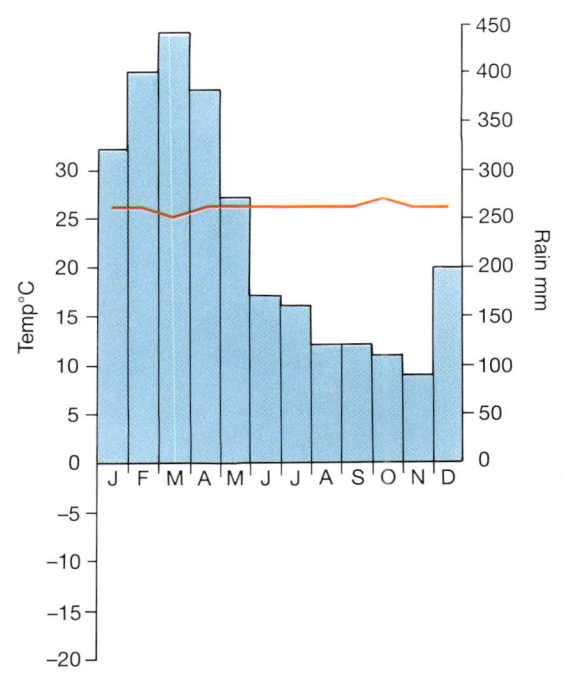

Fig 273 Climate graph of Belem

Fig 275 Tropical rain forest in Malaysia

Fig 274 Tropical rain forest

The British Climate and the Temperate Forest

The trees of the temperate forest are **deciduous** which means that they lose their leaves in winter. They do this for two main reasons: firstly, to save water (trees **transpire** (breathe out) water through their leaves and in the winter water may be in short supply because it is frozen); and secondly, to stop them from being damaged by wind, snow and frost. Some examples of trees found in the temperate forest are oak, elm, ash, willow and alder.

In the summer the canopy cuts out most of the light so only plants which like shade e.g. bracken and ivy grow on the forest floor. In the winter and spring light can get through and a number of flowers bloom before the trees get all of their leaves, e.g. primrose, bluebell and anemone.

Vast areas of the temperate forest in Europe and North America have been cleared in the past to make way for farming and settlement. For example, there is less than five per cent of Britain's original forest left. In many areas it only survives because of the work of conservation groups (Fig 278).

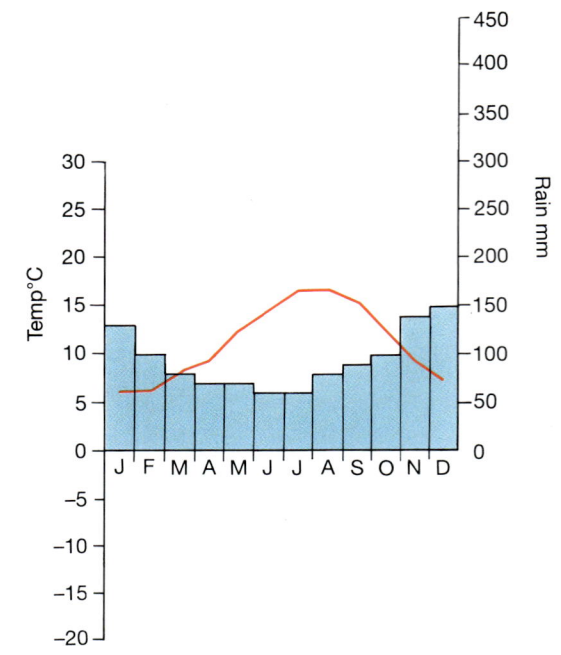

Fig 276 Climate graph of Brest

Fig 277 Temperate forest

Fig 278 (i) Wildlife Trust notice, Wistow Wood, Cambridgeshire
(ii) Wistow Wood

The Continental Climate and the Temperate Grassland

The temperate grassland is found in areas where it is too dry for trees to grow. Fires started by lightning, and animals grazing are also thought to play a part in keeping these grasslands free of trees because any young trees are burnt or eaten before they have a chance to become established.

The grasses have adapted to the hot, dry summers and the cold, snowy winters by either having long roots or by growing quickly in the spring when the snow melts. They grow up to a metre in height in the wetter parts of these regions, while in the drier parts they are rarely taller than 50 cm. They have a thick, matted system of roots which binds the soil together and prevents erosion in the dry, windy conditions. The problems of the Dust Bowl in North America illustrate the difficulties farmers have had in learning how to care for this environment (see Section 1.8).

As with the temperate forest, vast areas of the temperate grassland have been turned into farmland, although large areas do still remain (Fig 281).

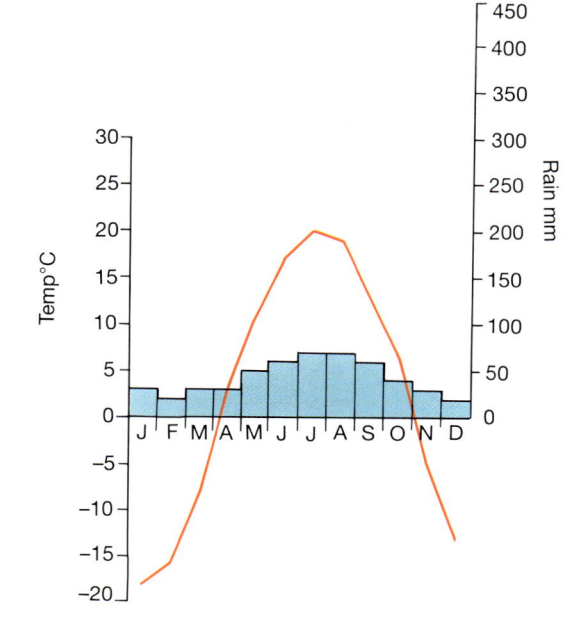

Fig 279 Climate graph of Winnipeg

Fig 281 Prairie Badlands National Park, South Dakota, USA

Fig 280 Temperate grassland

WEATHER, CLIMATE AND VEGETATION 6.6

ENQUIRY

1 For each of the three types of climate shown on Fig 271 describe where it is found. (Use the names of the continents in your descriptions; the part of the continent, e.g. north, south, central; the shape of the region, e.g. thin, long; and the size of the region.) Describe the similarities and differences between this map and Fig 272.

2 Describe the equatorial climate. How has the tropical rain forest adapted to this climate? Copy and label Fig 274 to show the main features of the tropical rain forest.

3 Describe the British climate. How has the temperate forest adapted to this climate? Draw a simple sketch of Fig 278 (ii) and label the following layers: litter; ground plants; shrubs/bushes; young trees; main canopy. What evidence is there that this photograph was taken in the spring?

4 Describe the continental climate. How has the temperate grassland adapted to this climate? Copy and label Fig 280. Add brief details/explanations to your diagram. In which countries are these temperate grasslands found — Prairies, Pampas, Veld and Steppes?

5 Which of the factors affecting vegetation in Fig 282 are not to do with climate?

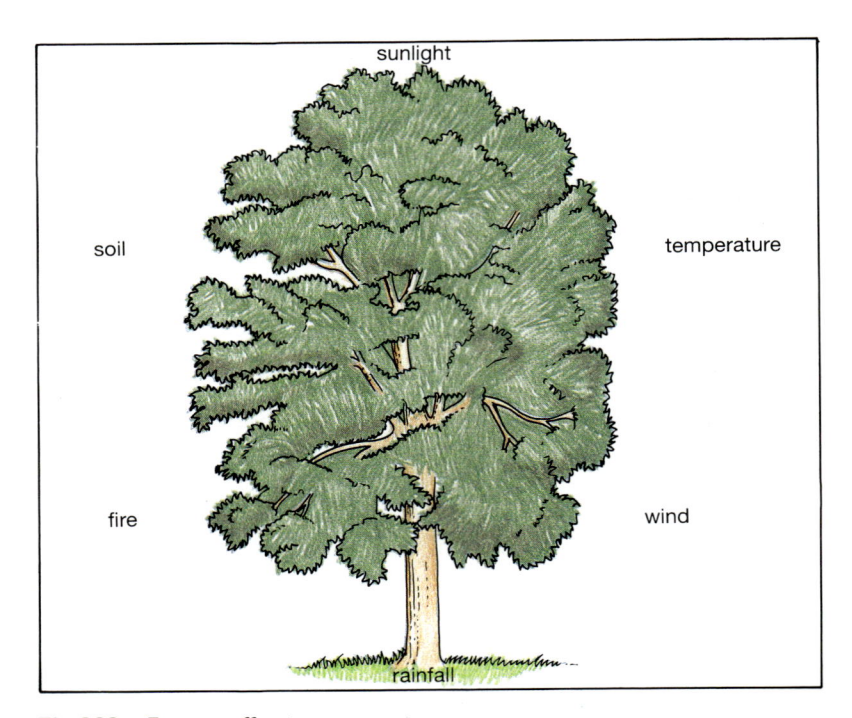

Fig 282 Factors affecting vegetation

6.7 What explains the world pattern of climate?

Latitude

As a general rule, temperatures get lower as you move away from the equator. This is for two reasons. Firstly, the sun's rays are concentrated onto a smaller area of the earth's surface. Secondly, they have to travel through a smaller amount of the earth's atmosphere so there is less chance of them being absorbed and/or reflected. These points are shown in Fig 283.

For example, the effect of latitude helps to explain why Belem has a hotter climate than Brest or Winnipeg.

Distance from the Sea

The sea heats up and cools down more slowly than the land. This means that in the summer places near the coast are cooler than places inland, whereas in the winter places near the coast are warmer than places inland (Fig 284).

For example, this helps to explain why Brest and Winnipeg have very different climates despite being on the same latitude: the sea helps to keep Brest neither too hot nor too cold, whereas the rapid heating and cooling of the land gives Winnipeg its big range of temperature.

Winds

Winds are also important in explaining the location of different types of climate. The prevailing (most common) winds affecting the three types of climate discussed in Section 6.6 are shown on Fig 290, page 132.

At the equator the North East and the South East Trade Winds meet. At the earth's surface they "cancel each other out", resulting in very light winds or no wind at all; this is the belt running round the earth known as the Doldrums. However, strong currents of air are found above the surface where these winds meet and these upward movements of air help to cause the almost daily convection storms (see page 117) which give places like Belem their very high rainfall.

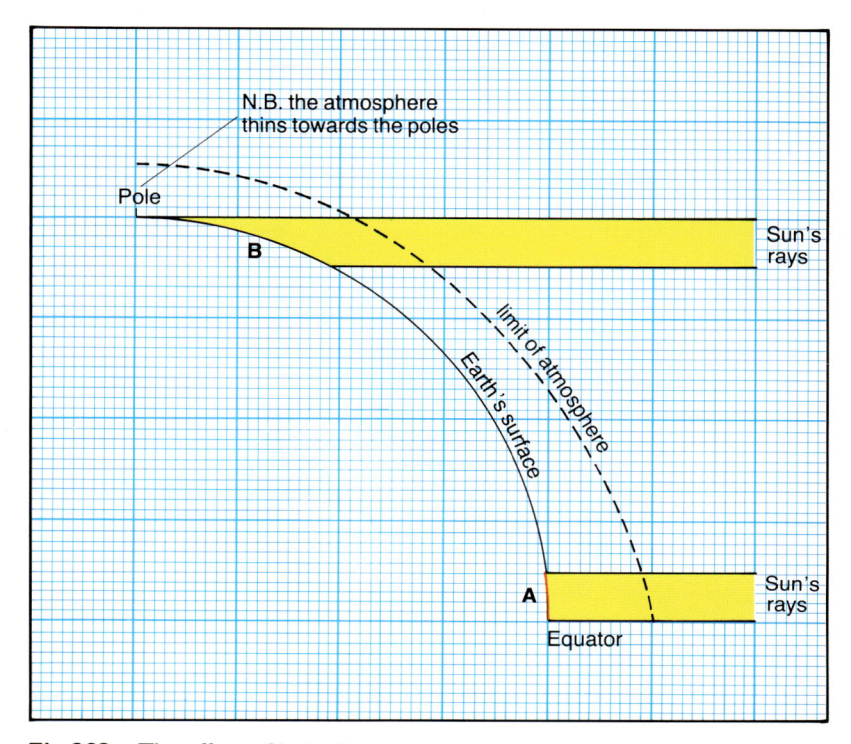

Fig 283 The effect of latitude on temperature

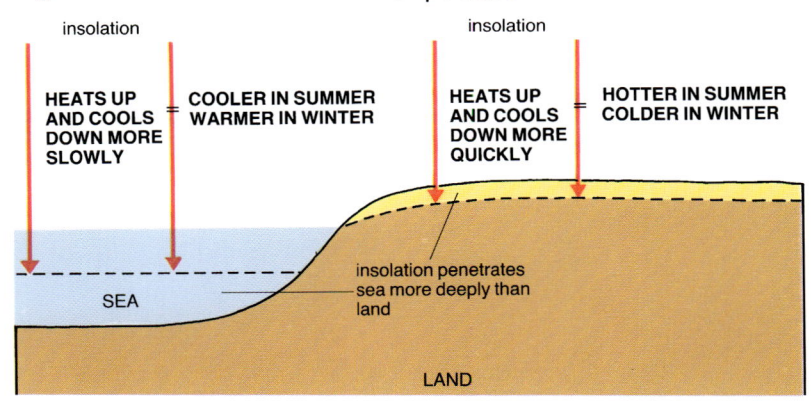

Fig 284 The effect of distance from the sea

All of the places with a temperate climate have prevailing winds which blow from the sea. These winds pick up the sea's moderating influence so they help to keep these regions neither too hot nor too cold. They also pick up moisture which keeps these places wet all year round. Depression rain is common because this is the zone where warm air from the tropics meets cold air from the poles (see pages 117 and 119).

WEATHER, CLIMATE AND VEGETATION 6.7

Month	J	F	M	A	M	J	J	A	S	O	N	D
Temp °C	13	13	13	13	13	13	13	13	13	13	13	13
Rain mm	120	130	150	190	30	50	20	30	80	130	100	100

Fig 285 Climate statistics for Quito

The prevailing winds in the continental interiors are from the west. They are very dry winds because, in North America, most of their moisture falls on the Rocky Mountains while in Europe most of their moisture falls on the coast. Also, by the time they have blown so far inland they have lost their moderating influence on temperatures.

Relief

Mountain ranges have a very big influence on climate. They force air to rise and as it does so it cools down at an average rate of 6°C for every 1000 metres; as a result, even places near the equator can have very low temperatures. For example, Quito in Ecuador has a similar latitude to Belem but it is at a height of 2812 metres compared with Belem's 24 metres. Quito, like Belem, has a low range of temperature but its average temperature is very much lower because of its altitude (Fig 285).

Mountain ranges are also the cause of **relief rainfall** (see page 117). The influence of the Rocky Mountains on rainfall is shown in Fig 286.

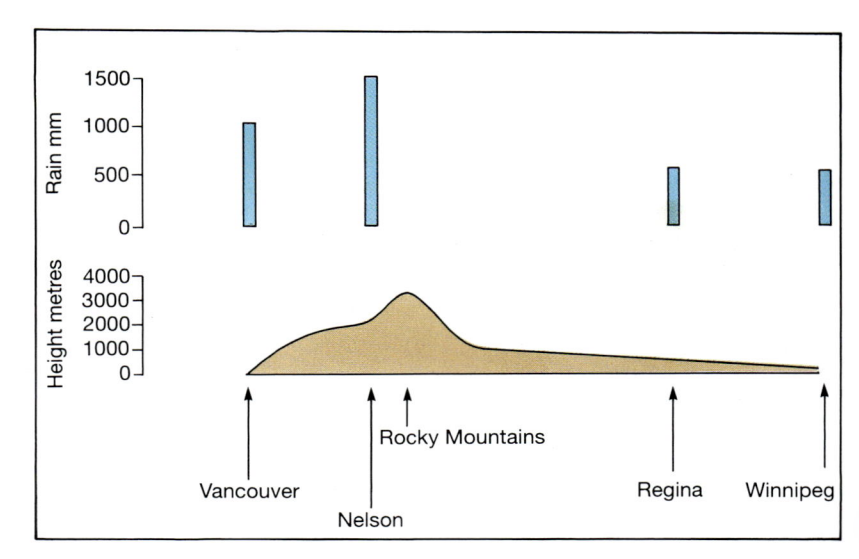

Fig 286 Rocky Mountains: relief and rainfall

Relief also influences **microclimate** and this can be very significant in mountainous regions. Aspect means the direction in which a slope is facing. In the northern hemisphere the south facing slope gets the sun and is therefore warmer than the north facing slope which is in the shade. This has a big influence on land use (Fig 287).

Fig 287 The effect of aspect

WEATHER, CLIMATE AND VEGETATION 6.7

ENQUIRY

1 How many small squares are the sun's rays concentrated on at the equator (A) and at the pole (B) in Fig 283?
2 What is the area of the earth's atmosphere (in small squares) which the sun's rays have to pass through at the equator (A) and at the pole (B) in Fig 283?
3 Use your answers to questions 1 and 2 to explain why latitude affects temperature. Give an example.
4 Explain why distance from the sea affects temperature. Give an example.
5 Match the three climate types on Fig 271, page 124, with the correct description from this list: mild winds blowing from the sea; gentle winds at ground level but strong currents of air above the surface; dry winds blowing across the land.
6 Explain how relief affects temperature. Work out the average temperature at Quito and compare it with the average temperature at Belem (see Figs 285 and 273 for the temperature statistics).
7 Explain why Regina is drier than Nelson on Fig 286.
8 How and why has aspect influenced land use in Fig 287?

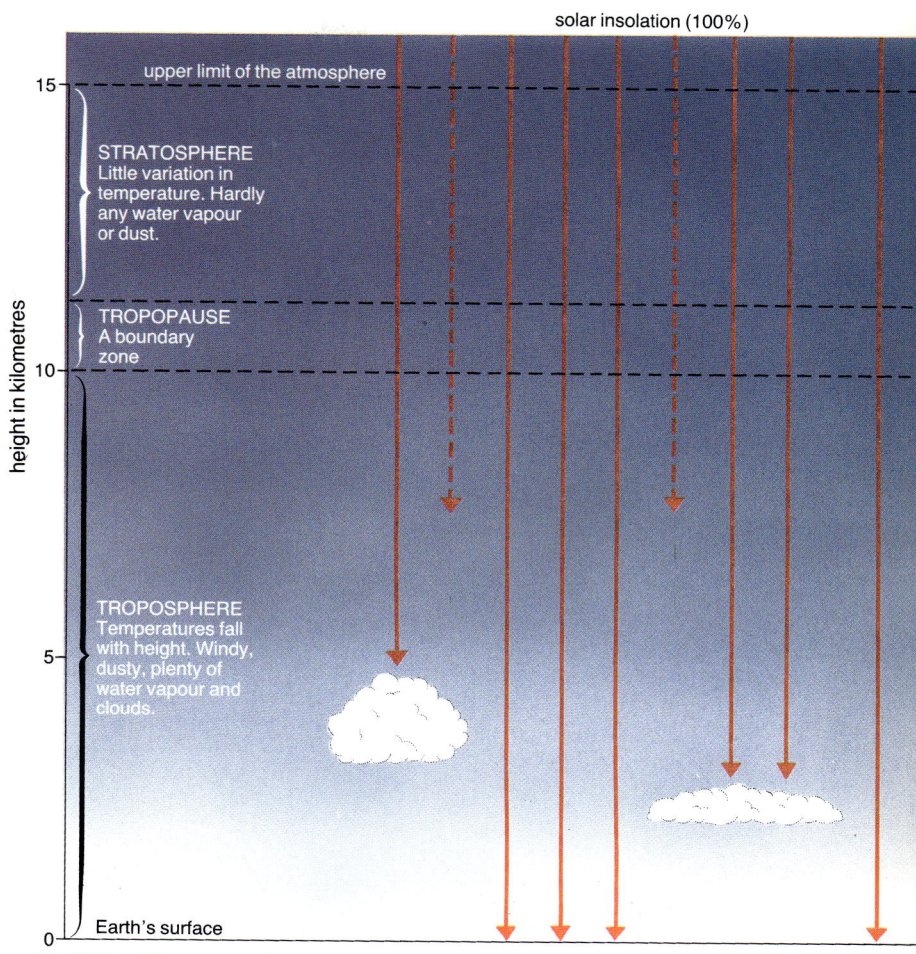

Fig 288 The atmosphere

Atmospheric Circulation

The lowest layer of the earth's **atmosphere**, the troposphere (Fig 288), is always on the move. Global winds carry heat and clouds across continents and oceans, and an understanding of these winds is important to an explanation of the world's different climates.

The theoretical pattern of atmospheric circulation (in the northern hemisphere) is shown in Fig 289. Warm air at the equator rises, causing low pressure. As it moves towards the pole it is deflected to the east by the rotation of the earth and because of this it runs out of energy and it sinks, causing high pressure. Winds then blow from this area of high pressure back to the low pressure at the equator.

At the pole cold air sinks, causing high pressure. As it moves towards the equator it meets warm air coming up from the tropics which rises, causing low pressure. This rising air spills to the north and the south and completes the three systems, or cells, of wind.

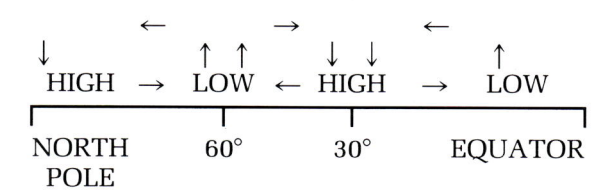

	←		→	↓ ↓	←	
↓		↑ ↑				↑
HIGH	→	LOW	←	HIGH	→	LOW
NORTH POLE		60°		30°		EQUATOR

Fig 289 Wind cells

This theoretical pattern would produce bands of pressure running round the earth, both north and south of the equator. With winds always blowing from high to low pressure and being deflected by the earth's rotation to the right in the northern hemisphere, and to the left in the southern hemisphere, there is also a theoretical pattern of global winds (Fig 290). However, the real pattern of atmospheric circulation (Fig 291) is more complicated than this for a number of reasons.

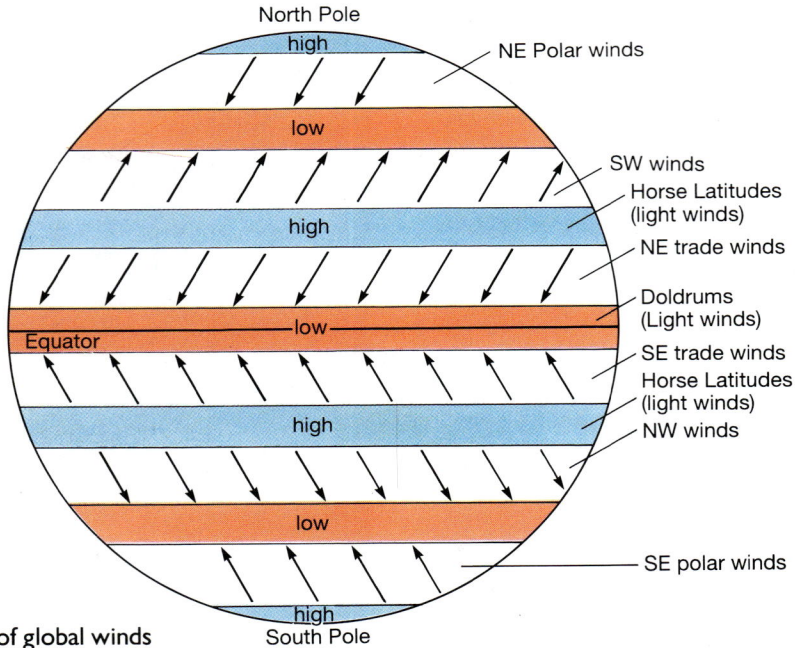

Fig 290 The theoretical pattern of global winds

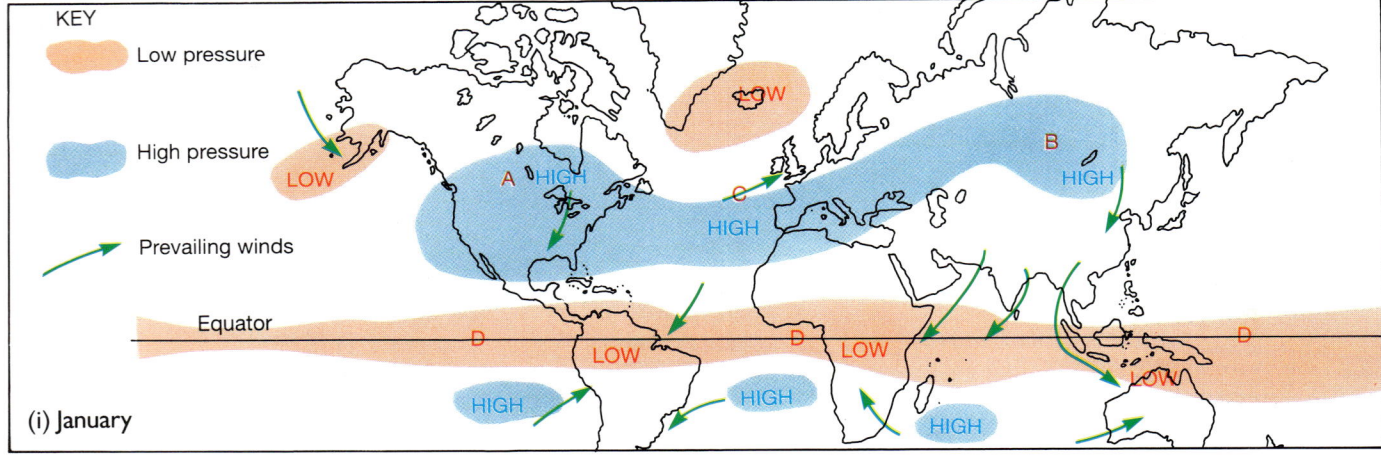

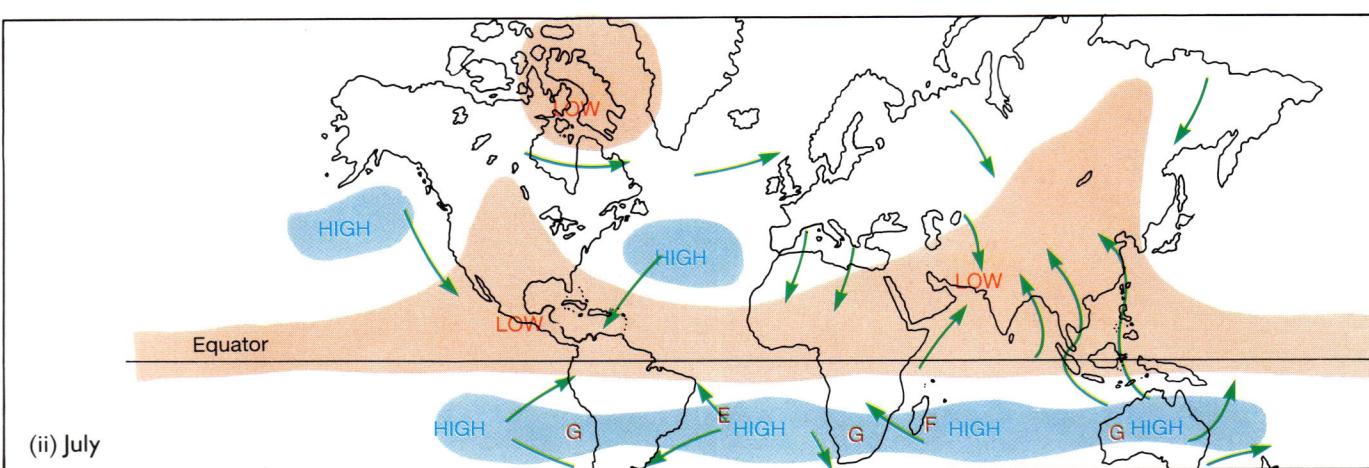

Fig 291 Pressure and winds

Firstly, high altitude winds, called **jet streams**, have been discovered. For example, the polar jet stream (Fig 292) is found at about 9 km above the surface and blows in an easterly direction with an average wind speed of 100 km per hour. It is the result of the collision between the polar air moving southwards and the tropical air moving northwards. It follows a meandering course with between two and six loops. It is very important to the climate of these latitudes because it controls the path taken by depressions (see page 119). They always begin at the poleward moving section of the jet stream and collapse when it turns to the south.

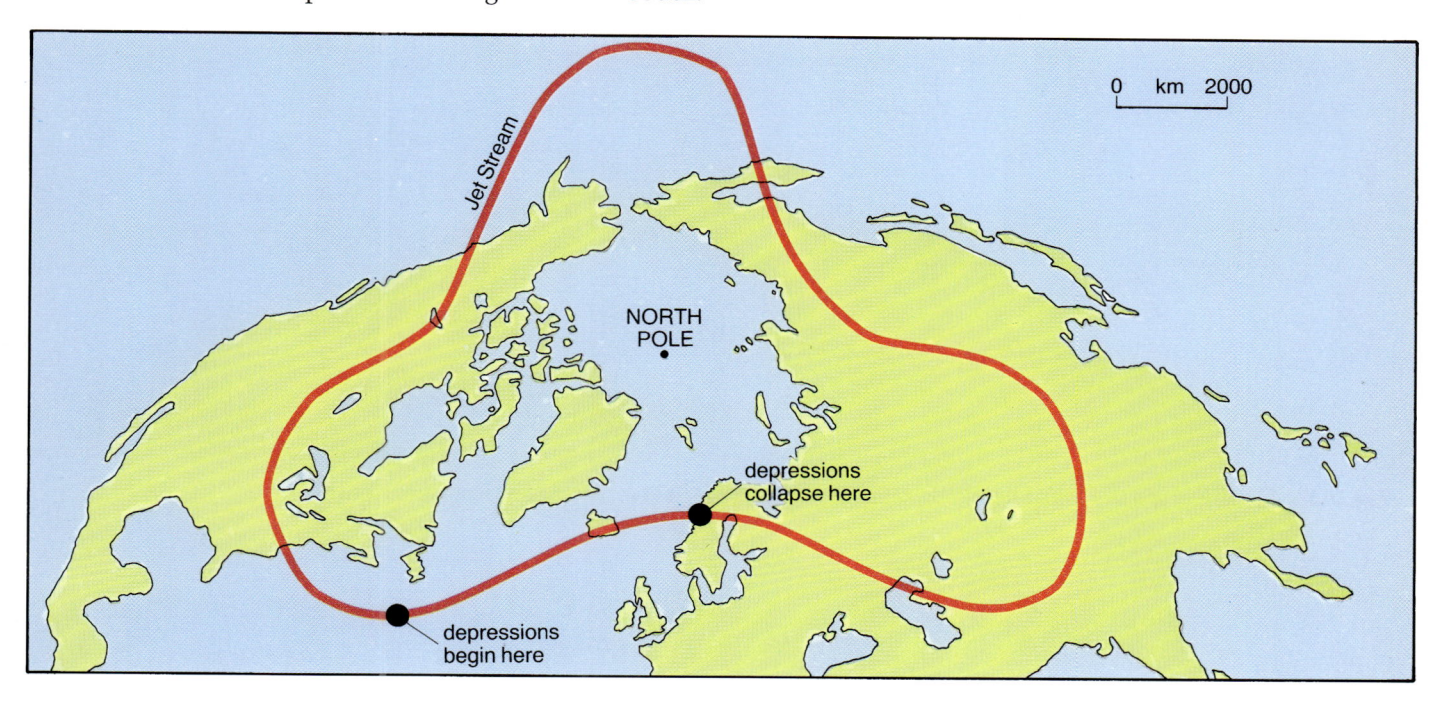

Fig 292 The polar jet stream

Secondly, the continents and oceans heat up and cool down at different rates. For example, the rapid heating of the continental interiors in the summer causes air to rise and low pressure to develop, while in the winter rapid cooling causes air to sink and high pressure to develop. These areas of high and low pressure, in turn, control the movement of winds.

The earth's major mountain ranges affect atmospheric circulation as well. For example, the Himalayas separate pressure systems and act as a barrier to winds.

Another major influence on atmospheric circulation is the apparent movement of the sun between the tropics because of the tilt of the earth's axis. As it moves it drags the belt of equatorial low pressure with it and this causes the other pressure belts to move as well.

There is a very clear relationship between pressure, winds and climate. The rising air at the equator which builds up towering cumulonimbus clouds is one of the main reasons for the equatorial zone's very high rainfall (see page 125). As the sun moves between the tropics it drags this belt of heavy rain with it. This gives the **savannah grasslands** to the north and south of the equatorial zone one rainy season (when the sun is overhead) and one dry season (when the sun is at the opposite tropic).

To the north and south of the savannah are the world's hot deserts. It is in these latitudes that the warm air from the equator is sinking. As it sinks it warms up and because it is sinking clouds cannot form so rain is unlikely.

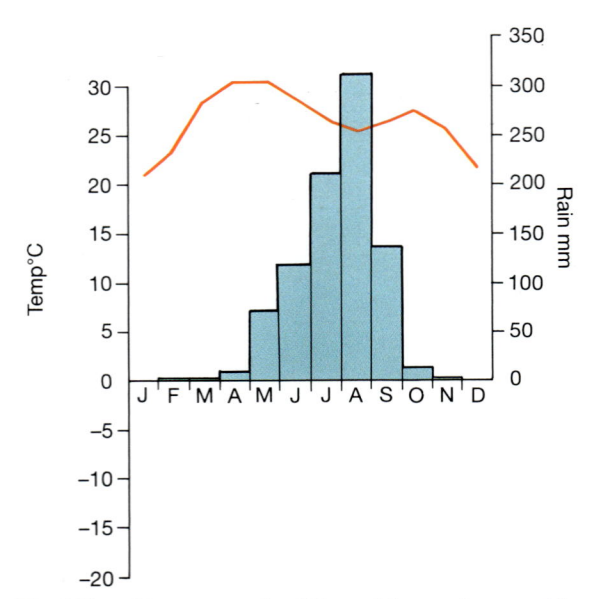

Fig 293 Climate graph of Kano, Nigeria (savannah)

Fig 294 Tsevo West National Park, Kenya

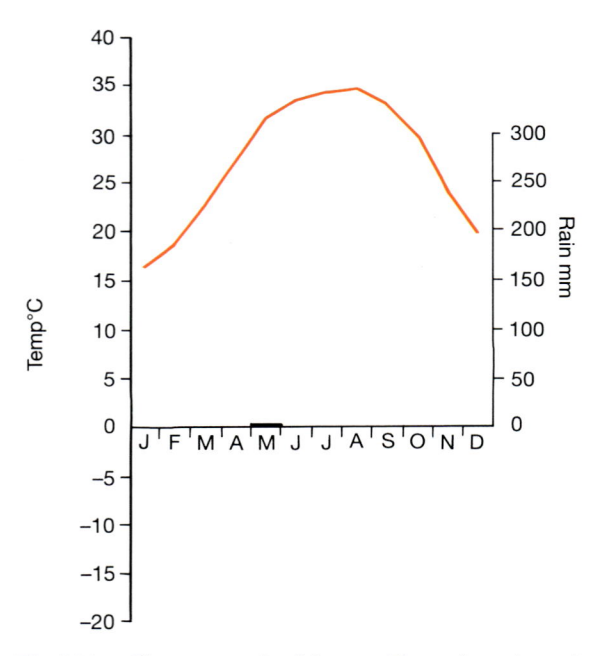

Fig 296 Climate graph of Aswan, Egypt (hot desert)

Fig 295 Hot desert, California

The **monsoon** climate affects a large part of Asia (see Fig 291). In the summer the Asian sub-continent heats up more quickly than the sea. As a result low pressure develops over the land and high pressure develops over the sea. Winds therefore blow from the sea to the land and bring the moisture for the monsoon rains. In the winter the situation is reversed. The Asian sub-continent cools down more quickly than the sea. As a result high pressure develops over the land and low pressure develops over the sea. Winds therefore blow from the land to the sea. They pick up very little moisture as they blow across the land so they produce very little, if any, rain.

Further away from the equator, the mid-latitude depressions form where the warm air from the tropics meets the cold air from the poles. In turn, these depressions are

WEATHER, CLIMATE AND VEGETATION 6.7

Fig 297 (i) Rainy season

(ii) Dry season

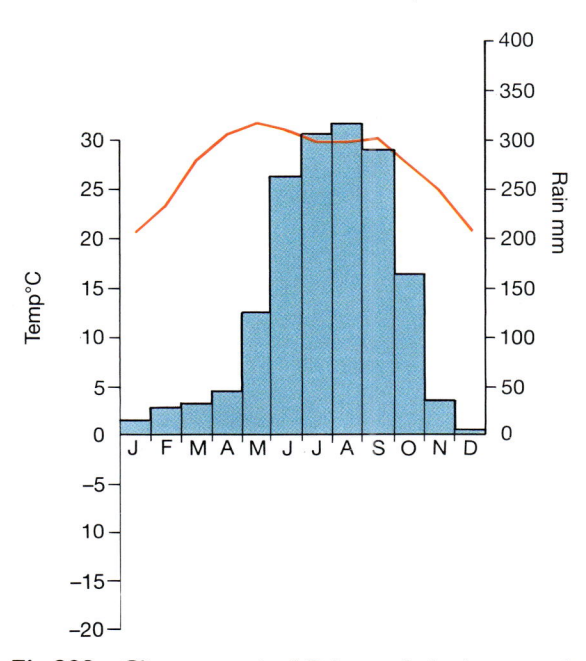

Fig 298 Climate graph of Calcutta, India (monsoon)

controlled by the polar jet stream. The weather associated with these depressions gives the British climate its main characteristics (see page 126).

The influence of the land is important to the climate of the continental interiors of North America and Europe/Asia (see page 127). The rapid heating and cooling of the land gives these regions their wide annual range of temperature. The high pressure which develops in the winter produces out-blowing winds and the low pressure which develops in the summer produces in-blowing winds. (This low pressure causes the North East Trade winds over eastern USA and Asia to disappear in the summer.)

Distance from the equator is the main influence on the climate of the polar regions — the subarctic, **tundra** and polar climates. Winters are long, summers are short and the air is so cold that it contains very little moisture. However, the fact that the air is sinking helps to ensure that **precipitation** is unlikely and the high pressure which develops mean out-blowing winds.

Fig 299 Tundra landscape

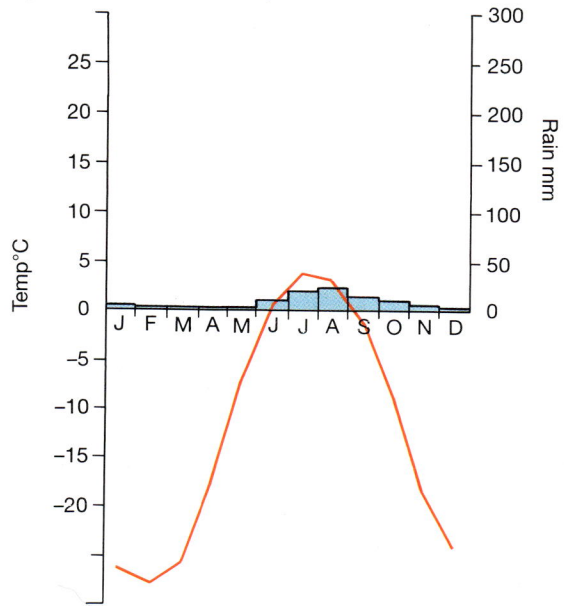

Fig 300 Climate graph of Barrow, Alaska (tundra)

WEATHER, CLIMATE AND VEGETATION 6.7

ENQUIRY

1. Study Fig 291 (i):
    a) Why are there large areas of high pressure at A and B?
    b) Give two reasons why the winds at C blow from the south west.
    c) What is the name of the low pressure belt D, and what are its characteristics?
2. Study Fig 291 (ii):
    a) Why does the equatorial low pressure belt extend further northwards than it does in January?
    b) Give two reasons why the winds at E and F blow from the south east, and what are they called?
    c) What is the name of the high pressure belt G, and what are its characteristics?
3. Use an atlas, Fig 271, page 124 and Fig 291 to complete these tasks:
    (i) Onto an outline map of the world mark on and label the following climate regions: equatorial climate; temperate climate; continental climate; the hot deserts (Californian, Atacama, Sahara, Namib, Kalahari, Arabian, Thar, Western Australian); savannah; the limit of the monsoon climate; and the tundra.
    (ii) For each of these regions except the monsoon region, add brief labels to describe its climate and to explain how it is influenced by pressure and winds.
4. Use Figs 291 (i) and (ii) to draw two sketch maps of the monsoon region, one showing pressure and winds in January and one showing pressure and winds in July. Add labels to explain the causes of the monsoon climate. Mark on the Himalayas and add a label to describe the effect they have on the winds of this region.

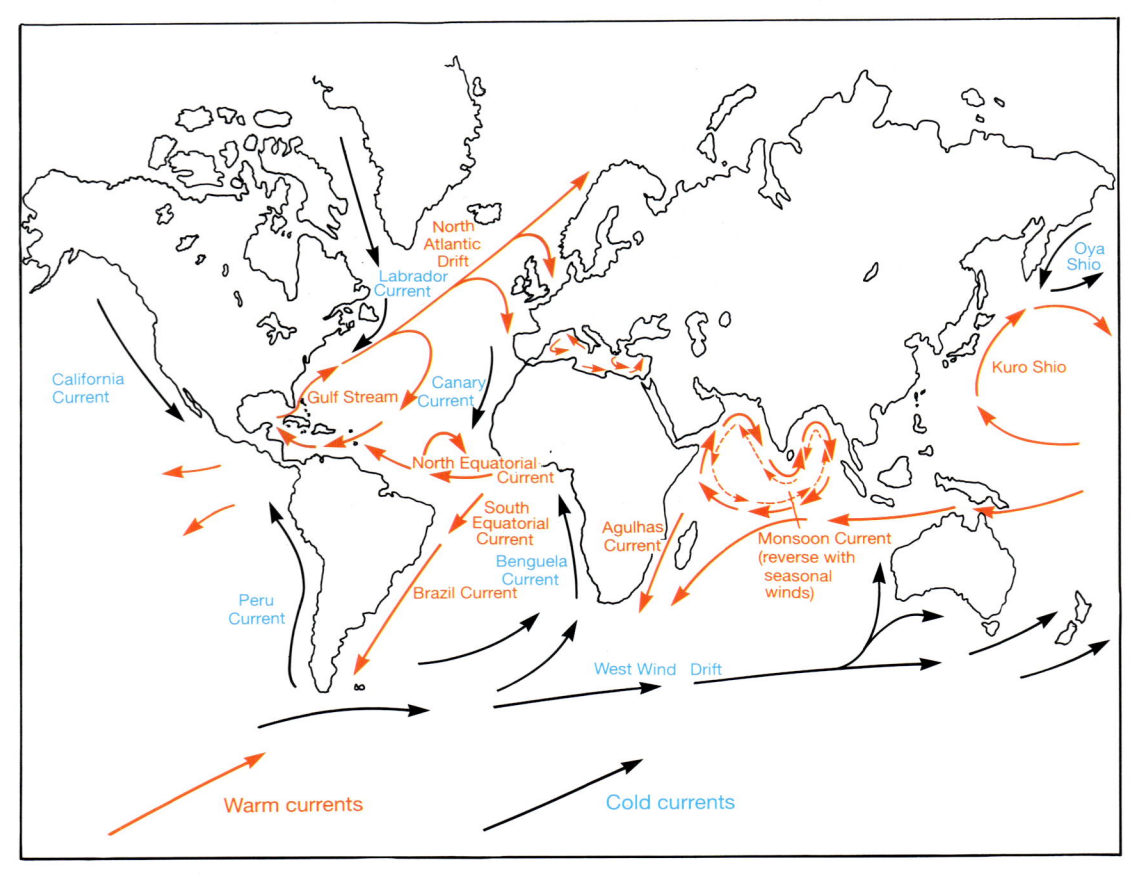

Fig 301 Ocean currents

Ocean Currents

There are three main causes of **ocean currents**. Most surface currents are caused by the prevailing winds. For example, the Gulf Stream is powered by strong south-westerlies and reaches speeds of up to 220 km per day. Most of the water re-circulates back into the Gulf of Mexico in a clockwise direction but some of it veers off towards Europe as the North Atlantic Drift (Fig 301).

Convection currents are caused by warm water from the tropics flowing towards the poles; there it cools down, sinks, and returns to the tropics along the sea bed.

Differences in salinity (the saltiness of the sea) can also cause ocean currents. For example, water in the Mediterranean is saltier than water in the Atlantic because of the high rate of evaporation and the low rate of input from rain and rivers. An increase in salinity causes an increase in density and this, in turn, causes surface water to sink. As surface water in the Mediterranean sinks a current of less salty water is dragged in from the Atlantic through the Straits of Gibraltar to takes its place, and the process is repeated.

The shape of the continents influences the circulation of ocean currents. For example, the Equatorial Currents pile up water against the coast of Brazil where it splits to form the North Equatorial Current and the Brazil Current (Fig 301).

Ocean currents influence climate because they affect the temperature of winds blowing across them. For example, the North Atlantic Drift is a warm current and it brings mild, wet weather to the shores of Europe, while the Labrador Current brings very cold weather to places on the same latitude in North America.

Ocean currents also help to explain the distribution of the hot deserts. To the west of these deserts are cold currents which cool down the prevailing westerly winds. As a result these winds deposit most of their rain over the sea.

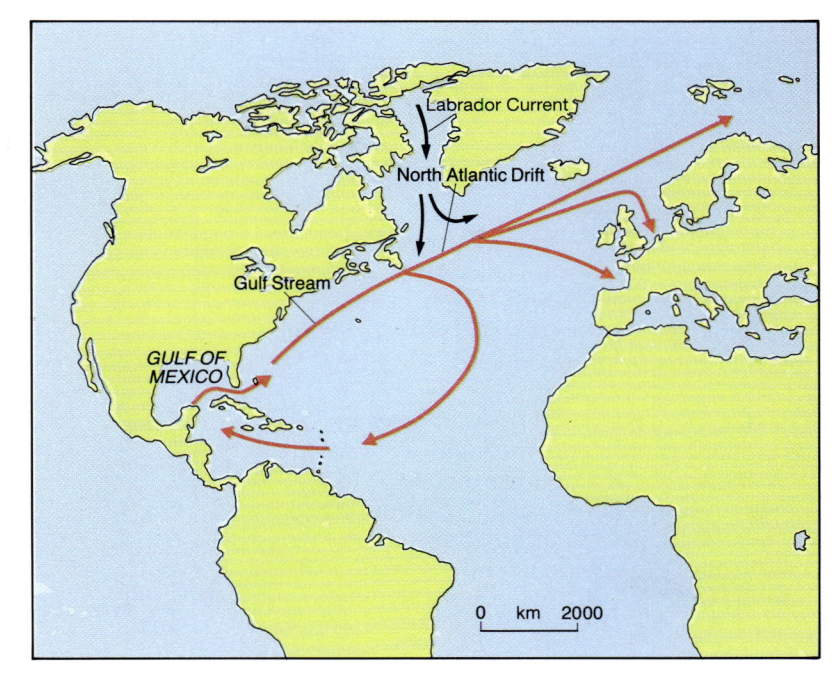

Fig 302 The North Atlantic Drift and the Labrador Current

ENQUIRY

1 Explain the causes of ocean currents.
2 Compare Fig 301 with Figs 290 and 291 (i) and (ii). Which winds account for the following ocean currents: the North Equatorial Current; the South Equatorial Current; and the West Wind Drift. (N.B. ocean currents do not always follow the direction of the prevailing wind exactly but they are given their direction (east-west or west-east) by it.)
3 Describe and explain the effect the North Atlantic Drift has on the climate of Western Europe.
4 Name the cold currents associated with the hot deserts listed in question 3, in the Enquiry on page 136. (If you completed the map for the Enquiry you could mark these currents onto it.) Briefly explain their significance.

6.8 Is climate to blame?

The terrible consequences of drought are rarely out of the news. For example, in 1984-5 30 million Africans were affected by drought, but despite a massive international relief effort the problem remains. Is climate to blame, or is it a problem we have made for ourselves?

In fact, large parts of the world have an unreliable rainfall and drought is a characteristic of a number of the world's major types of climate (Fig 303). Three regions where the rains sometimes fail — the monsoon, the savannah and the semi-arid desert fringes — are examined below.

The seasonal reversal of wind associated with the monsoon rains always take place (see Section 6.7), but it does not always produce a significant amount of rain. For example, since 1940 the monsoon in India has failed on at least ten occasions.

The reason for these failures is not fully understood. The moist winds blowing from the sea have to rise and cool down before they rain. This usally takes place in a series of depressions which track across Asia. Like the mid-latitude depressions, the path they take is controlled by a jet stream. Its path varies which is why sometimes the rains do not fall where they are needed. Conditions in the Indian Ocean, or to the north of the Himalayas, could be responsible for these variations.

The monsoon rains are vital to over half the world's population. If they do not come, or if they come at the wrong time, then the crops are ruined. Drought can quickly lead to famine because many of these countries are very poor (Fig 304).

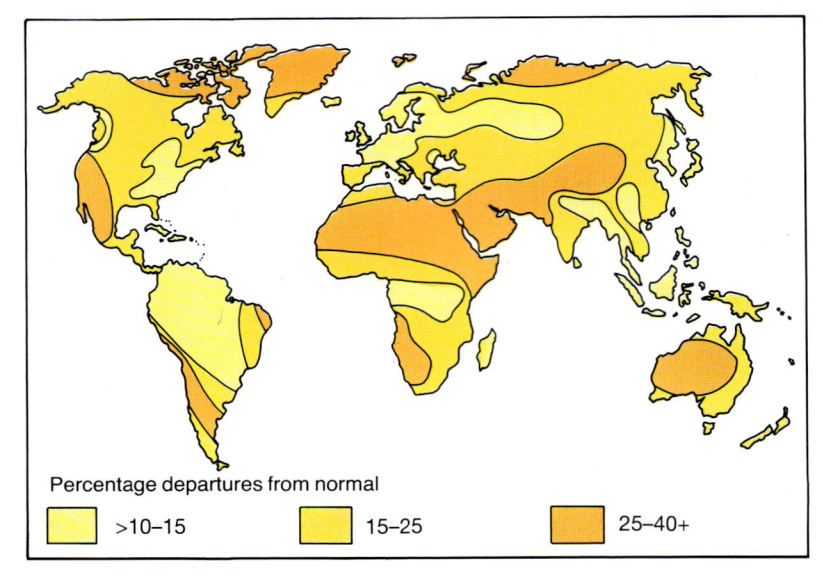

Fig 303 The world pattern of unreliable rainfall

Percentage departures from normal
- >10–15
- 15–25
- 25–40+

The **savannah** regions have one wet season and one dry season (see Section 6.7). However, there is a great deal of variation in the amount of rain from year to year. The size and intensity of the high pressure systems over the tropics, and changes in the pattern of ocean currents, appear to be responsible for this unreliability because they affect the position of the rain-bearing equatorial low pressure belt as it moves with the sun. Droughts are not uncommon; for example, Fig 305 describes the causes and consequences of the drought in the savannah of southern Africa in 1992.

Rain is least reliable in the semi-arid lands on the fringes of the hot deserts and this is where

Country	Income — GNP per capita per year US $	% of people earning a living from farming	Food supply — calories per person per day (average needed = 2400)
India	330	63	2229
Bangladesh	220	57	2037
Sri Lanka	500	43	2246
UK	16 750	2	3270
USA	22 560	3	3642
France	20 600	7	3593

Figure 304 Economic indicators, monsoon Asia and selected MDCs

WEATHER, CLIMATE AND VEGETATION 6.8

the risk of **desertification** — the process by which land becomes desert — is greatest. It is currently affecting 15 million acres a year on the margins of the Californian, Atacama, Sahara, Kalahari and Thar deserts.

Desertification in the Sahel

The problem is worst in the **Sahel**, a belt of land to the south of the Sahara where the desert is advancing in places by six kilometres every year (Figs 306 and 307).

The causes of this problem are complex and far from clear. There is some evidence of a change towards a drier climate in the Sahel. Statistics show that average annual rainfall has decreased since 1950. One suggestion is that this could be the result of global shifts in atmospheric circulation, with the equatorial low pressure belt not moving so far north, perhaps because of **global warming** (see Section 8.3). However, even if this change is permanent, it alone does not explain the relentless and rapid advance of the desert.

According to the aid agencies an area the size of Australia is now affected by drought, threatening 18 million people with starvation; and while there is not so far the acute famine experienced in the Horn of Africa, the possibility of a tragedy on an even larger scale is very much present.

What is especially alarming is that in all the countries affected — Zambia, Zimbabwe, Mozambique, Malawi, Lesotho, Swaziland and parts of South Africa — the drought is aggravating other serious problems and putting back the day when solutions may be found.

In Mozambique, ravaged by seemingly endless civil wars, the drought has set the peace process back and dealt the reeling economy another body blow. In Zambia, a country crippled and impoverished by decades of corruption and maladministration, the new "democratic" government needs both luck and skill to maintain popular support but finds itself struggling to keep its people alive. In Zimbabwe, the drought has shattered the fragile consensus that President Mugabe has generally enjoyed since independence, threatening stability.

The white minority in Zimbabwe probably numbers about 200,000 in a total population of 12 million; but white commercial farmers still occupy much of the most fertile and best watered land. The majority of blacks are peasant farmers still confined to what the British Colonial Administration designated as Tribal Trust Lands. These days they are called "Communal Lands"; and as their populations have grown, they have become increasingly overgrazed and degraded. Now, with seven years of poor rainfall and 18 months of no rainfall, their populations are destitute; their crops have totally failed and their cattle have died. According to the Red Cross, half a million people in southern Zimbabwe are at risk of starvation.

When I visited the Matibi Two Communal Lands near Chiredzi, I found the entire population of 80,000 living on grain handouts. The people have no income and if the food distribution ceases, we shall see again a mass migration of starving people, fleeing from empty bore-holes and withered harvests.

Perhaps the most depressing aspect of the whole picture in Zimbabwe is to see how the drought has aggravated social tensions.

When I spoke to one rancher about the misery on the nearby Communal Lands, he blamed the soaring black birth-rate: "They breed so fast, not even the Big A will take care of it" he said. For a moment, I was puzzled. The big A? Then the penny dropped. He was saying that even Aids could not kill enough people to solve what he perceived to be his country's biggest problem: too many blacks.

It was said in the presence of complete strangers, assuming that because of the colour of our skins we should automatically share their views. If they are prepared to say that Aids has not "done the job", I cannot avoid concluding that they are hoping that what Aids has not done, famine might achieve: that the drought may provide them with their "final solution".

The Guardian 14 September 1992

Fig 305 Africa's drought of despair

WEATHER, CLIMATE AND VEGETATION 6.8

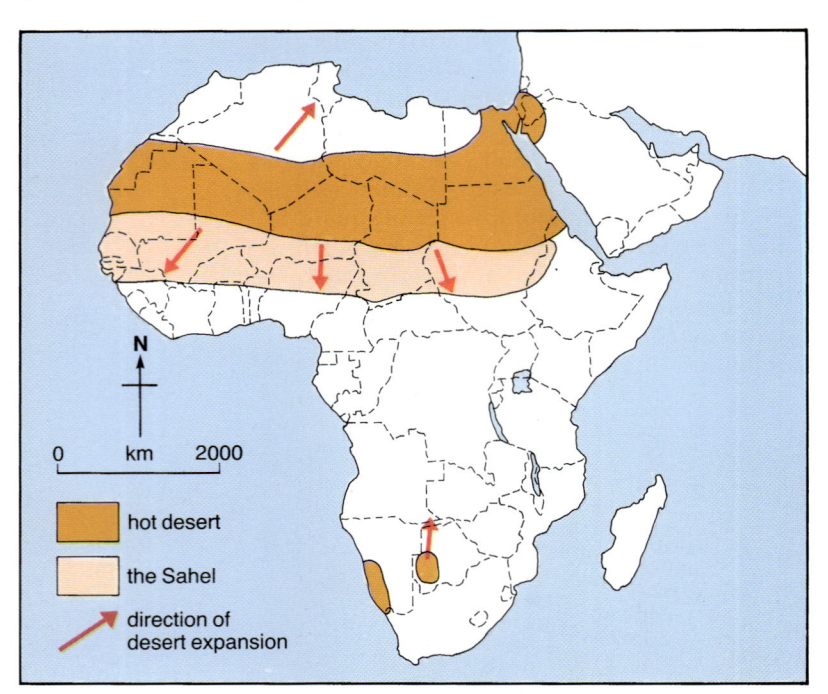

Fig 306 Desertification in Africa

Fig 307 Drought in the Sahel

Population pressure has almost certainly played its part. The traditional, farming systems of the Sahel are **slash and burn** and nomadic grazing. Both these systems give the land time to recover before it is used again, but they can support only low population densities.

In the last 30 years population growth rates in the countries of the Sahel have been high and this has placed an extra pressure on the lands. Fields have been given shorter rest periods and soil fertility and structure have suffered as a result; this, in turn, has caused lower crop yields and soil erosion. The number of livestock has been increased and this has led to overgrazing; this, in turn, means that the soil has lost its protective covering of vegetation and is liable to erosion.

A larger population has meant an increase in the demand for wood for fuel which has led to deforestation. This also leaves the soil unprotected, and the resource a farming community depends on is blown or washed away.

Changes in farming practices may also have contributed to the process of desertification. Settled agriculture with an emphasis on cash crops has been encouraged by many countries as a strategy for rural development. However, this already fragile environment requires very careful management if it is to be farmed intensively or problems of soil exhaustion soon set in.

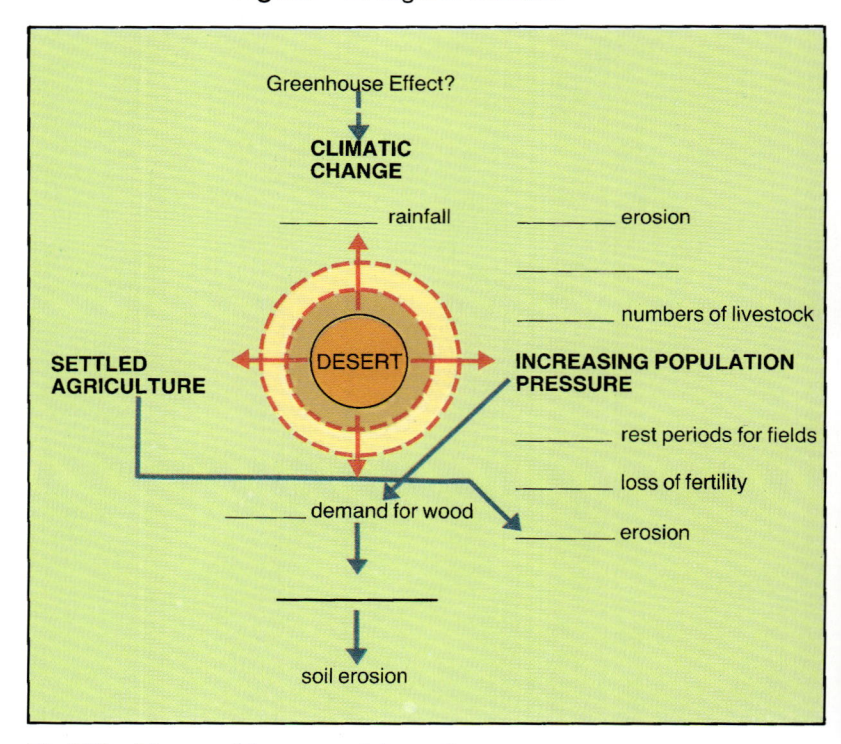

Fig 308 The possible causes of desertification

WEATHER, CLIMATE AND VEGETATION 6.8

The climate of the Sahel has changed in the past and there is evidence of the Sahara being both larger and smaller than it is at the present time. However, it is clear that our activities are at least partly, if not wholly, to blame for the present rate of desertification and it should therefore be possible to take some actions to improve the situation.

However, as in monsoon Asia, the countries of the Sahel are poor and the majority of the people are subsistence farmers. Perhaps not surprisingly, small-scale, inexpensive schemes which increase food production in a short period of time have been the most popular and the most successful ways of tackling the problem.

Reafforestation has taken place, wells have been drilled and small dams have been built. More recently, the use of "magic stones" has been developed (Fig 309). These are simply lines of stones running parallel to the contours of the land. They hold back rainfall which would normally run straight off the hard tropical surface, and give it time to sink in. The result is crop yields up by an average of 50 per cent. Stones are in plentiful supply and the only equipment needed is a simple level to get a correct alignment with the contours — Oxfam have developed one which costs only £3.50 to make.

Fig 309 Magic stones

ENQUIRY

1 Explain why rainfall in each of these three climate regions is unreliable:
   a) monsoon Asia;
   b) the savannah;
   c) the Sahel.
2 Use the statistics in Fig 304 to help you to explain why the failure of the monsoon rains can lead to famine in many countries of Asia.
3 Read Fig 305. What were **a)** the climatic and **b)** the human causes of the 1992 drought in southern Africa?
4 Use an atlas to help you name the countries which make up the Sahel in Africa.
5 Add labels to a copy of Fig 308 to complete an explanation of the possible causes of desertification. In particular, add extra arrows if you think factors are interrelated.
6 What sort of things could be done to slow down the rate of desertification?

ENERGY

ENERGY 7.1

7.1 Where does our energy come from?

The word energy is used in many different ways. If we are too tired to do our homework we say that we have run out of energy. Foods are advertised as being full of energy. When the price of petrol goes up the newspapers say that the cost of energy is rising. All these uses of the word energy have one thing in common: energy makes things work — us, our central heating, our cars.

Most sources of energy come from the sun. **Solar power** comes directly from the sun. Wood comes from trees which use energy from the sun to grow. Coal forms from the remains of trees so it, too, has come from the sun. Winds are caused by the sun heating up the earth's atmosphere.

Some types of energy are **renewable** which means that they will never run out; examples include solar power and wind power. Some resources are renewable as long as we are careful; for example, we will not run out of wood if we plant new trees and do not cut them down at a faster rate than they can grow.

However, other types of energy are non-renewable; for example, **fossil fuels** (coal, oil and natural gas) take millions of years to form, so once we have taken them out of the ground they are gone for ever.

ENQUIRY

1 Complete a copy of Fig 310 by drawing on arrows to show how the different sources of energy are linked to the sun.
2 Which types of energy on Fig 310 do not come from the sun?
3 A common form of energy used in homes in MDCs is electricity. This is a secondary energy source while the ones in Fig 310 are primary sources. What is the difference?
4 Divide the sources of energy in Fig 310 into renewable and non-renewable. (Set your answer out in a table.)

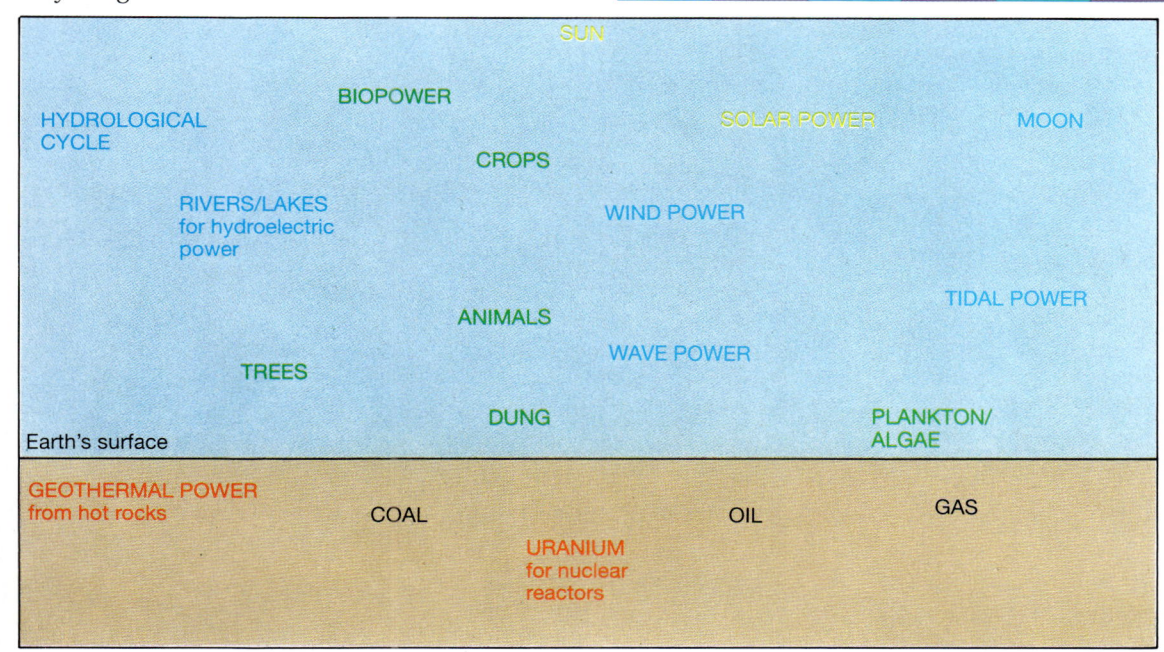

Fig 310 Sources of energy

Global Comparisons

There are big differences between MDCs and EDCs in the amount of energy they use and in the type of energy they use (Fig 311). These differences are even more significant when you bear in mind that three-quarters of the world's population live in EDCs.

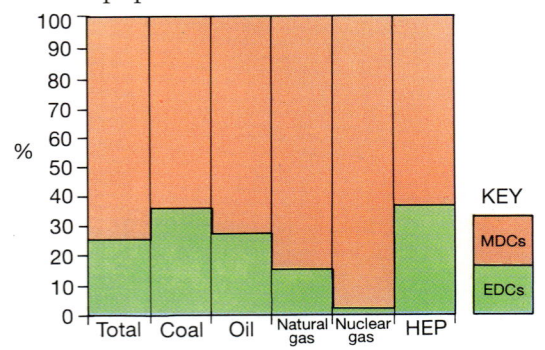

Fig 311 World energy consumption

The demand for large amounts of energy in Europe and North America began with the industrial revolution in the eighteenth and nineteenth centuries when coal was needed to power the factories and railways. Demand continues to rise as our homes, transport systems, industries and offices become more and more dependent on energy, particularly in the form of electricity. A striking statistic is that energy consumption per person in the UK is 87 times greater than in Bangladesh.

The majority of people in EDCs earn their living from the land. Very little work is mechanised and the most important sources of energy are human labour and animal power (Fig 312). Human power is also important in the growing cities. For example, few people own cars but bicycle rickshaws are a common sight in many Third World cities (Fig 313).

In the rural areas of EDCs wood is the energy source for 80 per cent of all requirements. Wood can be a renewable resource but the forests are being used up at a faster rate than they are growing; this is leading to widespread deforestation. The increasing scarcity of wood has forced many people in poor countries to make a greater use of dried animal dung as a source of energy. However, this means that they are not ploughing it back into the land, and as a result, a valuable fertilizer is lost and crop yields fall.

Of course, not all EDCs lack fossil fuels. For example, China and India have vast reserves of coal and there are major oil producers in all of the southern continents, even excluding countries from the Middle East; for example Venezuela, Nigeria and Indonesia. As EDCs set up manufacturing industries their need for energy rises, but most of them are unable to meet its cost.

An interesting attempt to cut down the need to buy oil has been made by the Brazilian Government. In 1975 they launched Proalcool, a plan to produce alcohol from home-grown sugar-cane and use it as a fuel instead of petrol in cars. In many ways the scheme has been a success: 25 per cent of all cars being built in Brazil are designed to run on alcohol and in 1984 8.8 billion litres of alcohol fuel were produced. However, there have been criticisms as well: sugar-cane is being grown in areas that once produced food; the effects of this fuel's exhaust fumes are not known; and many people doubt whether a poor country like Brazil should be trying to develop a car industry at all.

Fig 312 Animal power

Fig 313 Bicycle rickshaw

ENERGY 7.1

ENQUIRY

1. Describe the main differences in energy consumption shown in Fig 311.
2. Copy and complete Fig 314.
3. Draw scattergraphs to show the relationship between **a)** energy consumption and GNP and **b)** energy consumption and percentage of GNP earnt from manufacturing industry. Describe and try to explain the relationships. How might these figures change as the poorer countries of the world develop their economies?
4. Consider the Brazilian Government's "Proalcool" plan from the point of view of the following people. Would they be for or against it? Explain your opinions.
   - a subsistence farmer in an area chosen for sugar-cane production
   - a car manufacturer
   - a middle class family in Rio de Janeiro
   - a family living in a Rio shanty town.

	MDCs	LDCs
demand		low per person
farming	machine power	
transport		human power
heating/lighting	fossil fuels	

Fig 314 World energy comparisons

Country	Energy consumption per person, million tonnes of coal equivalent	Gross Domestic Product per person, $US	% of GNP earnt from manufacturing industry
UK	4.99	16 750	37
USA	9.96	22 560	29
Japan	4.15	26 920	42
France	3.97	20 600	29
Spain	2.53	12 460	39
Italy	3.68	18 580	33
Bangladesh	0.06	220	16
Brazil	0.77	2920	39
China	0.81	370	42
India	0.31	330	27
Kenya	0.11	340	22
Pakistan	0.28	400	26

Figure 315 Energy consumption, GNP and manufacturing industry

7.2 Oil — what impact does its use have on the environment?

Formation, Location and Extraction

Oil is formed mainly from the remains of miscroscopic plankton (plant life) found in the sea. When plankton die they sink to the sea-bed and if oxygen levels are low they only partly decompose. Other material may then fall onto the floor of the sea. The weight of this material compacts the remains and turns them into hydrocarbons. These are compounds of carbon and hydrogen, the chemicals which make up oil. It seems that heat is also important in bringing about this change. This heat could come from an area of underwater volcanic activity but temperatures increase nearer to the earth's core, anyway.

Oil can easily move through porous rocks (rocks with spaces between their grains). As a result it makes its way to the surface and escapes, unless it is trapped by impermeable rocks (rocks which do not let liquids or gases through). There are different types of oil trap and three of these are shown in Fig 316. Gas (which forms in a similar way to oil) and water are usually found with the oil.

The location of the world's main deposits of oil are shown in Fig 317.

Oil is extracted by drilling a pipe down to the rock where it is trapped. About 30 per cent of the oil usually comes up to the surface under its own pressure. Up to another 20 per cent can be recovered using a pump like the "nodding donkey" in Fig 318. It is possible to extract more of the oil than this, but chemicals or steam have to be pumped down to make it thinner and this can cost more than it is worth.

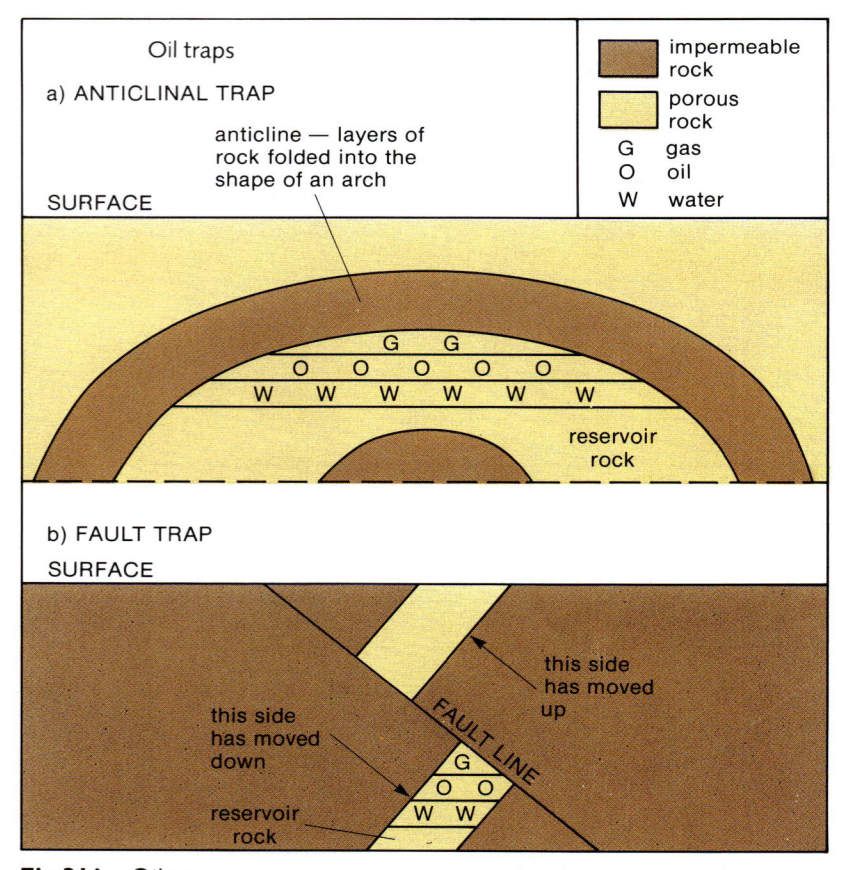

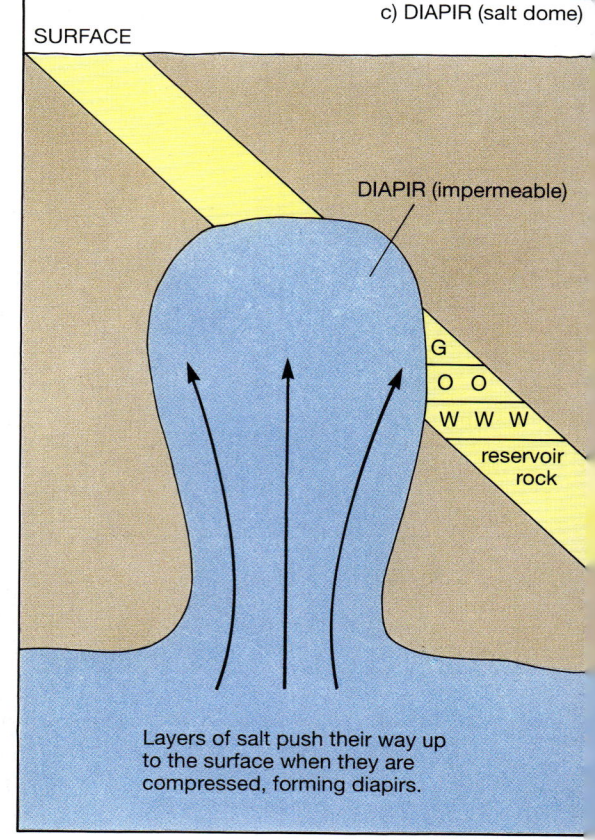

Fig 316 Oil traps

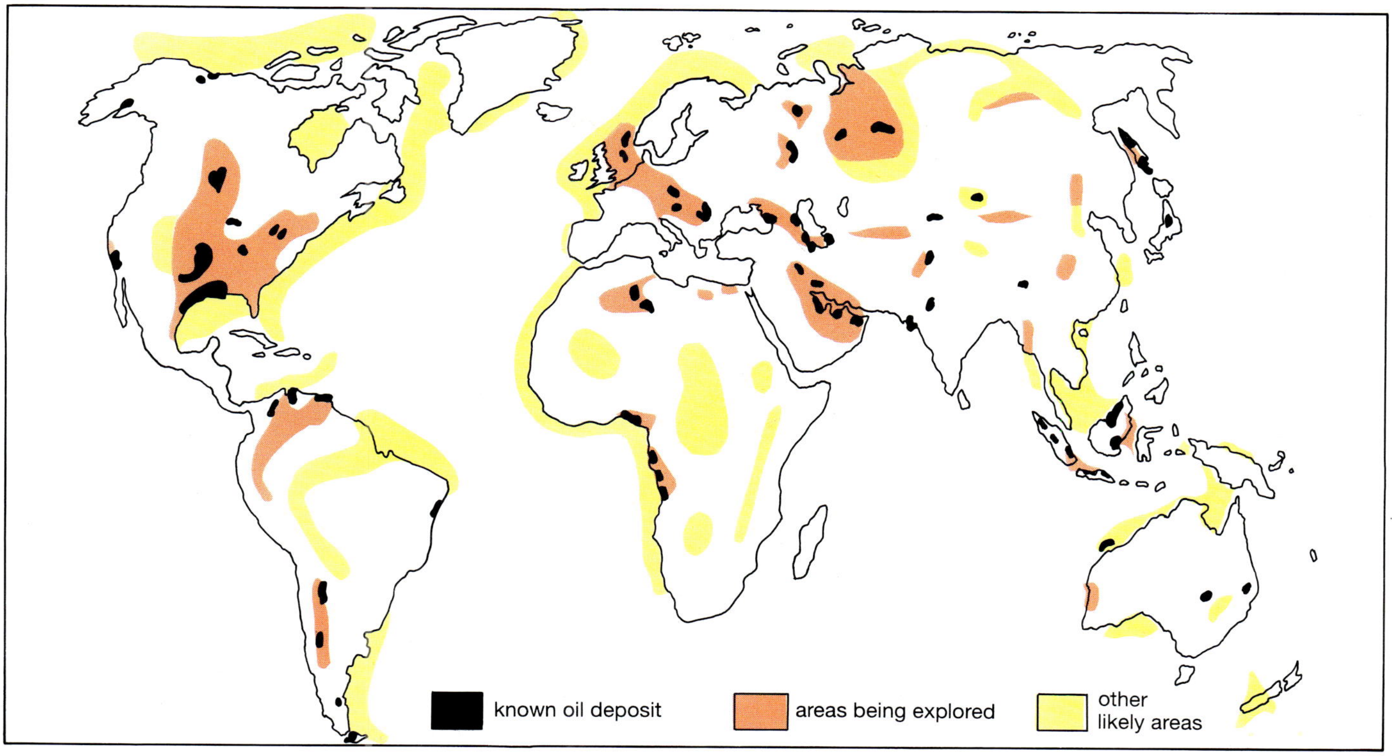
known oil deposit
areas being explored
other likely areas

Fig 317 The world's main oil deposits

The oil is sent to a refinery where it is processed in a distillation tower (Fig 319). It is heated and the various products separate out at different temperatures. About 3 per cent of this processed oil is used in the petrochemical industry to make, for example, plastics and synthetic fibres like polyester.

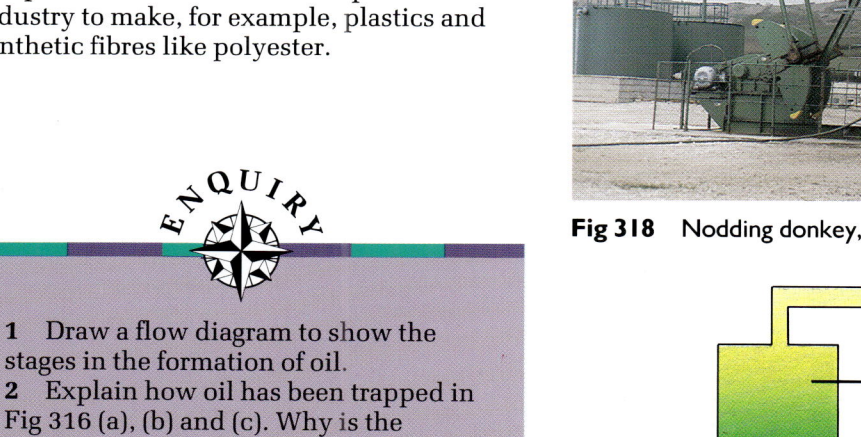

Fig 318 Nodding donkey, Kimmeridge Bay in Dorset

ENQUIRY

1 Draw a flow diagram to show the stages in the formation of oil.
2 Explain how oil has been trapped in Fig 316 (a), (b) and (c). Why is the sequence in the reservoir rock always water, oil, and natural gas?
3 Although Fig 317 does not tell us about the quantity and quality of oil which has been (or might be) discovered, what implication does it have for the statistics given in Fig 333, page 157?
4 Why is up to 50 per cent of the oil in a reservoir left underground?
5 Which of the products shown in Fig 319 are not sources of energy?

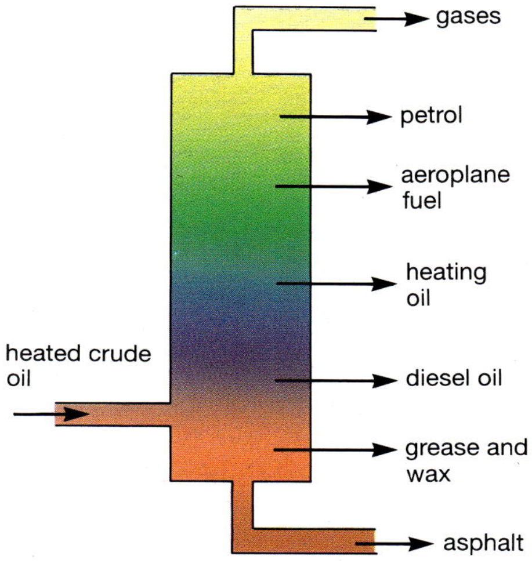
gases
petrol
aeroplane fuel
heating oil
heated crude oil
diesel oil
grease and wax
asphalt

Fig 319 Distillation tower

ENERGY 7.2

Fig 320 (i) Oil: production, consumption and trade

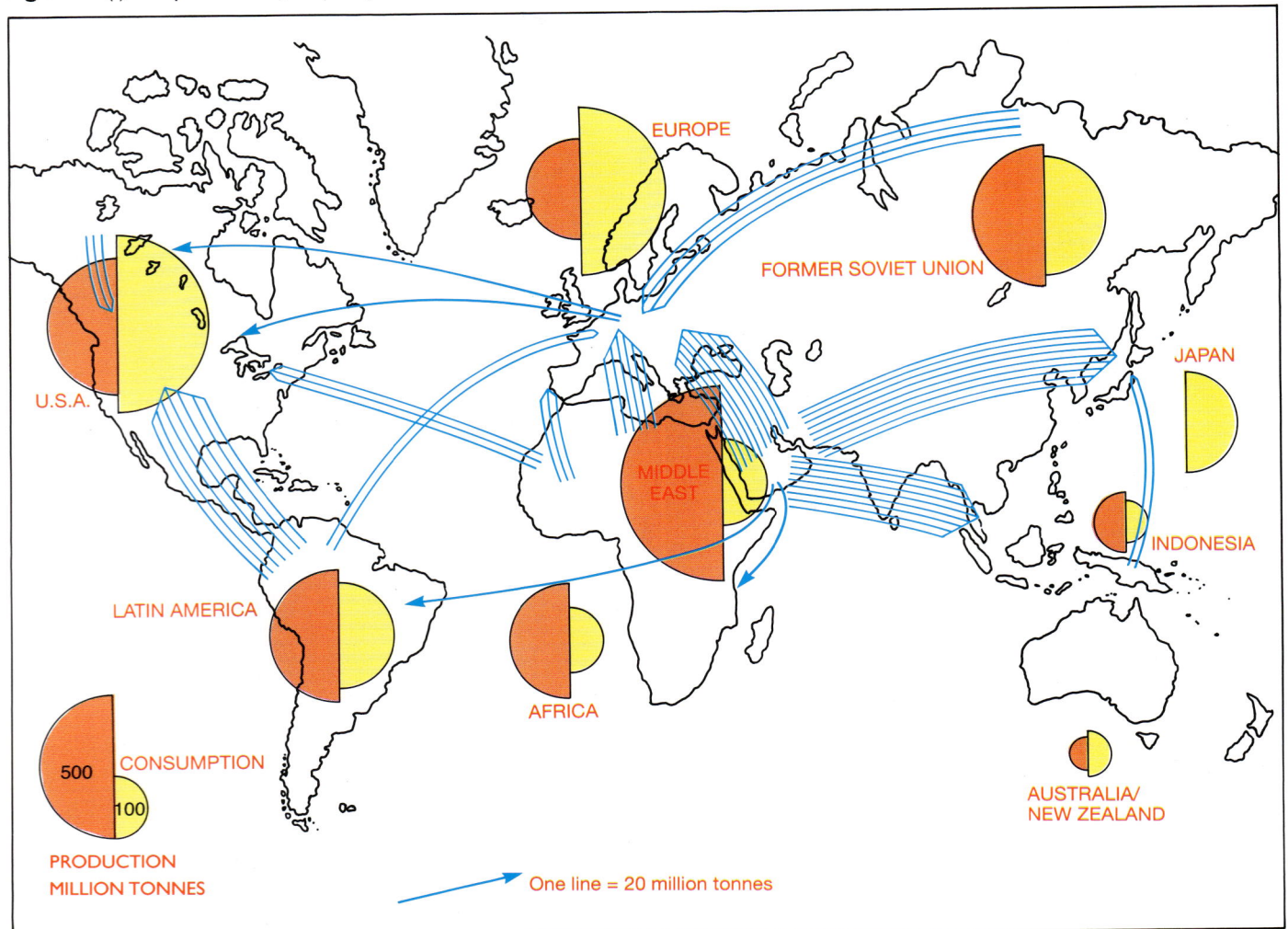

Map labels: EUROPE, FORMER SOVIET UNION, U.S.A., JAPAN, MIDDLE EAST, INDONESIA, LATIN AMERICA, AFRICA, AUSTRALIA/NEW ZEALAND

CONSUMPTION 500
PRODUCTION 100
MILLION TONNES

One line = 20 million tonnes

(ii) Main imports and exports of selected countries

Country	Main exports	Main imports
France	food, chemicals	crude oil
Italy	machinery	crude oil, food
Spain	machinery	crude oil
Germany	machinery, vehicles	crude oil, food
UK	machinery, chemicals	machinery, food
USA	machinery	vehicles, crude oil
Japan	iron & steel, motor vehicles	food, crude oil
CIS	crude oil	machinery
Mexico	crude oil	machinery
Nigeria	crude oil	vehicles, machinery
Venezuela	petroleum products, crude oil	chemicals, machinery
Brazil	machinery, animal foodstuffs	machinery, crude oil
Kenya	coffee, petroleum products	machinery, crude oil
Iran	crude oil	foodstuffs, chemicals
Saudi Arabia	crude oil	foodstuffs, machinery

ENERGY 7.2

Production and Consumption

There is an uneven balance between production and consumption of oil and this has led to a well-developed pattern of trade (Fig 320). Most of the major exporters are EDCs and most of the major importers are MDCs.

Before 1960 a large share of the profit from oil production in the EDCs went to the multinational oil companies of Europe and North America. However, in 1960 a number of these EDCs formed OPEC (the Organisation of Petroleum Exporting Countries) in order to negotiate a better deal. It has become a very important organisation — decisions made by OPEC can put the price of oil up or down and this affects the lives of all of us directly (e.g. when we buy petrol for our car) and indirectly (e.g. when the price of food goes up because the cost of transporting it to the shops has increased).

The countries of the Middle East have over 65 per cent of the world's reserves of oil and this makes them the most powerful members of OPEC. It helps to explain why the price of oil can be closely related to political events in this region (Fig 321).

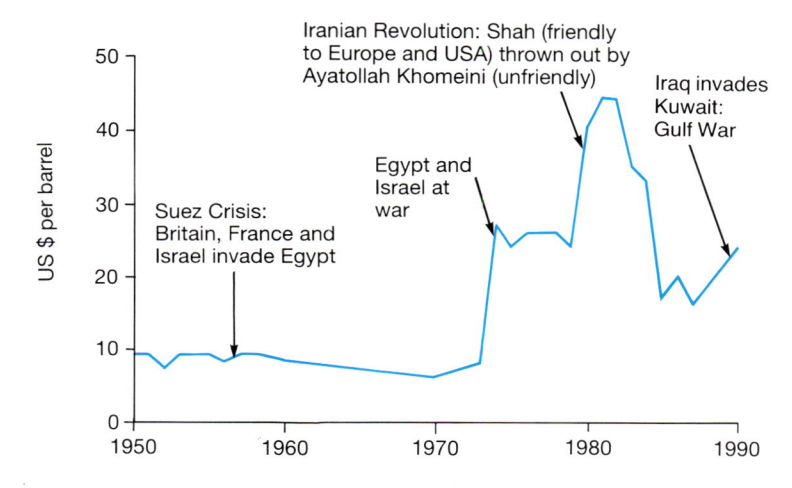

Fig 321 The price of oil

Oil and the Environment

The problems caused by our use of oil are shown in Fig 322. It can have an impact on people and the environment when it is extracted, when it is transported and when it is used.

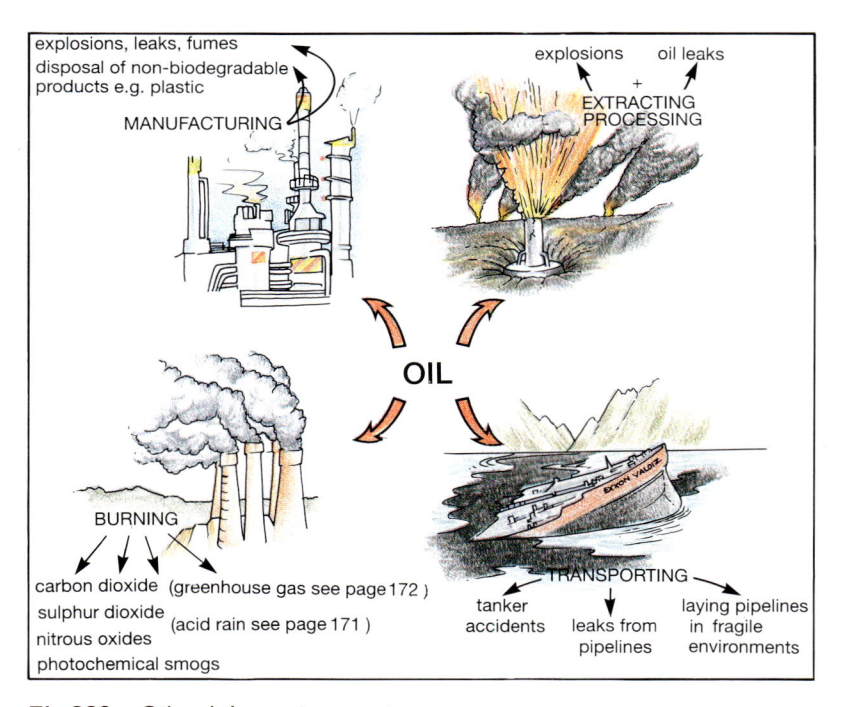

Fig 322 Oil and the environment

Great care has to be taken to reduce the risk of explosions at oil wells and processing plants, but accidents do sometimes happen. One of the worst was in 1988 when the Piper Alpha oil platform in the North Sea exploded and caught fire, killing 166 people.

ENQUIRY

1 Look at Fig 320 (i). Describe **a)** the world pattern of production and consumption of oil, and **b)** the world pattern of trade in oil. What is the relationship between these two patterns?

2 Look at Fig 320 (ii). What do you notice about the imports and exports of **a)** many of the MDCs and **b)** many of the EDCs, particularly in relation to oil and manufactured goods? What does this say about the importance of trade between MDCs and EDCs?

3 How and why has OPEC been of benefit to economically developing countries?

4 Which political events since 1960 can be related to oil price increases, and why? What problems do you think **a)** MDCs and **b)** EDCs will have to face when the oil runs out?

ENERGY 7.2

Fig 323 The *Braer* tanker disaster, 5 January 1993

(i) The *Braer*'s route

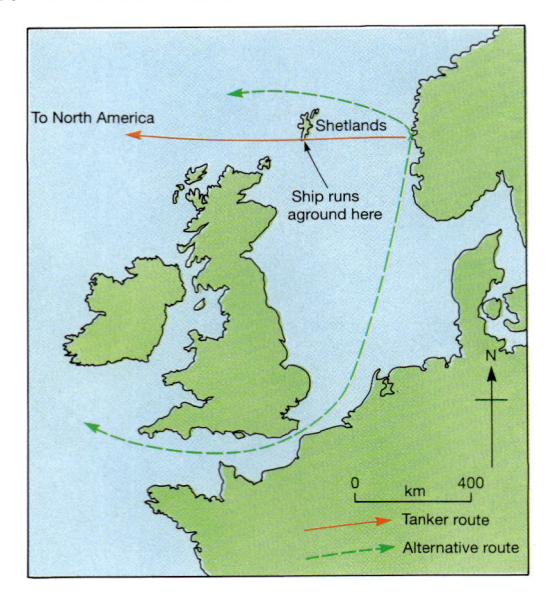

(ii) The accident
Where? Quendale Bay, southern tip of Shetland Isles
When? 5 January 1993
Why? — crew rescued too early. No-one left on board to secure a tow rope
— engine fault: ship lost power and drifted
— inexperienced crew
— short delay in requesting help
— weather: gale force winds
— route: too close to land
— tanker possibly not seaworthy

(iii) Oil and the food chain
— animals, e.g. otters eat fish
— shellfish, worms and shrimps eat polluted plankton
— fish eat shellfish, worms and shrimps
— humans eat fish
— birds, e.g. cormorants eat fish

(iv) Oil and people
Water supply: polluted by oil blown inland

Fishing: inshore fishing banned

Health: fumes cause sore throats, also possible long-term risks, e.g. cancer

Sheep grazing: grass polluted by oil blown inland

Salmon farming: fish affected directly and through the food chain

Tourism: beaches and cliffs polluted. Wildlife killed

Farming: crops contaminated by oil blown inland

(v) The outcome
Three months later:
— 2 000 tonnes of salmon worth £7 million was found to be unfit for humans to eat and sent to Norwegian mink farms instead.
— 10% of fishing industry affected
— 400 mile no-fishing zone south of the island
— food chain contaminated
— some people still with health problems
— worries about the tourist industry.

Tanker accidents have all too often been in the news. In 1989 the *Exxon Valdez* ran aground off the coast of Alaska when it hit a reef because of human error: 10 million gallons of crude oil spilled into the sea and over 1000 miles of coastline were polluted. In January 1993 the *Braer* ran aground off the coast of the Shetland Islands and an ecological disaster was feared (Fig 323). Storms stopped the salvage team from pumping the oil out of the tanker and after nearly a week of being battered by strong winds the ship broke up and spilled nearly all of its cargo. Fortunately, these same storms helped to break up the oil slick and this reduced the short term threat to wildlife. However, after only a fortnight traces of oil were being found in fish and experts were predicting that it could be 20 years before the area fully recovers.

Exhaust fumes from cars are a major problem in urban areas. The main gases given off are oxides of carbon and nitrogen and these can combine to form harmful chemicals such as ozone. For example, the photochemical smogs of Los Angeles (Fig 324) are the result of complex chemical reactions involving more than 12 000 tonnes of pollutants produced by the city each day. Particles and gases are unable to escape because Los Angeles is surrounded by hills on three sides and has very stable air.

Fig 324 Smog over Los Angeles

Oil and Technological Developments

All stages of the oil industry — production, transportation and processing — have seen many technological developments. These have been a response to the search for new reserves of oil, the desire to exploit it more economically and the need to protect the environment.

When oil was first discovered in the USA in the 1850s, wooden derricks were used to sink the wells and the prospectors relied on the oil coming up to the surface under its own pressure. When it became necessary to pump it out of the ground, simple but effective devices like the nodding donkey (Fig 318, page 147) were developed. More recently drilling rigs and oil platforms which can operate offshore in deep water, and which can withstand gale force winds and seas, have been built to exploit difficult but oil-rich environments like the North Sea.

In the early days of the industry, oil was transported in anything that was available. The first oil tanker carried only 2000 tonnes but as the world trade in oil grew, so did the size of tankers, and they can now carry as much as 450 000 tonnes. Pipelines, crossing land and sea, have also been built (see below).

Processing has also seen great advances. In the distillation tower (Fig 319, page 147) the lighter grades of oil, particularly petrol, are in greatest demand and ways of increasing their yield have been developed. There are also many new uses for oil, ranging from drugs to animal feed.

Oil in Alaska

When oil was discovered at Prudhoe Bay in north Alaska in 1968 (Fig 325), the industry was presented with one of its biggest challenges. The reserve was estimated to contain 9.6 billion barrels of crude oil — an enormous quantity — but Prudhoe Bay is north of the Arctic Circle and ice makes transport by tanker impossible for most of the year. The only way the oil could be exploited was by building a pipeline across Alaska to the port of Valdez on the warmer south coast from where it can be shipped to oil markets around the world (Fig 326).

However, the Alaskan environment made the construction of this pipeline extremely difficult. One of the main problems was that much of the ground is permafrost which means that it is permanently frozen except for its active layer — the top one or two metres which thaws in the short tundra summer.

When crude oil reaches the surface it is still at a very high temperature. If the pipeline had been built below ground, the warmth from the oil would have melted the permafrost and this would have resulted in the pipeline sagging and breaking. Consequently, for half its length the pipeline had to be built above ground, and in order to protect it from snow and ice it had to be covered with a 10 cm-thick insulating jacket (Fig 327).

Another problem was the extreme cold. Temperatures can drop to as low as ⁻60°C and because Prudhoe Bay is north of the Arctic Circle, for two months of the year the sun never rises. Working conditions are therefore very unpleasant and even the metal used to build the pipeline had to be tested to make sure it could stand up to the very cold temperatures.

The pipeline crosses areas liable to earthquakes and in these places special supports had to be built to stop it from breaking in two.

Caribou, the North American reindeer, also presented a big problem because the pipeline cuts across their migration route. In these areas it had to be built below ground even in permafrost. This required covering it with a refrigeration jacket (run by an electric motor) to stop the warm oil from melting the permafrost and removing the pipeline's support.

Despite all of these difficulties the pipeline was completed in 1977 at a cost of £4700 million and the oil field is currently producing 1.7 million barrels of oil per day. It is an excellent example of how technological developments have helped the oil industry to exploit a new reserve.

Fig 327 Trans-Alaska pipeline

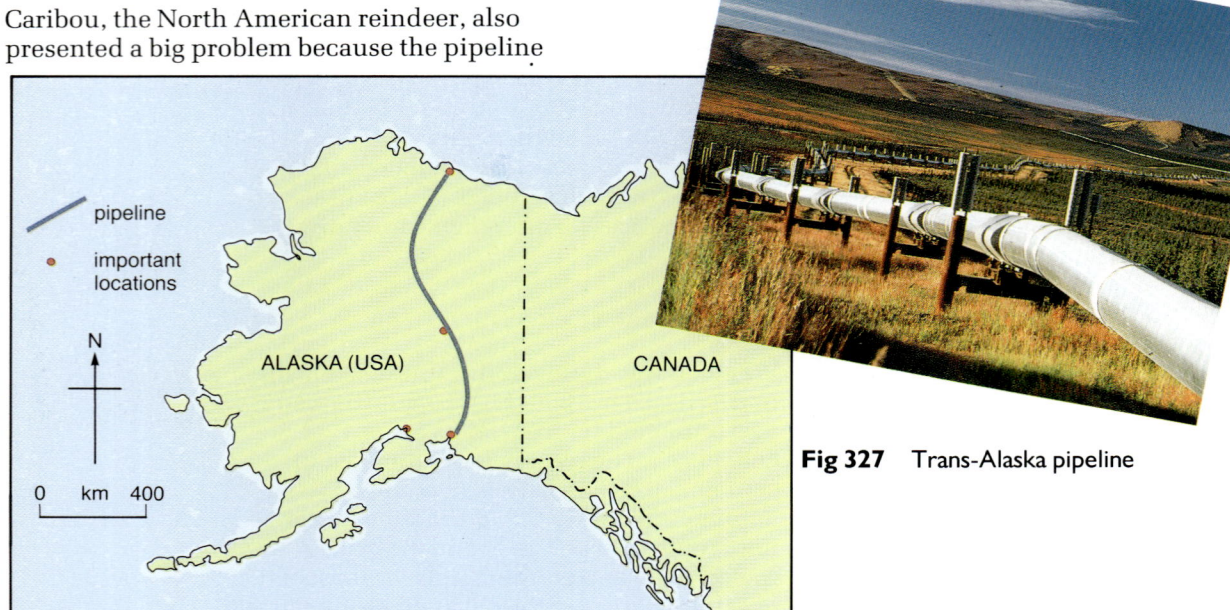

Fig 326 The Trans-Alaska pipeline: location map

Fig 325 Prudhoe Bay

7.3 Assessment task: *Oil and the environment*

Questions 1-5 are about the *Braer* tanker disaster.

1 Where did the accident happen and what was the area like before it was polluted? (Describe the physical environment, e.g. the sea and wildlife, and the human environment e.g. people, jobs.)

2 Why did the *Braer* choose a route which took it so close to the southern tip of the Shetland Islands? (Include at least two distances as part of your answer.)

3 Draw a flow diagram to show how oil pollutes the food chain.

4 List the possible causes of the *Braer* disaster in what you consider to be their order of importance. Explain your choice.

5 What effect has the *Braer* disaster had on the environment and the people of the Shetlands, and why?

Question 6 is about oil in Alaska. You will need an atlas.

6 Draw a large sketch map of Alaska. Mark onto it: Prudhoe Bay; Fairbanks; Anchorage; Valdez; the Arctic Circle; the Brooks Range; the Alaska Range; Mount McKinley; the Yukon River; and the Trans-Alaska pipeline. Add labels in appropriate places to explain the problems faced when building the pipeline, and briefly note the solutions.

Now reconsider the information in Section 7.2

7 What advantages and disadvantages has our use of oil brought? Which of the problems caused by our use of oil do you think we have most control over, and which do you think we have least control over? Has the development of technology protected the environment, or has it placed it at greater risk? Do you think that the world's oil resources should be managed differently in the future?

7.4 Hydroelectric power — what impact does it have on the environment?

Hydroelectric power (HEP) stations produce electricity from running water. The water is led to a turbine in pipes called penstocks (Fig 328). The turbine is connected to an electricity generator and power lines transfer the electricity to where it is needed.

The most important requirement for an HEP station is a constant supply of powerfully running water. Very few streams give this so most HEP stations are associated with the construction of a dam and a reservoir. This means that the water supply can be controlled.

A dam and reservoir have, in turn, their own special requirements:

- hard rock, so that the dam's foundations can be built securely;
- a steep sided valley so that the reservoir will fill up;
- plenty of water flowing into the reservoir to keep it topped up.

Fig 328 Penstocks, Sloy power station on Loch Lomond

Fig 329 An HEP station

ENERGY 7.4

HEP accounts for less than two per cent of the UK's electricity production. This is because the few good sites are mainly in the highland areas of the north and west where few people live and there are limits as to how far electricity can be transferred before its power begins to fade.

Consequently, HEP's effect on the environment in this country is small-scale. Some farmland (mainly rough grazing) has been lost; there is the noise from the turbines; and the reservoirs, dams, penstocks and electricity transmission lines have had an impact on the appearance of the landscapes where they have been built (Fig 330).

In other parts of the world HEP has had a bigger impact on the environment. The generation of large amounts of reliable and relatively cheap electricity has been a primary aim of many multi-purpose river management schemes. Many EDCs have attempted to harness their rivers because energy is vital to economic development; but there have been problems as well as benefits.

The Aswan Dam in Egypt is a good example of such a scheme. Almost all of Egypt is hot desert. 99 per cent of its 56 million people live in the Nile Valley next to the river which is the country's main source of water. Every year rain in the Ethiopian Highlands to the south swells the river. Before the Aswan Dam was built the Nile burst its banks every August, irrigating the flood plain and leaving a layer of fertile silt (see Section 2.2).

The main purpose of the Aswan Dam was to generate HEP and to irrigate thousands of hectares of desert, in order to encourage industrial and agricultural development. It cost more than US $1000 million: the USA decided not to help, but the USSR were keen to give assistance because it gave them an opportunity to be involved with the politics of the region. In the end they helped to build it, paid half the cost and lent Egypt the rest.

The project has undoubted advantages:
- it generates 25 per cent of the country's electricity;
- steel production increased from 304 000 tonnes in 1970, to 500 000 tonnes in 1980;
- 200 000 hectares of desert have been irrigated;
- the number of livestock has increased by one million;
- 30 000 more tonnes of freshwater fish are being caught each year.

Fig 330 Penstocks, Nant Cynydd, Snowdonia

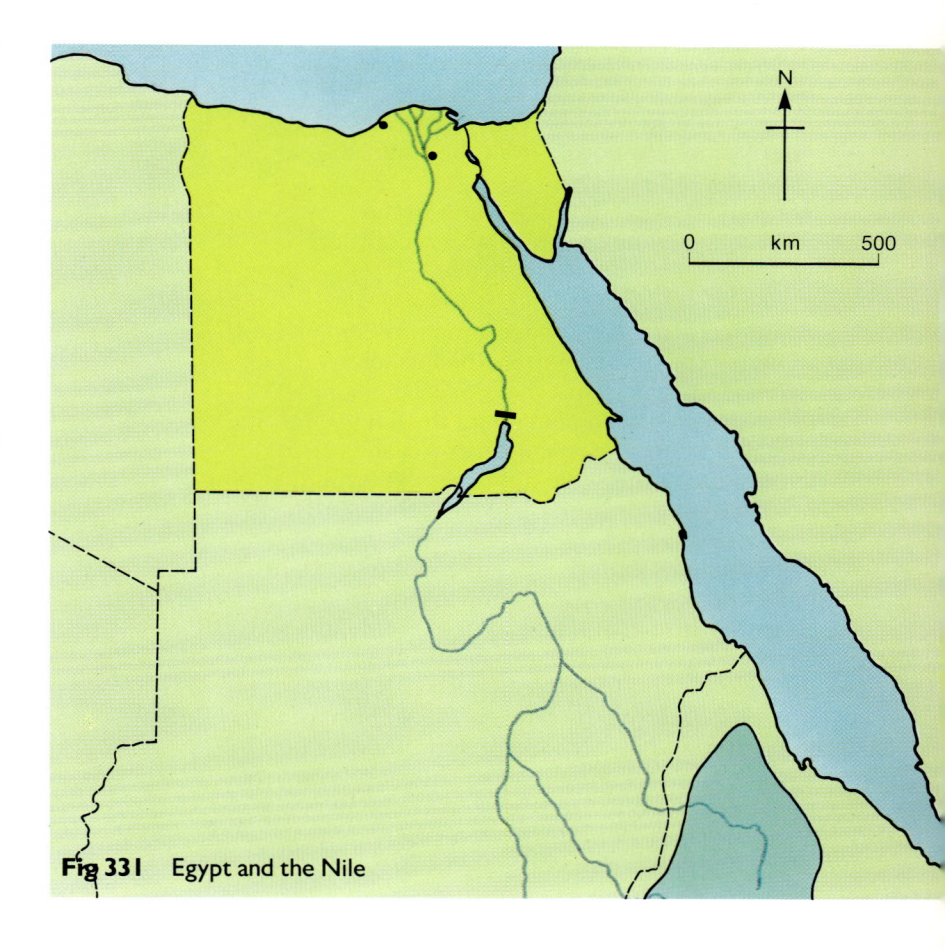

Fig 331 Egypt and the Nile

Fig 332 The Aswan High Dam

However, it has created a number of serious problems as well:
- the silt which used to fertilize the fields is now filling up the reservoir;
- this same silt used to flow out from the delta and feed a large sardine population but catches have fallen from 18 000 to 500 tonnes a year;
- in many places the banks of the river are wearing away because no new material is being added;
- the annual flood used to wash out to sea thousands of snails which carry the parasite bilharzia; these are now infecting the water supply all year round and over half of Egypt's population is suffering from the stomach disorders bilharzia causes;
- up to 50 per cent of the water in the reservoir is being lost through evaporation and seepage.

Egypt has also been left with the problem of repaying the money lent by the former USSR. This has meant that it has been necessary to use 20 per cent of the newly irrigated land to grow cotton as a cash crop for export, but at the same time the government is having to pay for imports of basic foodstuffs.

The problems experienced by the Aswan Dam have not stopped other countries from planning similar schemes. For example, the Chinese Government has recently approved the Three Gorges Dam on the River Yangtze. It involves building the largest HEP station in the world and it will control flooding which, in the past, has claimed many thousands of lives. However, the reservoir (which will be 375 miles long) will drown ten large towns and will require one million people to be moved.

ENQUIRY

1 Explain how an HEP station produces electricity.
2 What are the physical requirements of an HEP station?
3 Complete a copy of Fig 329 by adding the following labels: penstock, reservoir, dam, heavy rainfall, turbine/generator, power lines.
4 Use an atlas to help you to describe and explain the distribution of HEP stations in the UK. Why do they provide less than two per cent of the country's electricity requirement?
5 To what extent do you think the penstocks in Fig 330 spoil the appearance of the landscape?
6 Copy Fig 331. Label onto it the Ethiopian Highlands, Lake Nasser, the Aswan High Dam, the Nile, Cairo, Alexandria, the Mediterranean.
7 How has Egypt benefited from the Aswan Dam?
8 What impact has the scheme had on the environment?
9 What have been the other disadvantages of the scheme?
10 Find our more about the Three Gorges Dam. In the light of Egypt's experience, do you think China is right to go ahead with the scheme?

7.5 What will we use for energy in the future?

It is difficult to say exactly when the world's fossil fuels will run out. Some recent estimates are given in Fig 333 although a number of factors could push these dates further into the future:

- since many of the reserves are deep underground it is difficult to work out exactly how much they contain;
- new discoveries may be made;
- better mining and recovery methods could be developed (Fig 334);
- ways of conserving energy could reduce demand (Fig 335);
- alternative sources of energy could reduce demand.

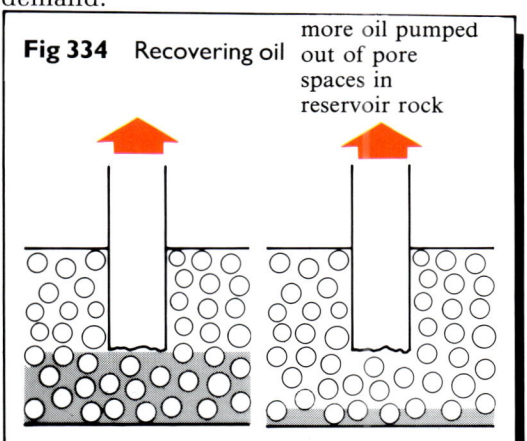

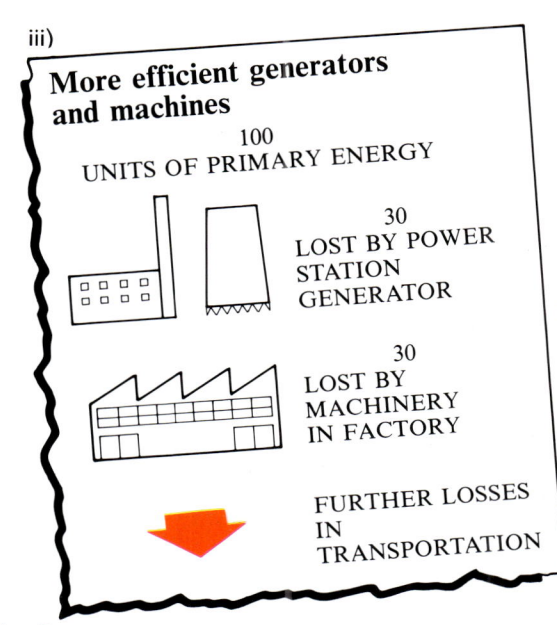

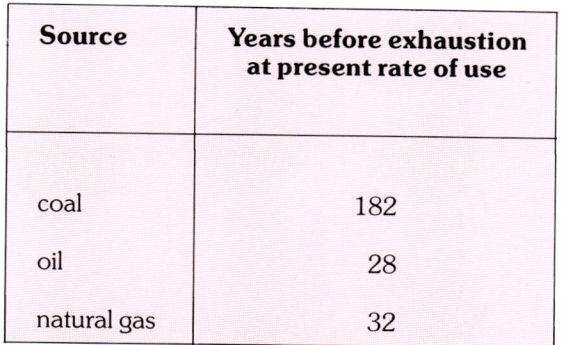

Source	Years before exhaustion at present rate of use
coal	182
oil	28
natural gas	32

Fig 333 World energy predictions

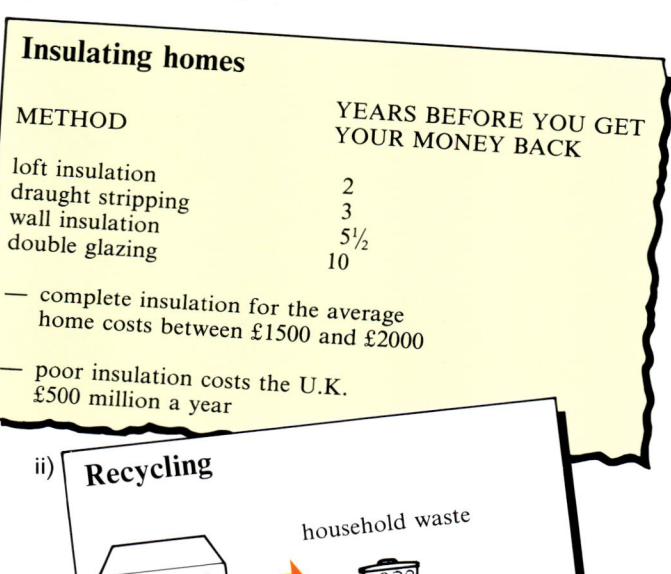

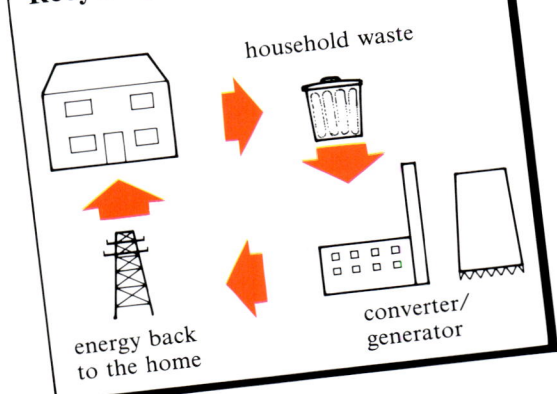

Fig 334 Recovering oil — more oil pumped out of pore spaces in reservoir rock

i) **Insulating homes**

METHOD	YEARS BEFORE YOU GET YOUR MONEY BACK
loft insulation	2
draught stripping	3
wall insulation	5½
double glazing	10

— complete insulation for the average home costs between £1500 and £2000
— poor insulation costs the U.K. £500 million a year

ii) **Recycling**

household waste → converter/generator → energy back to the home

iii) **More efficient generators and machines**

- 100 UNITS OF PRIMARY ENERGY
- 30 LOST BY POWER STATION GENERATOR
- 30 LOST BY MACHINERY IN FACTORY
- FURTHER LOSSES IN TRANSPORTATION

iv) **greater use of renewable energy sources**

SOURCE	1973%	1978%	1984%
oil	41	40	35
natural gas	16	16	17
coal	25	25	27
nuclear	1	2	3
renewables	17	17	18

(world figures)

Fig 335 Conserving energy

Of course, "world" predictions are misleading because stocks in some countries will run out much sooner than in others. For example, North Sea oil may be completely exhausted by the year 2020 but Saudi Arabia's oil reserves will last for another 100 years at their current rate of production.

ENQUIRY

1. According to the estimates given in Fig 333, how old will you be when the world's supplies of **a)** oil and **b)** natural gas run out? In which year will coal run out?
2. Explain why it is difficult to predict when non-renewable energy sources are going to run out.
3. How much primary energy (in total) is wasted by generators in power stations and machines in factories?
4. Why do you think many people do not insulate their homes properly?
5. What seems to be the main problem with all the different ways of conserving energy shown in Fig 335?
6. Explain how the following ideas would save energy:
   — car drivers sharing lifts to school;
   — keeping windows closed;
   — buying a thick jumper;
   — making train fares cheaper;
   — going to bed an hour earlier than usual in cold weather.
7. Which of these two statements do you most agree with, and why?

   "We shouldn't worry about using up our non-renewable sources of energy because necessity is the mother of invention."

   "We should be doing everything possible to make our non-renewable sources of energy last longer — if we don't, future generations will suffer."

Alternative Sources of Energy

In recent years there has been a growing interest in renewable sources of energy mainly because of concern about fossil fuels running out, and because of a better understanding of the threat fossil fuels and nuclear power pose to the environment. Research has concentrated on **solar power** (power from the sun), **wind power**, wave power, **tidal power**, **geothermal power** (power from the earth's heat), and **biopower** (power from plants, crops and organic waste). These sources of energy share major advantages; for example, they will not run out and most of them have little impact on the environment. However, there are disadvantages as well, such as the high cost of their development and the fact that most of them can only be harnessed to produce electricity.

Solar power uses the sun's energy directly either to heat water (e.g. for a central heating system) or to produce electricity. In the UK solar panels can be installed in houses for water heating (Fig 336). In France an experimental solar furnace has been built at Odeillo: a huge mirror concentrates the sun's energy to produce steam which can be used to generate electricity as in a normal power station.

Fig 336 Solar panels, Milton Keynes

ENERGY 7.5

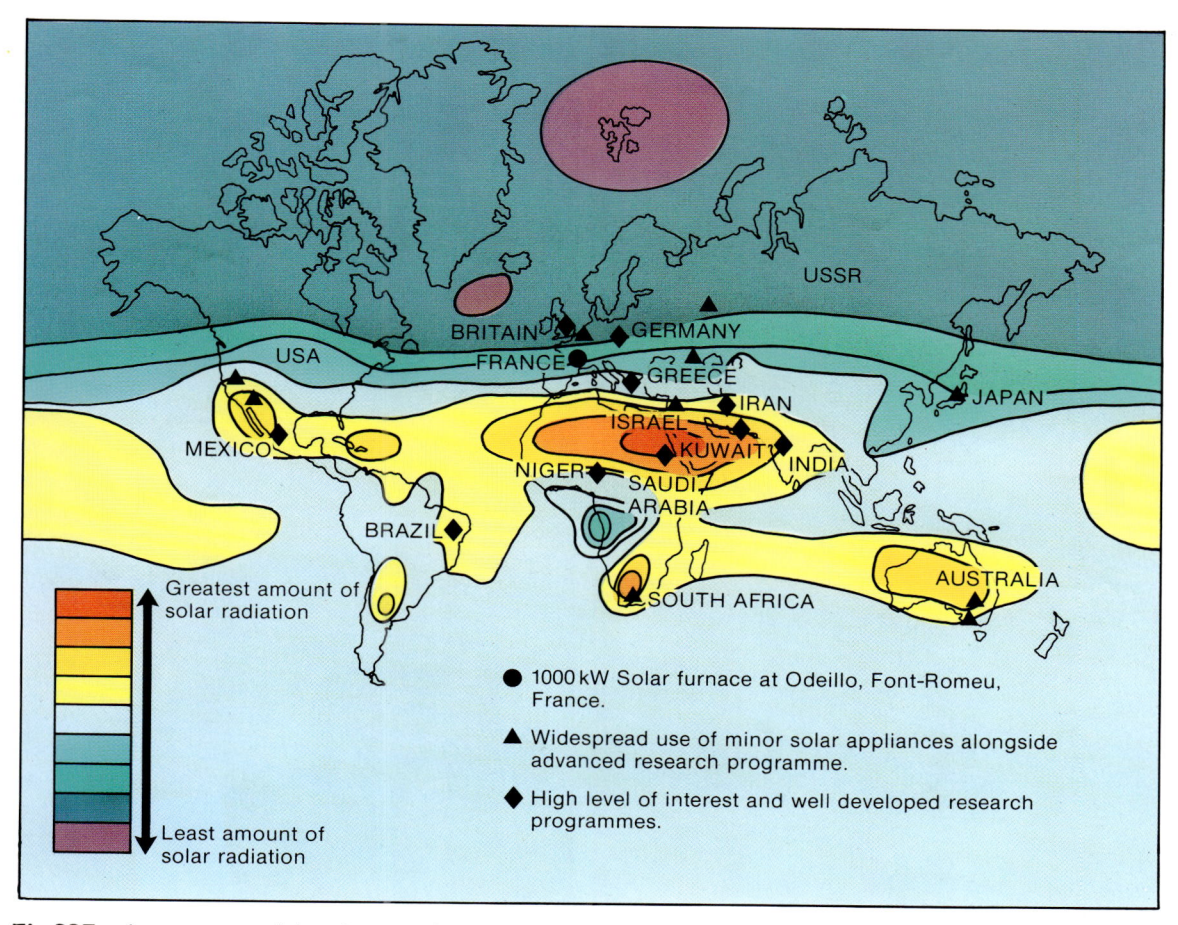

Fig 337 Average annual distribution of solar radiation

The wind is one of our oldest sources of power. In nineteenth century Britain 10 000 windmills were in use for grinding corn and powering machinery. More recently, different types of wind generators have been built to produce electricity (Fig 339). The lone wind generator in Fig 338 provides electricity for Wood Green Animal Shelter in Cambridgeshire, while at Carmarthen Bay in South Wales there is an experimental windfarm (a group of wind generators).

Many sites offer great potential for wind power but there are drawbacks. The obvious problem is the unreliability of the wind. The generators are noisy which could make windfarms unpopular near settlements. Their appearance is also a concern, especially as many of the sites are in relatively unspoilt areas.

Tidal power, like wind power, has been used for many centuries; for example, London Bridge was fitted with water wheels which were turned by the tide in medieval times. The same principle is used today but the wheel is connected to an electricity generator; an example is shown in Fig 340.

Fig 338 The wind generator at Wood Green Animal Shelter, Cambridgeshire

ENERGY 7.5

i) traditional windmill — 25 metres

ii) small electricity pylon — 30 metres

iii) large electricity pylon — 50 metres

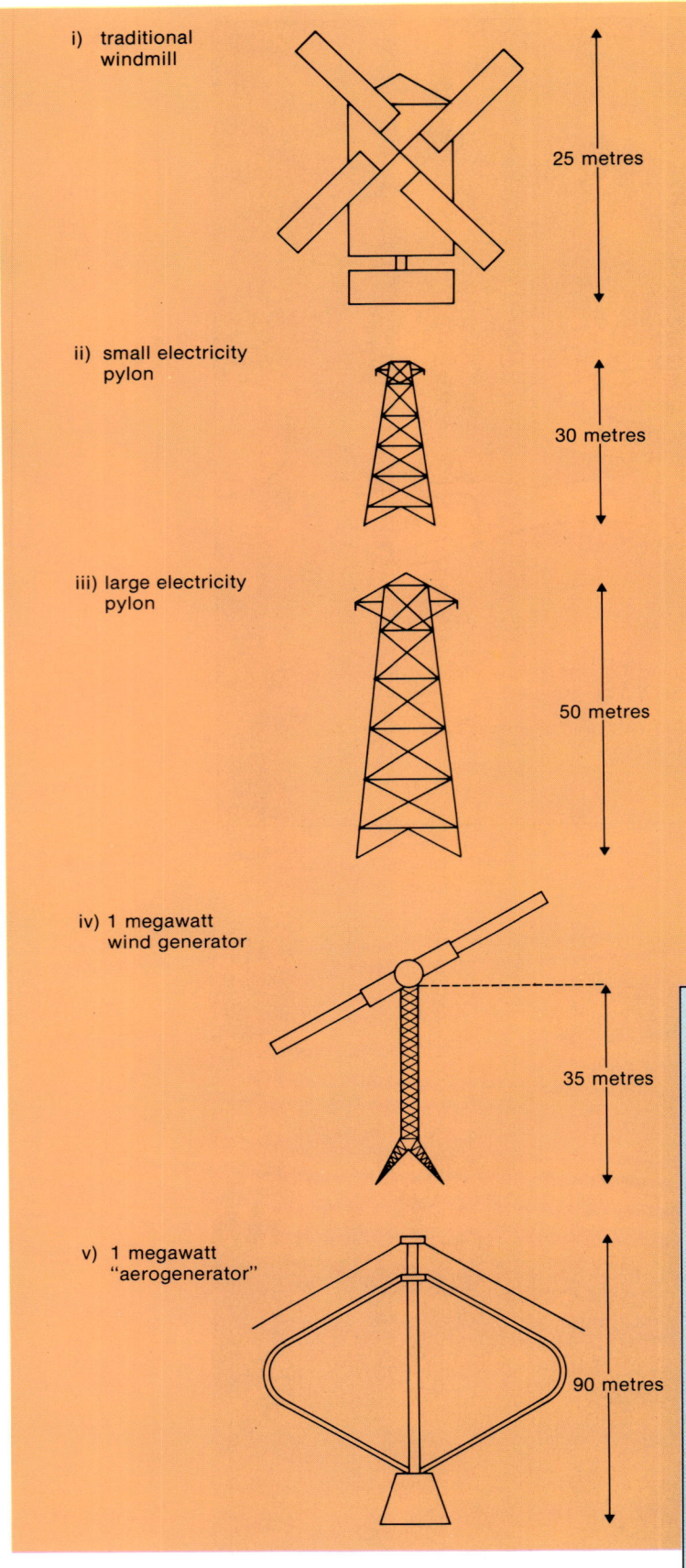

iv) 1 megawatt wind generator — 35 metres

v) 1 megawatt "aerogenerator" — 90 metres

Fig 339 Wind generators

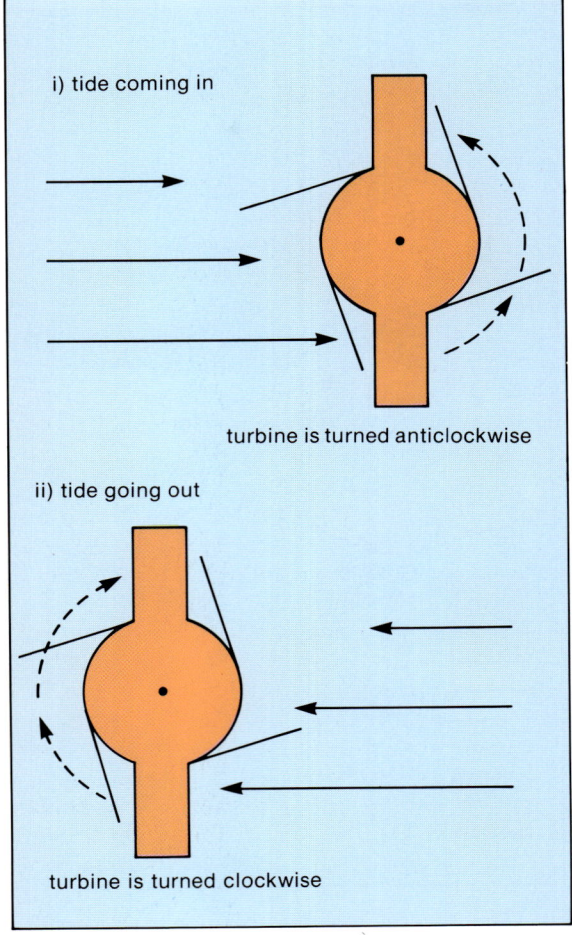

i) tide coming in

turbine is turned anticlockwise

ii) tide going out

turbine is turned clockwise

Fig 340 Tidal power generator

Fig 341 Tidal energy sites

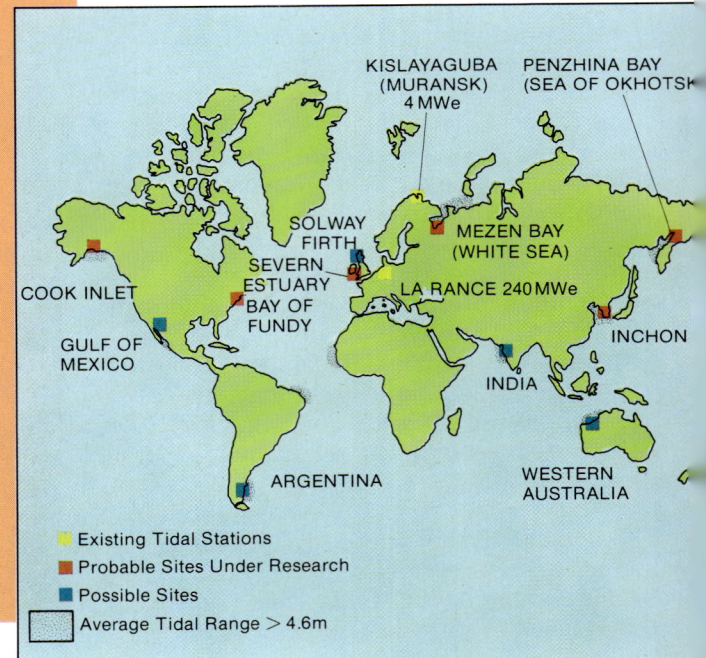

KISLAYAGUBA (MURANSK) 4 MWe
PENZHINA BAY (SEA OF OKHOTSK)
SOLWAY FIRTH
MEZEN BAY (WHITE SEA)
SEVERN ESTUARY
LA RANCE 240 MWe
COOK INLET
BAY OF FUNDY
INCHON
GULF OF MEXICO
INDIA
ARGENTINA
WESTERN AUSTRALIA

- Existing Tidal Stations
- Probable Sites Under Research
- Possible Sites
- Average Tidal Range > 4.6m

ENERGY 7.5

The map (Fig 341) shows possible sites for tidal stations. A good site is one where there is a large tidal range which means that the difference between high tide and low tide is great. The map also shows that only a few tidal stations exist today — and they are very small. In Britain the Severn Estuary is considered to be the best site as it has one of the largest tidal ranges in the world. However, the cost of building a tidal station would be £4 billion and it would take up to 20 years to construct. Also, the Severn Estuary is polluted by waste from the Avonmouth Industrial Area and by 47 million gallons of sewage a day. At the moment, this pollution is washed out to sea by strong tidal currents.

Biogas, one type of biopower, is given off when organic matter decomposes; for example, animal waste gives off methane and this can be harnessed to produce energy. At Eye in Suffolk, a small power station generates electricity by using gas given off by chicken droppings. In EDCs biogas converters like the one in Fig 342 offer a relatively low-cost source of energy. Slurry from cattle is swept into the converter and the gas is used for lighting and cooking. The residue can also be used as a fertilizer.

Fig 342 Biogas converter

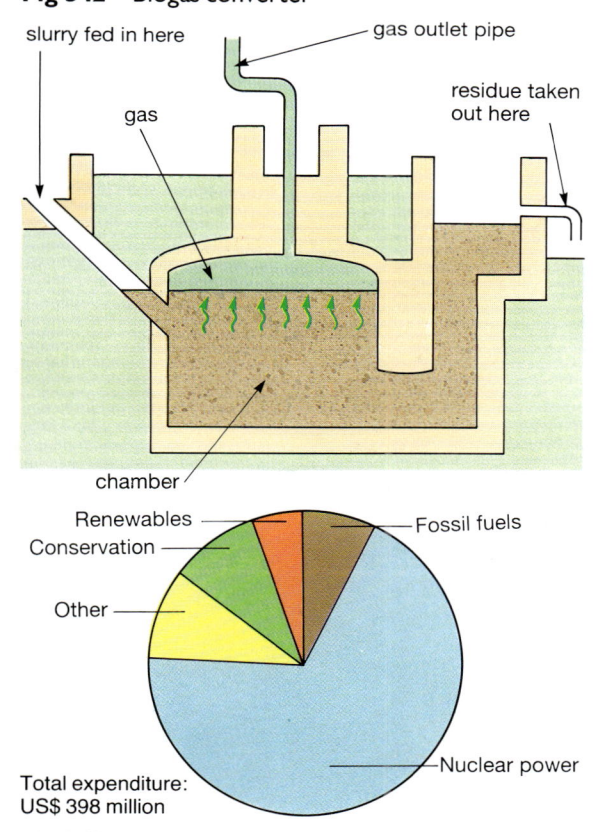

Fig 343 Spending on energy research in the UK 1988

ENQUIRY

1 Study Fig 337. Describe and explain the average annual distribution of solar radiation. In which areas of the world is solar power likely to be most useful? Explain why.

2 List those countries making widespread use of solar appliances. Are the majority of these countries MDCs or EDCs? Try to explain your answer.

3 Peak demand for electricity in the UK is during the evenings in the winter. What implications does this have for solar power in this country?

4 What do you think are the main problems facing the development of wind power?

5 **a)** On a world map mark on and label the following countries: UK, France, USSR (CIS/Russian Federation), Canada, North Korea, South Korea, USA (including Alaska), Argentina, Australia and India.
b) Using the information given on Fig 341 mark on:
 • existing tidal stations;
 • tidal stations under research;
 • areas of large tidal range.
c) Give your map a key and title.
d) Compare your map with a map of world population density in an atlas. Which of the tidal energy sites are a) near to and b) a long way from large centres of population? Overall, how useful do you think this source of energy could be.

6 Why could biogas converters be of great value to EDCs?

7 Fig 343 shows spending on energy research in the UK in 1988. What is your reaction to the amount spent on renewable sources of energy?

8 Choose either wave power or geothermal power. Find out about it and write an account using the following headings: what it is and how it works; where it is found or could be developed; its advantages and disadvantages; and how important it could become in the future.

ENVIRONMENTAL ISSUES

8.1 What are we doing to the land?

Sand and Gravel Extraction in East Anglia

A **quarry** is a place where stone is extracted (taken from) the ground. Many quarries in this country produce **aggregate** — crushed rock, sand and gravel — mainly for building. Aggregate is very heavy so it is expensive to transport and this explains why building firms try to use local material. Fig 344 shows that the most suitable aggregate in East Anglia is sand and gravel.

A great deal of the sand and gravel in East Anglia was deposited (dumped) by water when the ice sheets melted at the end of the Ice Age (see Section 3.1). This explains why there are so many gravel pits in river valleys. It is usually found near the surface in layers a few metres thick.

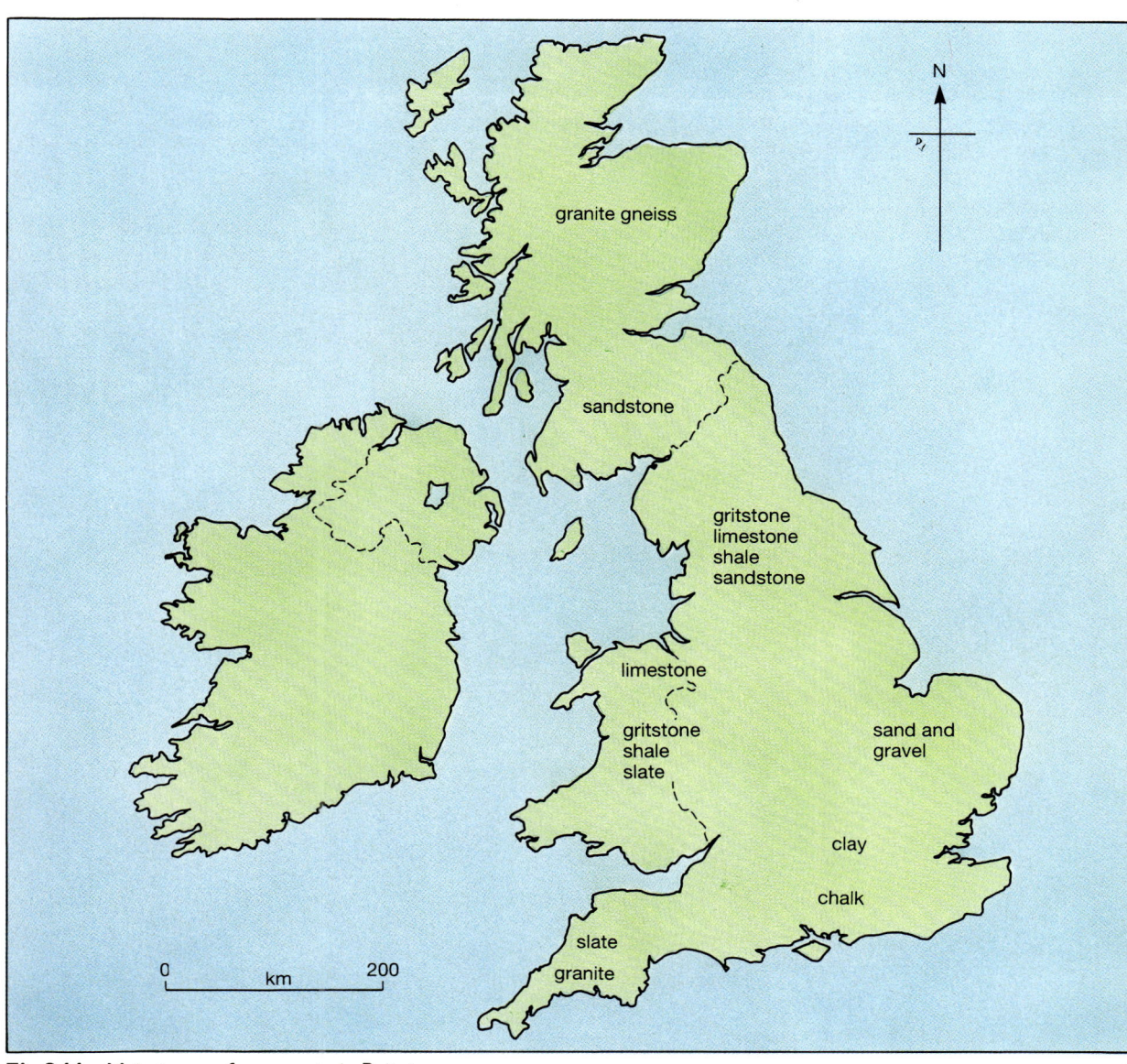

Fig 344 Main types of aggregate in Britain

ENVIRONMENTAL ISSUES 8.1

If a company wants to open up a new quarry it has to get permission from the local planning department. It has to draw up a plan which covers all stages of the quarry's life. If the site is of archaeological interest it has to arrange for a survey to be carried out (Fig 345). It has to say how it is going to cut down noise and pollution while the quarry is being worked. Finally, it has to say what will happen to the land when the sand and gravel have been dug out.

Quarrying the sand and gravel is quite straightforward. First, the soil is removed and put to one side (Fig 346). Then an excavator scoops out the material and drops it onto a conveyor belt (Fig 347). This takes it to the processing plant where it is washed, graded and stored in separate piles (Fig 348). It is usually transported to its final destination by lorry.

Decisions about what happens to a quarry when the sand and gravel has been extracted have the biggest impact on the environment. In the past they were usually left to fill up with water. However, these days there are so many excavations and they are on such a large scale that too much land would be lost if this was the only strategy.

Fig 345 Archaeological dig on the site of a new gravel pit

Fig 346 A mound of top soil

Fig 347 Excavator and conveyor belt

Fig 348 Processing plant and stockpiles

ENVIRONMENTAL ISSUES 8.1

When the quarry is being worked the main problems are noise, dust, traffic and the appearance of the stockpiles. Surrounding a quarry with an earth bank called a screening bund cuts down noise and hides the quarry from view. The bund can be planted with trees (Fig 349). The layout of the quarry can also help; for example, when lorries reverse a warning signal sounds which disturbs nearby houses, but the site can be arranged so that the lorries follow a one-way system and do not have to do any backing up.

Fig 349 Bund surrounding a quarry

Whenever possible, the land is returned to agricultural use by putting back the soil which was removed at the start of the excavation (Fig 350). However, there are very often drainage difficulties because the land is at a lower level than it used to be. Drainage schemes can sometimes solve this problem, or the level of the land can be raised by using it for waste disposal before it is restored. Some pits have been turned into nature reserves (Fig 351). Others have been used for leisure and recreation (Fig 352).

Fig 350 Gravel pit restored to farmland

Fig 351 Little Paxton Nature Reserve

Fig 352 Hinchingbrooke Country Park

ENVIRONMENTAL ISSUES 8.1

In 1988 320 million tonnes of aggregate were used in the UK. Demand is increasing and if current trends continue this figure will have risen to 505 million tonnes by 2011. East Anglia is one of the fastest growing regions of the country (its population grew from 1.4 million in 1951 to 2.25 million in 1991) and there is a great deal of concern about the impact of providing more and more aggregate from the region's own supplies of sand and gravel.

Some alternatives have been suggested. Aggregate from quarries in Scotland could be imported by boat. Sand could be dredged from the sea (1½ million tonnes of aggregate were provided in this way for the building of Sizewell B nuclear power station in Suffolk). Waste from slate quarries in Wales, and from china clay quarries in Cornwall, could be transported into the region by rail. What is certain is that if we want new roads and buildings some difficult environmental decisions will have to be made.

ENQUIRY

1. What are the main types of aggregate used in **a)** Scotland, **b)** Wales and **c)** East Anglia?
2. Draw a flow diagram to show the main stages in the quarrying of sand and gravel.
3. How does a quarry affect the environment when it is being worked, and what can be done to reduce its impact?
4. Which of the uses for disused quarries mentioned in this section do you think is best, and why?
5. What are the advantages and disadvantages of the alternative sources of aggregate for East Anglia? (Think of the place where the material would be coming from, as well as the place it is going to.)

ENVIRONMENTAL ISSUES 8.2

8.2 What are we doing to the sea?

The sea covers 70 per cent of the earth's surface. It has always been a source of food and increasingly it has been used as a dumping ground for the waste products of industrial society. It used to be thought that the sea was so vast that we could do little to harm it, but in the last 20 years **overfishing** and pollution have become serious problems in many parts of the world.

Human impact is greatest on the continental shelf; this is where most of the fish live and it is where most of the pollution stays (Fig 353). The oceans appear to be under less threat than coastal waters but we do not, as yet, know what they can cope with.

Overfishing

Fish are a **renewable resource** as long as stocks have time to recover through natural breeding after they have been fished. However, fishing grounds have been under increasing pressure for two main reasons. Firstly, demand for fish (25 per cent of which is turned into animal feed) has gone up; for example, the world marine fish catch in 1950 was 20 million tonnes but this had risen to 85 million tonnes by 1990. Secondly, fishing methods have improved; for example, sonar searches can locate the fish and nets covering an area of two square kilometres can take out an entire shoal.

In the 1960s and 1970s herring stocks in the North Sea virtually disappeared, and in the

Over the past ten years we have seen the near-disappearance of some species, like sprats, and the re-emergence of others — principally herring — after tough conservation measures.

Now the once mighty haddock, mainstay of the British white fish industry — concentrated almost entirely in Scoland — is at risk.

Haddock stocks have suffered from the increasing sophistication of fishing — principally the strength of the new vessels — up to 800 horsepower — which can haul much larger nets. Take the Lothian Rose, a fairly typical trawler owned by seven members of the Clark family, which usually operates from Peterhead, now Britain's biggest fishing port. Her modern wheelhouse, incorporating two sonars, two echo sounders, two radar scanners, and an automatic navigation system, underlines that the "luck factor" long since disappeared from fishing. It is a highly targeted business.

The young skipper, Linus Clark, is disarmingly honest. "You can criticise who you want, but there is no one else to blame but the Scots for cleaning up the haddock," he says. "The past year has been disastrous. But we have to keep on fishing to meet our commitments."

In these circumstances, he described a 40 per cent quota cut next year — the British fleet will be allowed to catch no more than 54,380 tonnes — as "modest".

The Guardian

Fig 354 The disappearing haddock

late 1980s the same thing seemed to be happening to the haddock (Fig 354). Stocks of nearly all traditional food fishes are falling worldwide.

```
Cross section
           Continental
           shelf (up to                Ocean         Ocean
           200 metres deep)            basin         trench        Ocean
land                    Continental slope (5–6 km deep) (11 km deep) ridge
```

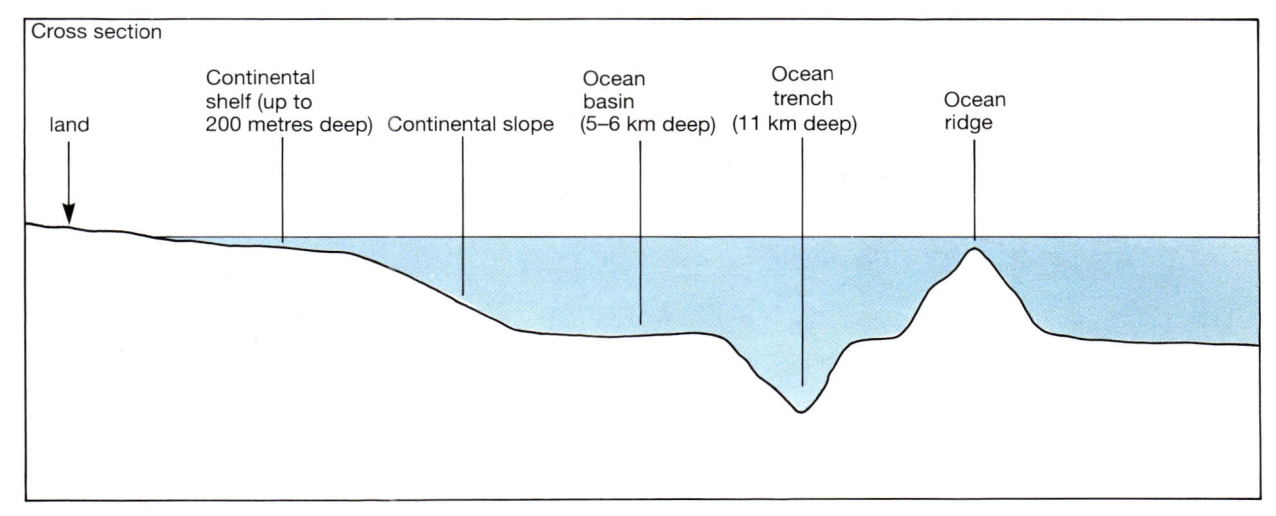

Fig 353 A cross section of the ocean floor

There are things which can be done to solve this problem. Nets can be designed so that young fish can escape. **Quotas** can be set to limit the amount of fish which can be caught; restrictions can be placed on where countries are allowed to fish; and limits can be set on the number of days boats are allowed out to sea. International agreements are very important if such measures are to work but they can be difficult to achieve and to put into effect (Fig 355). Fish farming can be developed; for example, over 300 salmon farms have been set up in Scotland in the last ten years and have helped to meet the demand for the North Atlantic salmon at a time when it was in danger of being virtually wiped out (Fig 356).

Pollution

The sea is polluted in a number of ways. There are accidents like the *Exxon Valdez* and the *Braer* disaster (see Section 7.2) but most of the 600 000 tonnes of oil which gets into the sea each year is dumped illegally by ships cleaning out their tanks. Many types of waste product are deliberately discharged into the sea by factories, power stations and sewage treatment works. Rivers also carry waste which has been dumped into them, (Fig 357) as well as agricultural fertilizers which have been washed out of the soil by rain, and this eventually reaches the sea.

The North Sea suffers from all of these problems. It is at risk because it is surrounded on three sides by some of the world's major industrial nations; it is relatively shallow; and the pattern of currents means that it takes two to three years for water to circulate back out into the Atlantic Ocean. (Fig 358).

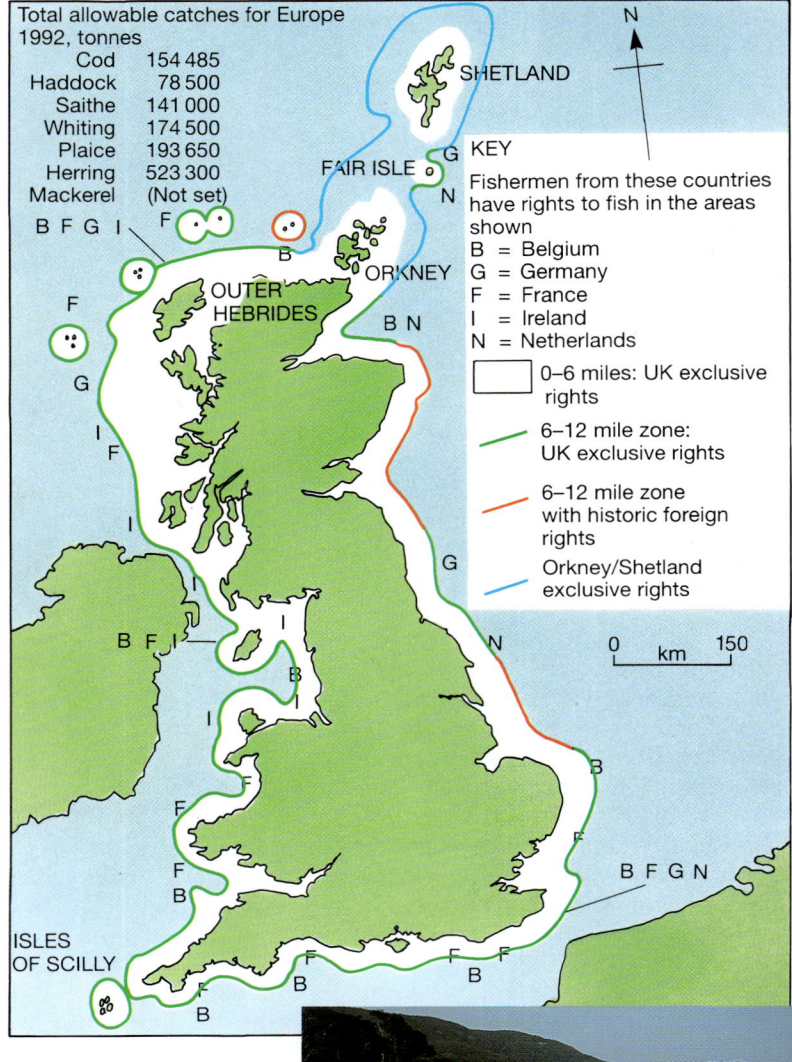

Total allowable catches for Europe 1992, tonnes
Cod	154 485
Haddock	78 500
Saithe	141 000
Whiting	174 500
Plaice	193 650
Herring	523 300
Mackerel	(Not set)

KEY
Fishermen from these countries have rights to fish in the areas shown
B = Belgium
G = Germany
F = France
I = Ireland
N = Netherlands

0–6 miles: UK exclusive rights
6–12 mile zone: UK exclusive rights
6–12 mile zone with historic foreign rights
Orkney/Shetland exclusive rights

Fig 355 Fishing rights

Fig 356 Salmon farm, Loch Craignish

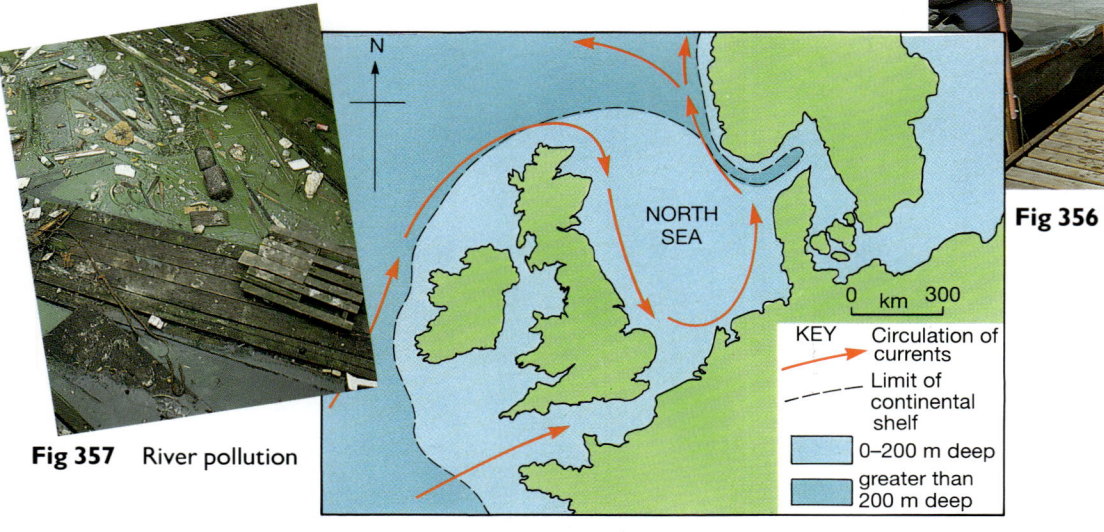

Fig 357 River pollution

Fig 358 The North Sea: location map

KEY
→ Circulation of currents
--- Limit of continental shelf
0–200 m deep
greater than 200 m deep

ENVIRONMENTAL ISSUES 8.2

Many industries have located on its shores so that they can dispose of their waste products easily. For example, Tioxide, who make pigments for paint, set up on the Humber in 1947 and built a pipeline out into the estuary for waste disposal. However, by 1986 20 square kilometres of the estuary was almost totally lifeless. They have now extended their pipeline further out to sea but life is returning to the affected area only slowly.

One of the waste products from coal-fired power stations is fly ash. This can be made into bricks or used for road building but it is cheaper to dump it. Until recently the Blyth power station on Tyneside was getting rid of two barge loads a day out at sea. Fly ash is not poisonous but it smothers the sea floor so that nothing can grow or live there. An area of 18 square kilometres has been badly affected; it will take 10 to 15 years for the area to recover.

Rivers are a major source of pollution; for example, in the mid-1980s the River Elbe was discharging ten tonnes of heavy metals and three or four tonnes of toxic chemicals a day into the North Sea. These poisons enter the food chain and either kill marine life or make it vulnerable to disease (Fig 359). PCBs (chemicals used as coolants and insulators in industrial equipment) brought into the sea by rivers, have been linked to the decline in the seal population of the Dutch coast. Agricultural fertilizers washed into the sea cause an increase in the growth of algae; this deprives the water of oxygen and can lead to the death of fish and other marine life. Huge growths of algae were blamed for £120 million worth of damage to the Norwegian fishing industry in 1988.

As with overfishing, something can be done about pollution. Some countries have already banned the discharge of untreated sewage and the dumping of sewage sludge and industrial waste. Some countries have placed stricter limits on the discharge of chemicals into rivers; for example, the amount of pollution in the River Elbe has declined since the mid-1980s and as a result pollution levels in that part of the North Sea have gone down. Unfortunately, because so many heavy metals — which will never break down — have already been dumped, the fish stocks remain vulnerable to bacteria and viruses.

However, not all countries have taken such measures. One reason is that pollution control is expensive and some countries face bigger bills than others because they have more dirty industries. This makes international agreements all the more important: countries need to understand each other's problems and they need to agree a common course of action.

At the third North Sea Conference in 1990 the UK agreed to stop dumping industrial waste by 1993 and to stop the discharge of untreated sewage and the dumping of sewage sludge by 1988. All countries agreed to reduce by half the levels of 37 important chemical pollutants by 1995. However, no agreements were reached on pollution from agricultural fertilizers and radioactive waste from nuclear power stations.

Organisations like Greenpeace mount high-profile campaigns to draw attention to the problem of sea pollution (Fig 360). Conservation groups help to keep beaches

Fig 359 Flounders suffering from bacterial/viral infections

clean and tidy. As individuals we can be concerned and informed: does your local beach, or the one you visit on holiday, meet EU standards? – if not, find out why not.

Fig 360 Greenpeace in action off Barcelona

ENQUIRY

For *either* overfishing *or* pollution:
1   Describe the causes of the problem.
2   Explain the consequences of the problem.
3   Explain why international agreements are important to solving the problem, but often difficult to achieve.
4   Say how you think our seas should be managed: for example, do you think fishing in the North Sea should be banned completely for a period of time, or do you think pollution should be reduced by closing down dirty industries?

8.3 What are we doing to the atmosphere?

When we burn **fossil fuels** — whether it be in a thermal power station in order to generate electricity, in our car engines, or to fuel our central heating system — gases and particles are released into the air.

Sulphur dioxide and nitrogen oxides combine with water droplets in the atmosphere to produce **acid rain**. This can kill trees and vegetation and pollute rivers and lakes (Fig 361).

The UK is Europe's worst exporter of acid rain. It releases 11 times as much sulphur dioxide as it receives from other countries, largely because of its heavy reliance on coal-fired power stations. Much of this pollution is carried by the prevailing south-westerly winds to Norway and Sweden. These countries blame the UK for the declining health of their forests, streams and lakes.

However, the problem is not quite as simple as it seems. Recent years have also seen an increase in the number of conifers grown in north-west Europe. These trees increase the acidity of the soil that they are growing in. Water trickling through the soil will carry this acidity with it into streams and lakes, so this could also add to the acid water problem.

There is no doubt, though, that this type of pollution could be reduced if power stations and factories fitted filters to their equipment. However, there is a price to pay — in Germany it was estimated that to fit filters to all power stations and maintain them would increase electricity prices by 20 per cent.

Fig 361   Acid rain

The burning of fossil fuels (and to a lesser extent wood) releases 18 billion tonnes of carbon dioxide (CO_2) into the atmosphere every year. CO_2 is the most important of the "greenhouse gases" which trap heat re-radiated by the earth and which are responsible for the "greenhouse effect" (Fig 362). These gases get their name because they act like the glass of a greenhouse which lets short-wave radiation from the sun through but traps long-wave radiation; this is why the greenhouse heats up.

The other greenhouse gases are shown in Fig 363. Chlorofluorocarbons (CFCs) are used in some aerosol sprays and foam packaging. (CFCs also damage the ozone layer in the stratosphere. It protects us from harmful ultraviolet radiation which, among other things, can cause skin cancer.) Methane comes from vegetation rotting under water e.g. in a paddy field and from cattle manure. Nitrous oxides are given off by organic and inorganic fertilizers.

Until recently, the carbon cycle enabled the earth to maintain a steady amount of CO_2 in the atmosphere (Fig 364). Animal life breathes in oxygen and breathes out CO_2. Half of this CO_2 dissolves in the top layers of the oceans and supports life like plankton. The other half is breathed in by plants and converted into vegetable tissue. This traps the carbon but releases the oxygen, allowing it to go through the cycle again. When the plants die and decay some of the CO_2 is released back into the atmosphere while the rest is stored, e.g. in fossil fuels.

This cycle has now been upset. Figure 365 shows the increase in CO_2 in the atmosphere since 1958 and its predicted level by 2050. If there is more CO_2 in the atmosphere more heat will be trapped and temperatures will increase: this is the process known as global warming.

There is already evidence that temperatures have risen by 0.5°C since 1900. However, the regional effects of global warming are very difficult to predict, simply because we do not yet know enough about how the weather system works. Wind belts and ocean currents would shift, and with them the rain belts. Some places would benefit but others would become hotter and drier — desertification could become an increasing problem.

Global warming would be uneven. The greatest increase in temperature would be at

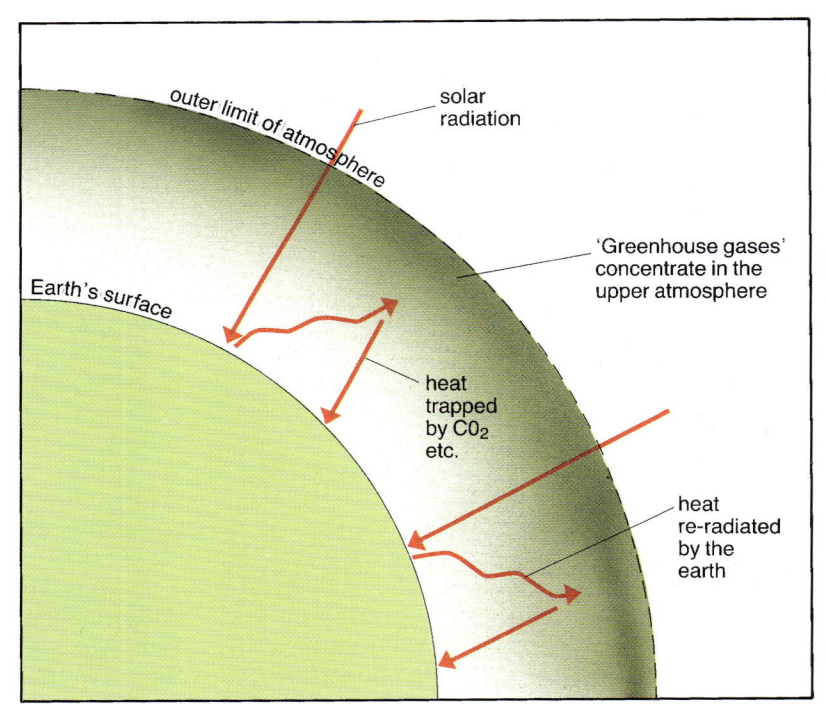

Fig 362 The Greenhouse effect

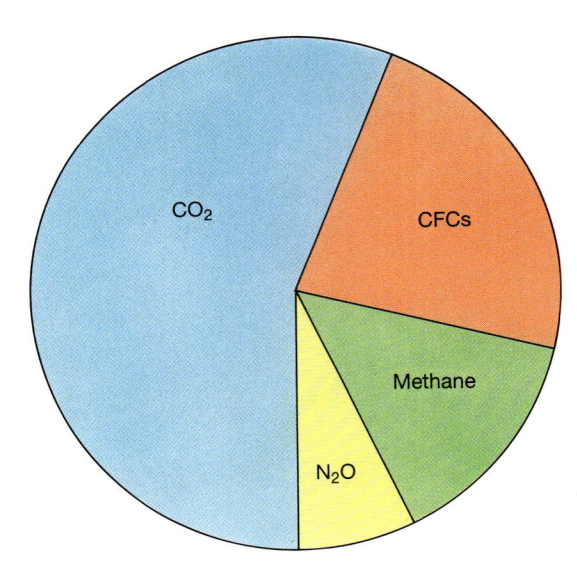

Fig 363 The Greenhouse gases

the poles and this would cause the ice sheets to melt. As a result, sea-levels would rise. The 2050 prediction would produce an increase in sea-level of between 0.5 to 1.5 metres. This has major consequences for low-lying areas the world over, but particularly in EDCs which are less able to afford flood protection schemes.

An increase in CO_2 would cause overall plant growth to increase, but some plants respond to CO_2 more than others. Experiments have

ENVIRONMENTAL ISSUES 8.3

Fig 364 The carbon cycle

shown that weeds which grow alongside subsistence crops in EDCs such as maize and sorghum, unfortunately do much better than the crops.

There are several ways in which this problem could be tackled. Conventional power stations are a major source of CO_2; they could be replaced with nuclear power stations but these bring with them their own problems. Forests could be planted to absorb the CO_2, but it has been estimated that 250 000 acres of trees is needed for an average power station. CFCs could be banned. Saving energy would cut consumption of fossil fuels.

At the Earth Summit in Rio de Janeiro in 1992 it had been hoped that governments would agree to reduce output of greenhouse gases to 1990 levels by the year 2000; however, the USA refused to attend unless time limits and amounts were removed from the treaty (see Section 8.5).

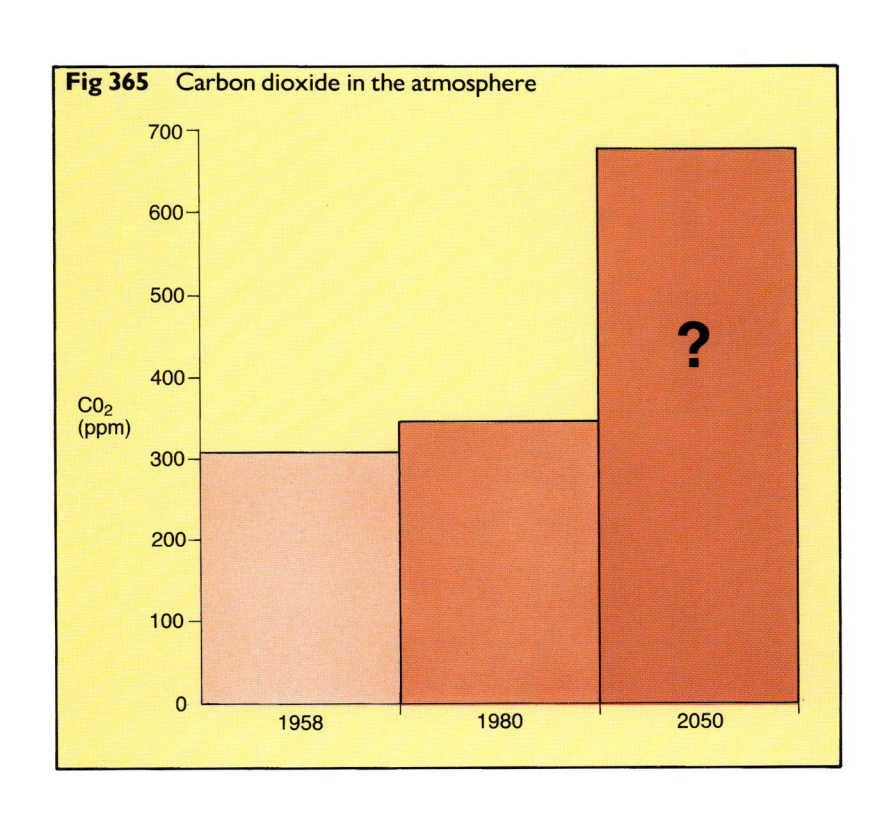

Fig 365 Carbon dioxide in the atmosphere

ENVIRONMENTAL ISSUES 8.3

ENQUIRY

1 Copy Fig 361 and add the following labels in their correct place:
— acid rain falls on Scandinavia;
— rain-bearing winds are blown across the North Sea;
— the gases mix with water droplets in the atmosphere;
— trees and lakes die;
— conifers increase soil acidity;
— power stations release sulphur dioxide and nitrogen oxides into the air.

2 Design a large poster to explain what is meant by global warming. Include its causes, its consequences and what could be done about it.

3 Describe the main findings of the Observer/Harris "Greenhouse effect" opinion poll (Fig 366). Can you explain any of the results? (Consider, for example, how the different age groups answered the questions.) Choose one of these sets of statistics and present them in an appropriate manner.

4 Why is international co-operation needed to solve the problems caused by atmospheric pollution?

Awareness of the Greenhouse effect

	Sex		Age				Total
	Male	Female	18–24	25–44	45–64	65+	
Yes	95%	90%	90%	95%	93%	89%	92%
No	4%	8%	7%	4%	5%	11%	6%
Don't know	1%	2%	4%	1%	2%	0%	2%

Worry over the Greenhouse effect

	Sex		Age				Total
	Male	Female	18–24	25–44	45–64	65+	
Very worried	26%	30%	30%	31%	28%	22%	28%
Little Worried	48%	47%	48%	54%	42%	43%	48%
Not worried	24%	20%	22%	14%	27%	33%	22%
Don't know	2%	3%	0%	2%	3%	2%	2%

How much is Government doing?

	Sex		Age				Total
	Male	Female	18–24	25–44	45–64	65+	
Far too Little	46%	37%	50%	43%	27%	36%	41%
Rather too Little	36%	40%	39%	40%	38%	35%	38%
About Right	10%	13%	5%	10%	15%	16%	12%
Too Much	1%	1%	0%	1%	2%	1%	1%
Don't know	7%	8%	6%	6%	8%	12%	8%

Will you help by paying more for fuel?

	Sex		Age				Total
	Male	Female	18–24	25–44	45–64	65+	
Yes	58%	55%	63%	63%	55%	39%	56%
No	31%	32%	26%	26%	35%	45%	32%
Not sure	11%	13%	11%	11%	10%	16%	12%

Will you change life to protect the Earth?

	Sex		Age				Total
	Male	Female	18–24	25–44	45–64	65+	
Yes	62%	61%	69%	68%	63%	41%	61%
No	27%	29%	26%	23%	26%	41%	28%
Not sure	11%	10%	5%	8%	12%	18%	11%

Fig 366 Attitudes towards the Greenhouse effect

ENVIRONMENTAL ISSUES 8.4

8.4 What are we doing to the forests?

The world's forests are a renewable resource, as long as they are replanted and given time to grow. However, vast areas of forest have been cleared to make way for farming and settlement. This process — called **deforestation** — is taking place at an ever increasing rate and in recent years it has become an issue of global concern.

Deforestation in Britain, as in many other European countries, began in prehistoric times and there is now very little of its original forest left. What remains is still under threat; for example, 40 per cent of its ancient woodland has been cleared in the last 40 years.

However, deforestation is more of an issue in EDCs because the rate of clearance is so great: for example, 7 per cent of the tropical rain forest (Fig 367) is being cleared every year which is equivalent to an area the size of Britain.

Deforestation in the Tropical Rain Forest

There are three main reasons why this is taking place:

- To provide farmland for settlers. For example, there are more than 2.5 million landless people in Brazil and one solution has been to clear land in the Amazon rain forest for smallholdings.

- To provide land for cattle ranches. For example, two-thirds of the Central American rain forest has been cleared since 1950 to make way for beef cattle. Nearly all of the land is bought by multinational companies or rich landowners and nearly all of the meat is exported to make hamburgers in MDCs.

- To exploit valuable timber reserves. Timber exports earn EDCs about US $8.7 billion a year. Hardwoods such as teak and mahogany are particularly valuable. EDCs need export earnings for many reasons including the repayment of loans and debts.

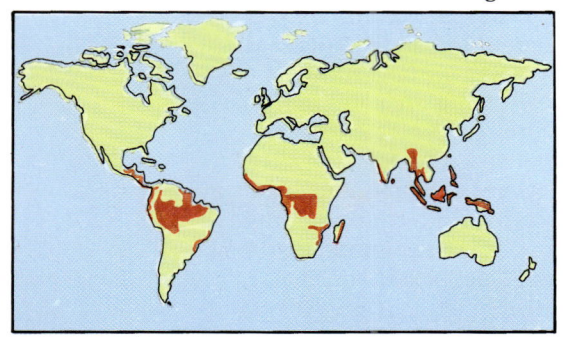

Fig 367 World distribution of tropical rain forest

Fig 368 Tropical rain forest, Thailand

Fig 369 Tropical deforestation

However, clearing the tropical rain forest presents a number of environmental problems. We are only just beginning to understand some of these but their significance is regional and global, as well as local.

The lush tropical vegetation suggests a rich soil but this is not necessarily the case (Fig 370). Where soils are poor the rain forest ecosystem survives by storing most of its nutrients in the trees and plants themselves (see Section 6.6). When a tree dies it quickly decomposes in the hot, humid conditions and the nutrients which are released are almost immediately taken up by the shallow roots of living trees and plants. When the forest is cleared this cycle is broken. Any nutrients in the soil are quickly washed away. This leaves the land infertile, liable to erosion and useless for farming.

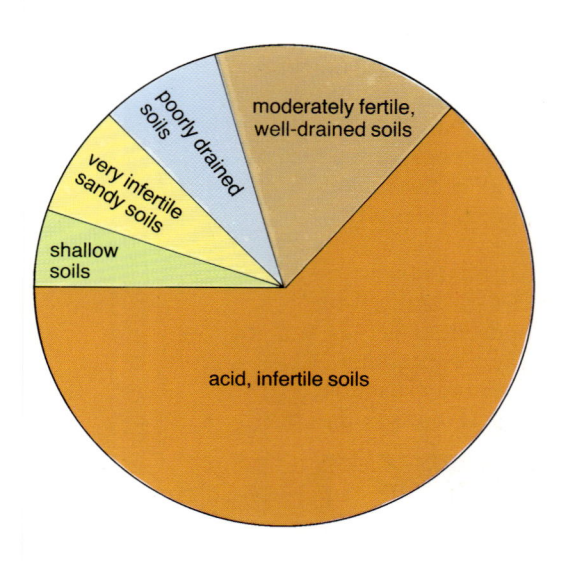

Fig 370 Soil fertility in the tropics

Where the soils are most fertile and contain most of the nutrients, deforestation still leads to soil erosion because the land is exposed to the heavy tropical rains. In the Malaysian forests it has been discovered that even selective logging (taking only certain types of trees in limited numbers) is a problem because the vehicles used to pull the trees out of the forest compact the soil; as a result surface runoff has increased and this has caused soil erosion.

Nearly half the world's animals and plants live in the tropical rain forest and the present rate of clearance means that two species become extinct every hour. An enormous genetic pool is being lost to science. Its value is easy to demonstrate: many of our medicines came originally from the tropical rain forest and only recently scientists were able to develop a drug to fight leukaemia from a rare tropical plant, the rosy periwinkle.

Clearing the rain forest breaks the carbon cycle and increases the amount of carbon dioxide in the atmosphere. This contributes towards global warming (see Section 8.3) and could therefore have global consequences.

Rain forest clearance upsets the hydrological cycle. The rain forest acts like a giant sponge by intercepting and storing rainfall. When it is cleared surface runoff increases dramatically. This can lead to soil erosion and to flooding as has already happened, in Bangladesh, for example.

Another example of deforestation upsetting the hydrological cycle is the threat faced by the Panama Canal (Fig 371). The canal system is fed by water from Gatun Lake. In the four month dry season the lake is kept full by water seeping out from the rain forest. However, deforestation is increasing surface runoff in the wet season and reducing the catchment area's ability to act as a reservoir for the dry season. The water is also bringing more silt with it. Unless this issue is tackled, the canal, which is very important to international trade and vital to the Panamanian economy, could run out of water for at least part of the year.

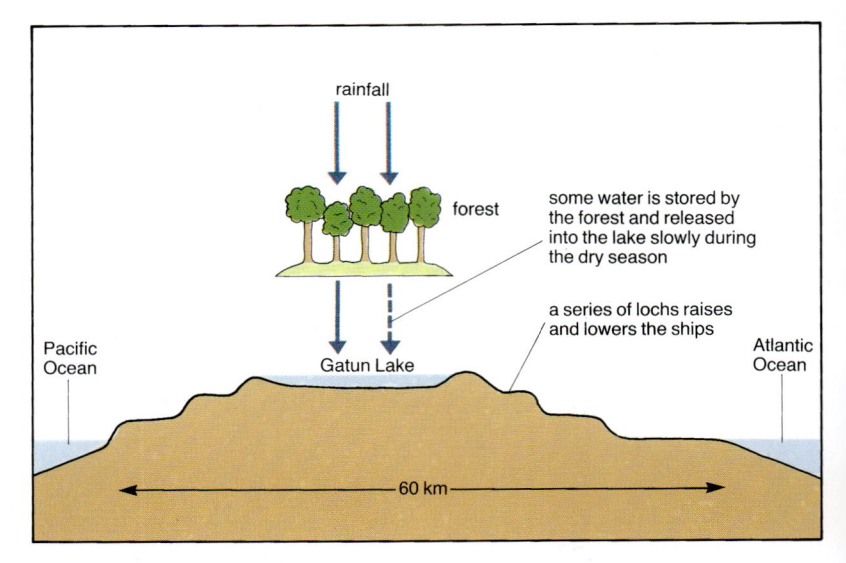

Fig 371 The Panama Canal system

ENVIRONMENTAL ISSUES 8.4

Deforestation in Brazil

Amazonia — the Amazon rain forest — is Brazil's largest but least populated and least developed region (Fig 372). However, its reserves of timber, its mineral wealth and its potential for farming have made it a target for development, particularly in the last 50 years.

The traditional farming system of the Amazon — slash and burn — is well-adapted to the rain forest ecosystem. An area of forest is cleared by cutting and burning. Large tree stumps are left in and this gives the soil some protection. The ash from the burning provides nutrients. After a few years, when the fertility of the soil begins to fall, the clearing is abandoned and a new one is made. However, this type of land use can only support a low population density and there are fewer than 200 000 Amazonian Indians living in this way.

In 1945 the Brazilian Government set up a development agency to encourage farming in Amazonia. Many migrants, especially from the north-east of the country, were attracted by grants and the opportunity to run their own farm. However, for most of them the move was not a success: they were given land that was difficult to farm; there were not enough supply posts; the government-provided houses often lacked a water supply, let alone electricity; and they were cut off from services such as health and education.

The building of the Trans-Amazonia Highway in 1968 which was supposed to act as a growth corridor did little to help the situation. It has attracted very few colonists and many of the settlements which have been built are very isolated even though they are on the highway.

This lack of success led to a change of strategy. As part of Brazil's Second National Development Plan, 15 "growth poles" were identified as places where development would be concentrated. They were to exploit different aspects of Amazonia's wealth (Fig 374) with targets being set for ranching, timber, mining and farming.

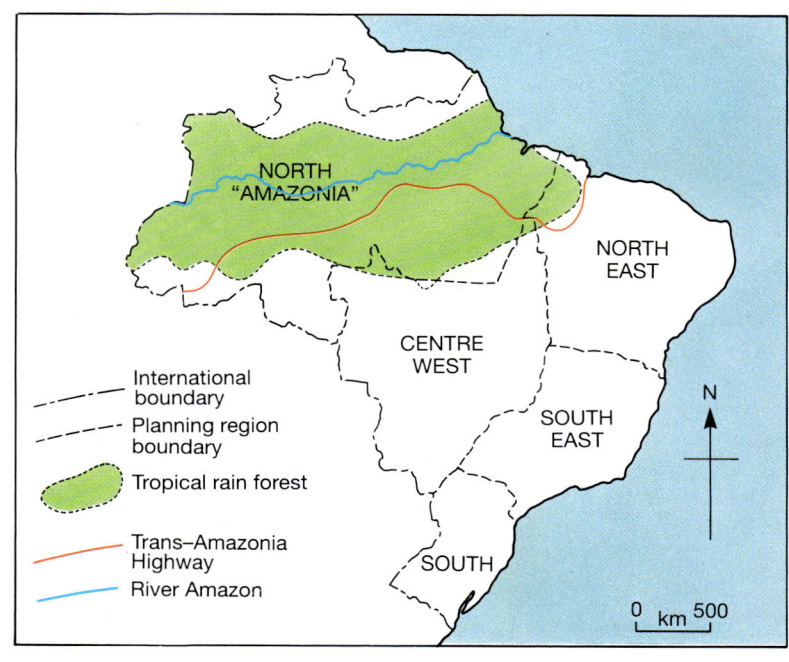

Fig 372 Amazonia — location map

Fig 373 Trans-Amazonia highway

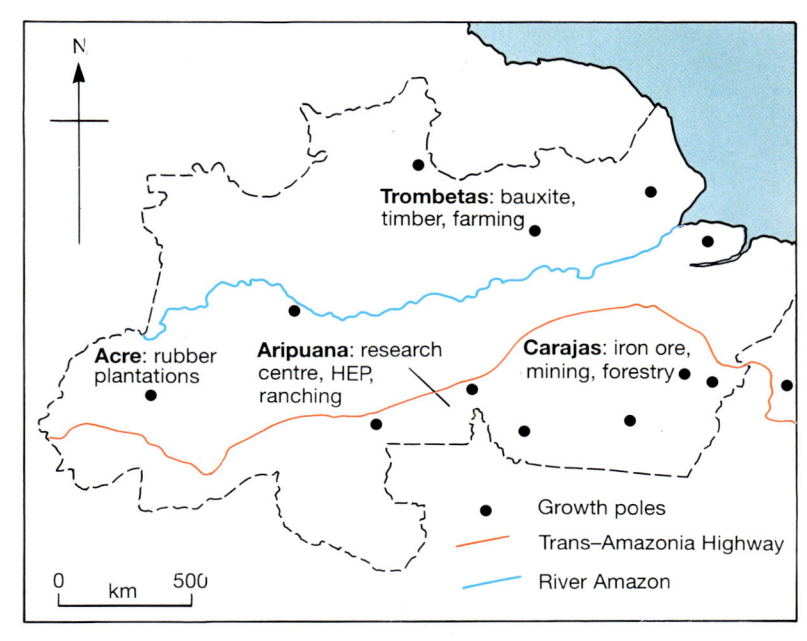

Fig 374 Amazonia's growth poles

Fig 375 Brazilian cattle ranch

Of all the activities encouraged by the government, ranching has had the biggest impact on the rain forest. In 1987, and again in 1988, over 20 million acres of forest were burnt, mainly to clear land for cattle. Six billion dollars in subsidies have been paid to the ranchers and the target set in 1975 of five million cattle has been exceeded. In ecological terms the policy has been a disaster: vast areas of the rain forest have been destroyed and, because the soil soon becomes exhausted, there has been widespread soil erosion. Even in economic terms it has been far from a success: 1 in 3 of the ranches has been abandoned; 1 in 2 has never sold a cow; and most of the profits have gone to land speculators and multinational companies, not the government.

Logging has also claimed millions of acres of rain forest. The valuable hardwoods are widely scattered and the rain forest has been indiscriminately felled in order to reach them. Mining, roads, dams and railways have also led to the destruction of the rain forest.

What could and should be done about it?

In the long term there is little, if anything, to be gained from the destruction of the tropical rain forest, either for the countries directly involved or for the world as a whole. However, there are many aspects to the problem and there are no easy solutions.

It is unrealistic to expect EDCs not to develop their natural resources. For example, 60 per cent of Brazil's population live below the poverty line and it has the world's largest foreign debt: it has to develop its economy and the rain forest is a potential source of wealth.

It is therefore important that the rich world helps the poor world and there are many ways in which this could be done. Debts could be written off. Levels of aid could be increased. Higher prices for rain forest products could be paid. Help and advice could be given to governments for the establishment of development projects.

There are things we as individuals could do to help. We could use softwood instead of tropical hardwood. We could buy hardwoods only from sustainably managed forests. We could treat wood more carefully and re-use it rather than throw it away.

With so many countries involved, international agreements are important to any solution. This explains why "A declaration on forests" was on the agenda of the Earth Summit in Rio de Janeiro in 1992 (Section 8.5); but so far agreements have had a limited effect.

Given that, with careful management, the rain forest is a renewable resource, it should be possible to combine sustainable rain forest development with the other types of development EDCs will inevitably want to make. This will give EDCs — and the rest of the world — a resource for the future, but at the current rate of clearance, time is running out.

ENQUIRY

1 Why is the tropical rain forest being cleared?
2 Why is the rain forest ecosystem so easily damaged?
3 Explain two of the problems tropical deforestation is causing.
4 Draw a diagram to show the traditional farming system of the Amazon rain forest.
5 Why did the first attempts to settle farmers in Amazonia largely fail?
6 Why did the Brazilian Government set up growth poles? List two examples.
7 What impact has ranching had on the Brazilian rain forest? Has it been an economic success? What other activities have affected the rain forest?
8 Make a list of **a)** the ways in which rich countries could help poor countries to conserve their forests and **b)** the things we as individuals could do to help. What are the disadvantages of these strategies?
9 We have already cleared our forests. Do we have any right to ask EDCs not to clear their forests?

8.5 Can the earth cope?

Ever-increasing demands are being made of the earth's natural resources. The world's population has risen dramatically this century and even the lowest estimate for the middle of the next century means a further big increase (Fig 376). People want to improve their standard of living and this takes on a greater significance because only a quarter of the world's population live in the richer countries of the north but they consume 15 times as much as the poorer countries of the south; other global comparisons are given in Fig 377. Modern technology allows us to extract and process natural resources at a far greater rate than ever before.

One view of this situation is that we have always been able to cope in the past and that there is no reason why we should not be able to cope in the future. For example, China's population has doubled in the last 40 years but it has kept pace with this increase (Fig 378). Between 1975 and 1985 it improved grain production by 100 million tonnes and it is now self-sufficient. Average food consumption has gone up by nearly 50 per cent. Production of soybeans and livestock (for protein) and fruit and vegetables (for vitamins and minerals) has also increased at record rates and as a result **malnutrition** (the wrong balance of food) has almost been wiped out.

Fig 379 Farming in China

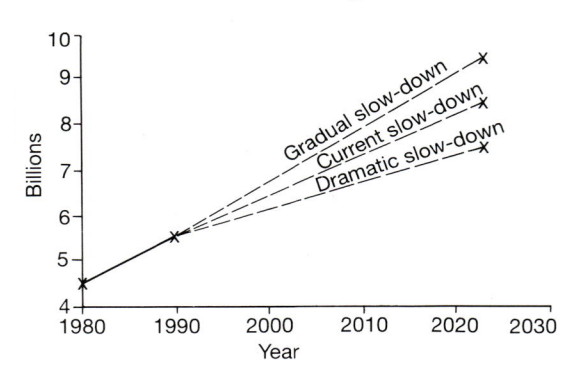

Fig 376 World population — growth and estimates

The rich north	The poor south
has 86% of world industry	has 14% of world industry
consumes 80% of energy	consumes 20% of energy
consumes 70% of fossil fuels	consumes 30% of fossil fuels
has 90% of cars	has 10% of cars
uses 350–1000 litres of water per day per person	uses 20–40 litres of water per day per person

Fig 377 Global comparisons

Population:	1 165 million
Population density:	315 per square mile
Natural increase:	1.3%
GNP (per capita):	370 US$ per annum
Food value:	+3 (0 = average)
Food production improvement since 1971:	+16 (0 = stayed the same)

Fig 378 China: vital statistics

ENVIRONMENTAL ISSUES 8.5

An alternative point of view is that there are real signs that the earth is close to breaking point: for example, a quarter of the world's population is undernourished and a further quarter is malnourished; some of our resources, like oil, will run out sooner rather than later; CO_2 emissions are changing our climate; and the ozone layer is being destroyed.

Sustainable Development

Concerns about the environment, and a recognition that a no-growth policy is unrealistic because poorer countries will inevitably want to catch up with richer countries, has led to the idea of sustainable development — development of a type and scale with which the earth can cope. It has five main requirements which are explained below:

Fig 380 Hunger

1 The stabilisation of the world's population. This is vital, but it will not be easy to achieve. One problem is that not all countries want to stabilise their populations. In a recent United Nations survey 19 countries said that their natural rate of population increase was too low and 11 countries with rates of 3 per cent or more per annum said that it was satisfactory (Fig 381). A larger population could be a political advantage because it could give a country greater international influence, and it could also provide a larger army. Similarly, an increasing population provides a growing labour force and a larger home market.

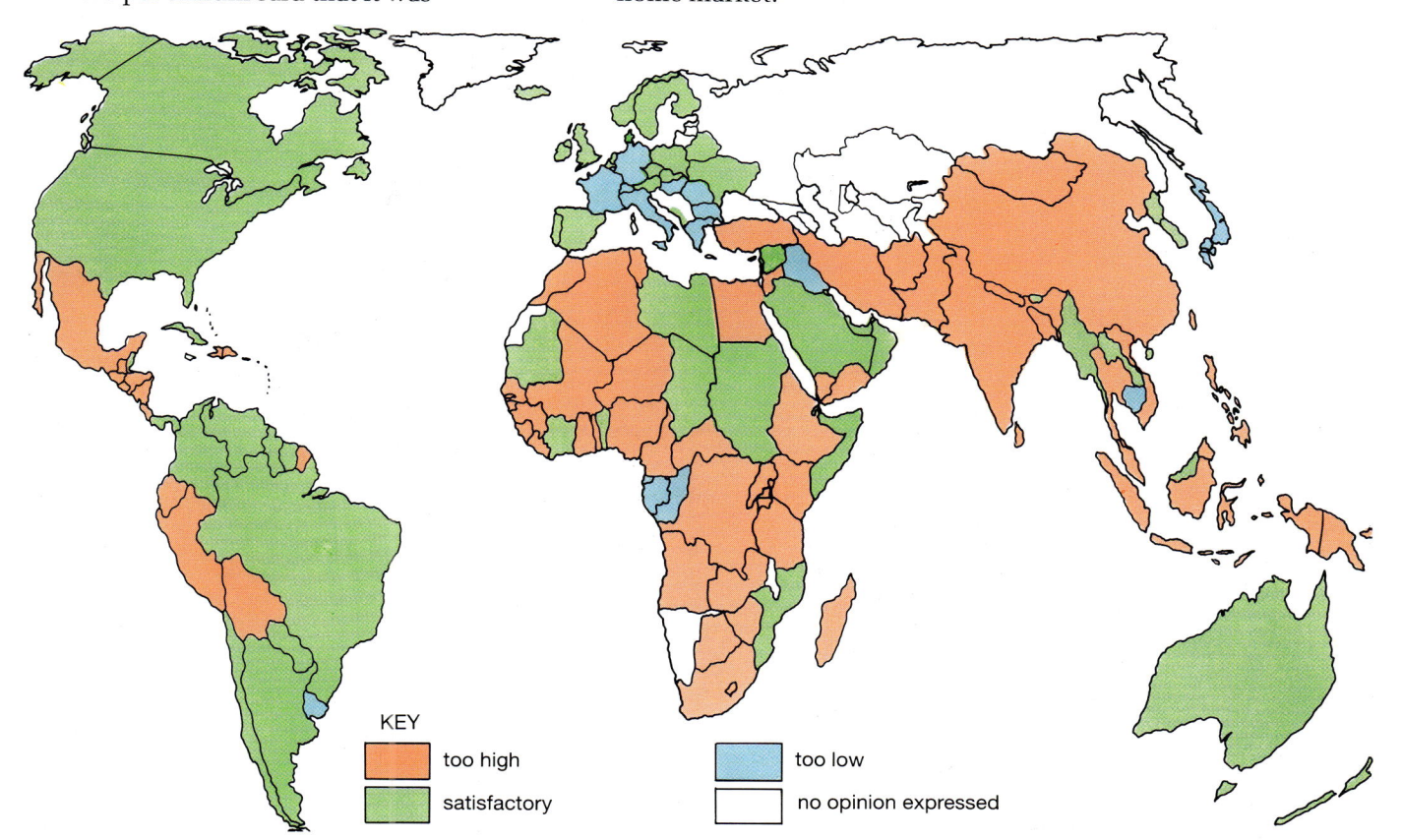

KEY
- too high
- satisfactory
- too low
- no opinion expressed

Fig 381 What do governments think of population growth?

ENVIRONMENTAL ISSUES 8.5

The major problem, though, is how EDCs can bring their populations under control. China has had some success with its strict "One Child" policy, and rates of increase in other EDCs have declined. However, many others (including India, the world's second most populated country) have had less success.

2 An economic value being placed on the environment. An "environment tax" could encourage us to use resources more carefully and could make money available for environmental protection. However, there are many potential problems in introducing such a tax. In 1992 the Austrian government placed an environment tax on imports of rain forest hardwood, but the strongest opposition came not from the consumers who were faced with higher prices, but from the Malaysian government which was worried that the move could reduce imports.

3 The curbing of atmospheric pollution. Acid rain, the threat of global warming and damage to the ozone layer have made this a priority. Again, though, there is a cost to be paid: for example, it is estimated that reducing CO_2 emissions to an acceptable level could require an oil price rise of 50-100 per cent. Many EDCs could be badly affected and in need of considerable help because they have invested in fossil fuel technology, usually with the assistance of MDCs, in an attempt to modernise their economies.

4 Controlled economic growth. Some economic growth is seen as necessary in order to tackle poverty and to create the wealth to deal with the environmental problems. The difficulties are in identifying how much growth is necessary and in deciding where it should be concentrated: MDCs do not want to see their living standards fall but EDCs have the most ground to catch up.

5 The setting up of binding international agreements. Without these, sustainable development stands no chance of success. What one country does affects another, whether it be a decision about imports of endangered species or the building of a new power station.

The Earth Summit

The need for such agreements led to the Earth Summit in Rio de Janeiro in June 1992 (Fig 382). It was organised by the United Nations and it took 2½ years to plan. The agenda for the summit proved to be very controversial (Fig 383). The USA refused to attend until time limits and amounts for the reduction of CO_2 emissions were removed from the treaty. Brazil and Malaysia opposed the declaration on forests so that in the end it was not made legally binding. However, 130 world leaders did attend; new money was donated by the rich countries to the poor via a special UN fund, the Global Environment Facility; and, most importantly, it was agreed that the issues raised at the summit should stay on the political agenda.

Fig 382 Earth Summit 1992

1 World convention on climate: measures to avoid global warming
2 Biological diversity treaty: commit countries to protecting habitat
3 A declaration on forests: to combat deforestation
4 Agenda 21: an action plan setting out the practical steps necessary for sustainable development
5 Earth Charter: a statement by governments confirming their support for sustainable development

Fig 383 The Earth Summit's agenda

ENVIRONMENTAL ISSUES 8.5

What could we do about sustainable development?

There are things which we as individuals could do to help. We could make sure that our politicians know that we take development issues seriously. Ideas for saving energy and for helping to conserve the tropical rainforests have already been mentioned in Sections 7.5 and 8.4. We could make better use of recycling facilities (Fig 384); we could buy environmentally-friendly products; and we could use recycled paper.

Fig 384 A recycling facility

ENQUIRY

1 To what extent do you think population growth is the main reason for the ever-increasing demands being made of the earth's natural resources? Explain your answer.

2 The experience of China suggests that perhaps the earth could cope with a further significant increase in population. Can you think of anything else which could support this point of view?

3 Define what is meant by sustainable development. List its five main requirements and for each of them explain one problem or disadvantage.

4 Describe and comment on the information given in Fig 381. What implications does it have for the policy of population stabilisation?

5 The agreements signed at the Earth Summit contained few firm details. Can its very considerable expense (for example, 24 million sheets of paper were used in documents and reports!) be justified?

6 A number of ways in which we as individuals could help the policy of sustainable development are listed above. Can you think of any others?

7 Reconsider the arguments for and against sustainable development. Do you think the MDCs in particular are prepared to make the sacrifices necessary to make the policy a success? Do you think they should make these sacrifices?

8.6 Assessment task: *The earth's future*

This task involves designing a large poster. You will need at least an A3 sheet of paper. It does not matter if you are not very good at drawing: you can use labels, flow diagrams, photographs, newspaper cuttings etc. The issues covered in Section 8 should form the basis of your work but you may wish to find out more about some of them.

Your poster should show the following:
a) The impact of quarrying and two ways in which the land can be restored.
b) The threat to the sea from human activity and some of the possible solutions.
c) The ways in which the atmosphere is being damaged and how it could be prevented
d) The conflicts between preservation of the rainforest and economic development in Brazil.
e) The reasons for the increasing demand being placed upon the world's resources.
f) Why international agreements are necessary if global problems are going to be solved.
g) The meaning of sustainable development; its advantages and disadvantages; and what we as individuals could do to help the earth's future.

Analysis of Statements of Attainment

In view of the current review of the National Curriculum and the development of new orders for Key Stage 4, it was felt that it would be confusing to retain any reference to present Key Stage 4 requirements in the text. An analysis of statements of attainment has therefore been omitted from this book. However, any teachers who would like guidance on how the book relates to current Key Stage 4 criteria can write for a free copy of the Statements of Attainment Analysis. Please state which of the two Discover books your request relates to and contact:

The Geography Editor
Hodder & Stoughton Educational
338 Euston Road
London
NW1 3BH

GLOSSARY

abrasion erosion caused by rock fragments being rolled or hurled against the land by water, ice or wind.

acid rain rain which has been polluted by (mainly) sulphur dioxide and nitrogen oxides.

aggregate crushed rock, sand and gravel used mainly for building.

air mass a large region of air with the same characteristics throughout, e.g. temperature.

anticyclone an area of high pressure with (in the northern hemisphere) clockwise winds.

aquifer a layer of rock which contains water.

aspect the direction a slope is facing in relation to the sun, i.e. towards it or away from it.

atmosphere the layer of gases which surrounds the earth.

attrition rock fragments being knocked against each other and breaking up into smaller pieces.

bay an indentation (opening) in the coastline, eroded by the sea.

biopower energy which comes from organic matter, e.g. gas from animal dung.

boulder clay (till) a glacial deposit of angular rock fragments in a mass of clay.

bulldozing erosion carried out by the sheer power of ice as it moves.

canopy the top layer of leaves and branches in a forest.

cliff a steep rock face, at the coast or inland.

climate the overall pattern of weather for a place from season to season.

concordant coastline a coastline where rock structure is parallel to the sea.

cone the hill or mountain made by a volcano.

coniferous trees which stay in leaf all year round.

conservation preserving resources and/or the environment.

convection rain the result of air rising because it has been heated.

corrie (cwm, cirque) the bowl-shaped hollow where a glacier begins.

crag and tail a hard outcrop of rock (crag) which has protected a soft outcrop of rock (tail).

crust the solid outer layer of the earth.

Dalmatian coastline a series of long, thin islands separated by narrow strips of sea.

deciduous trees which lose all of their leaves, usually in the winter.

deforestation clearing large areas of trees.

delta a low-lying area of land deposited at the mouth of a river.

deposition the dumping of material by water, ice or wind.

depression an area of low pressure with (in the northern hemisphere) anti-clockwise winds.

desertification the process by which land becomes a desert.

differential erosion less resistant rocks being worn away at a faster rate than more resistant rocks.

discharge the amount of water flowing past a given point in a river in a certain amount of time (it is usually measured in cubic metres per second, cumecs).

discordant coastline a coastline where the rock structure is at right angles to the sea.

drumlin a low, streamlined hill of boulder clay.

dry valley a valley which no longer has a river flowing in it (common in limestone regions).

earthquake when the ground moves and shakes.

EDCs the poorer, economically developing countries of mainly South America, Africa and Asia.

epicentre the place on the surface above where an earthquake starts.

erosion the wearing away of the earth's surface by water, ice and wind.

erratic a rock which has been transported by a glacier to an area where it does not belong.

fetch the distance of water across which the wind blows before it meets the coast.

fjord a glaciated valley which has been drowned by the sea.

flood plain the land the river spills onto when it bursts its banks.

focus the place in the crust where an earthquake starts.

fossil fuel sources of energy formed from the remains of animal and vegetable matter, e.g. oil and coal.

front the place where two air masses meet.

gabion a steel cage filled with rock used to protect the coastline.

GLOSSARY

geothermal energy which comes from hot rocks and fluids from inside the earth's crust.

glacier a slow-moving river of ice.

global warming an increase in the temperature of the earth's atmosphere because of a build up of greenhouse gases.

GNP Gross National Product is the amount a country earns in a year.

groyne a wooden fence built out into the sea to stop longshore drift and to protect the coastline.

hanging valley a tributary valley which has been left high above a main valley at the end of the ice age.

headland a band of rock jutting out into the sea.

hydraulic action erosion carried out by the sheer power of running water.

hydroelectric power (HEP) energy from running water.

hydrograph a line graph which shows the discharge of a river over a period of time.

hydrological cycle water moving from the oceans, to the atmosphere, to the land, and back to the oceans.

igneous rocks these are formed when hot, molten rock cools down and solidifies.

impermeable a rock which water cannot get through.

infiltration the rate at which water sinks into the soil.

interception this is when precipitation is caught by leaves etc, before it can reach the ground.

interlocking spurs the hills a river winds between in its upper section.

isobar a line joining places of equal pressure.

jet stream a high-speed, high-altitude wind.

karst the name given to limestone landscapes.

land restoration putting land back to use after, for example, it has been quarried.

levee the naturally-formed raised bank of a river, usually found in its lower section.

limestone pavement flat, bare surfaces of limestone broken up into blocks (clints) by gaps (grykes).

longshore drift the movement of material along a beach because of waves arriving at an angle to the shore.

magma molten rock under the earth's surface.

malnourishment the lack of adequate nutrition resulting from insufficient food or an unbalanced diet.

MDCs the richer, more developed countries of mainly North America, Europe and Australasia.

meander a loop or bend in the course of a river.

metamorphic rocks these are formed when existing rocks are changed by heat and/or pressure.

microclimate the climate of a small area caused by local factors such as aspect.

monsoon a seasonal wind affecting many parts of Asia.

moraine material deposited by a glacier.

mouth the place where a river meets the sea.

natural hazard a threat to people caused by a natural event, e.g. a flood.

non-renewable resource a resource which will run out because there is a limited amount of it, e.g. oil.

ocean current a stream of water moving in the ocean.

outwash plain the material deposited by the meltwater streams flowing away from the snout of a glacier.

overfishing catching so many fish that their numbers go down or stocks disappear completely.

ox-bow lake a crescent shaped lake formed when the neck of a meander is cut off.

penstock the pipes which take the water to the turbine in an HEP station.

permeable a rock which water can get through because it is porous and/or pervious.

pervious a rock which water can get through because it has cracks in it.

plate a piece of the earth's crust.

pollutant anything which contaminates or spoils the environment.

porous a rock which water can get through because it has spaces between its grains.

pot-hole a small depression found in the bed of a river.

prairie (steppe, pampas, veld) a temperate (neither too hot nor too cold) region of grassland found in mid-latitudes, e.g. central North America.

precipitation all forms of moisture reaching the ground, e.g. rain, drizzle, snow, hail.

quarry a place where stone is taken from the ground.

quota a limit set on the amount of something, e.g. the amount of fish which can be caught.

raised beach a former beach which is now at a higher level than the sea because the land has risen or the sea has fallen.

recycling re-using materials, rather than dumping them, e.g. paper, wood, steel.

GLOSSARY

relief rain (orographic) the result of air being forced to rise by mountains.
renewable resource a resource which will not run out, e.g. the sun, or will not run out as long as we are careful, e.g. trees.
resource anything which is of use to people, e.g. oil, wood.
resurgence the place where a stream reappears in a limestone region.
ria a V-shaped river which has been drowned by the sea.
ribbon lake a long thin lake found in a glaciated valley.
river basin the area drained by the river and its tributaries.
river terrace an area of flat land on the side of a river valley.
roche moutonnée an outcrop of rock shaped by a glacier, with one gentle and one steep side.
Sahel a belt of land to the south of the Sahara which is suffering from desertification.
savannah a hot region of grassland which borders the tropical rain forest.
scars steep, bare rock faces.
sediment cell a unit of coast and sea around which material circulates.
sedimentary rocks these are formed from fragments of other rocks, the remains of plants or animals, or chemicals which have built up in layers.
slash and burn a traditional farming system in the tropical rain forest which involves clearing land by cutting and setting fire to it.
soil a mixture of mineral matter, organic matter, water and air.
solar power energy which comes directly from the sun.
solution rocks dissolving in water.
source the place where a river begins.
spit a beach deposit which has grown out into the sea.
stewardship managing the earth so that it has a long-term future.
striation a scratch caused by glacial abrasion.
sustainable development development with which the earth can cope.
swallow hole (sink or pot-hole) the place where a stream disappears underground in a limestone region.
throughflow water moving through soil.
tidal power energy which comes from the flow of the tide.
transpiration vegetation losing water through its leaves.
transportation the movement of eroded or weathered material by water, ice or wind.
tropical rain forest the hot, wet forest of the equatorial region.
tributary a smaller stream or river joining a large stream or river.
truncated spur an interlocking spur which has been eroded by a glacier.
tsunami a wave started by an underwater earthquake.
tundra a cold, treeless region found at the Arctic Circle.
undernourishment not having enough food to eat.
wave-cut platform the area of rock in front of a cliff eroded by the sea.
weather the day-to-day changes in temperature, rainfall etc.
weathering rocks breaking down where they are because of contact with the earth's atmosphere.
wind power energy which comes from the force of the wind.

INDEX

abrasion 25, 27
acid rain 171
aggregate 163
air masses 118
alternative sources of energy 157–161
anticyclones 121
aquifers 59
arêtes 70
aspect 130
Aswan Dam 40, 155–156
atmosphere 131
attrition 25
barchan 28
bays 92
bay-bars 96
beaches
    formation 93
    surveys 94–95
Beaufort wind scale 111
bedding planes 7
biopower 158, 161
bluffs 54
boulder clay 75
braiding 56
Brazil
    deforestation 177–178
    energy 144
bulldozing 27
canopy 125, 126
carbon cycle 173
CARBONIFEROUS LIMESTONE, Section 4 82–89
China 180
Chlorofluorocarbons (CFCs) 172
cliffs 91
climate
    British Isles 115–116, 126
    continental 127
    definition 109
    equatorial 125
    factors affecting 129–131
    monsoon 134, 138
    savannah 133, 138
    tundra 135
    world distribution 124
clints 86
composite cone 10
concordant coastline 106
cone 10
coniferous tree 171
conservation 157
continental climate 127
convection currents 8
convection rain 117
core 5

corries 70
crag and tail 72
crust 5
Dalmatian coastline 97
deciduous trees 126
deforestation 175–179
delta 57
deposition 25, 52, 74, 93
depressions 119–120
depression rain 117
desertification 139–141
differential erosion 105
discharge 50
discordant coastline 105
drainage density 46
drainage patterns 46
drought 138–141
dry valleys 85
Dust Bowl, USA 34
EARTH, Section 1 4–37
earthquakes
    cause 12–13
    distribution 15
    prediction 14
Earth Summit 173, 178–179, 182
ENERGY, Section 7 142–161
ENVIRONMENTAL ISSUES, Section 8 162–184
epicentre 12
equatorial climate 125
erosion 25, 52, 70, 91
erratics 74
eskers 75
estuary 97
Etna 11
fetch 26
fjords 73
flood plains 55
fluvio-glacial deposition 75–76
focus 12
fold mountains 17
fossil fuels 143
freeze-thaw 20
frontal rain 117
fronts 119–120
gabions 99, 101
geothermal power 158
glacial movement 69
glaciers 27, 67
global warming 139, 172
gorges 53, 86
greenhouse effect 172
groynes 25, 101
grykes 86
hanging valleys 71
hazards

coastal floods 99–100
droughts 138–141
earthquakes 12–13
river floods 40–42
volcanoes 10
headlands 92
hot spots 19
hydraulic action 25
hydroelectric power (HEP) 78, 154–156
hydrograph 40, 50–52
hydrological cycle 43
ICE, Section 3 66–81
Ice Age 67–68
ice caps 67
ice sheets 67
igneous rocks 6
impermeable rocks 50, 59, 63, 85
infiltration 32, 48, 50
interception 48, 50
Isle of Purbeck, Dorset 103–107
isobars 119
isostatic readjustment 98
Japan 14
jet streams 133
kames 75
kame terraces 75
karst 83
Kenya
    soil erosion 35–37
    water supply 60–62
Kielder Water 63–64
land reclamation 164–165
lava
    acid 10
    basic 10
Leninakan 13
levees 56
limestone pavements 86
loess 28
longshore drift 25
magma 6, 10, 14
Malham, North Yorkshire (land use & management) 88–89
malnutrition 180
mantle 5, 16
meanders 54
Mercalli scale 12
metamorphic rocks 7
microclimate 109
Mississippi delta 57
monsoon climate 134, 138
moraine 27–74
mouth (of a river) 39
mushroom rock 28

natural hazard (see hazard)
Nile
    delta 57
    flooding 40
non-renewable resources 43, 143
Norfolk coast 99–102
ocean currents 137
oil 146–153
onion-skin weathering 20
open V-shaped valleys 55
orographic rainfall 117
outwash plain 76
OS maps
    glaciated uplands 80–81
    rivers 65
overfishing 167–168
ox-bow lakes 55
Panama Canal 176
Pangaea 8
penstock 154
permeable rocks 50, 59
pervious rocks 83
plates 8–9
plucking 27
pollution
    acid rain 171
    global warming 139, 172
    oil 150
    sea 168–170
population growth 180
porous rocks 83
pot-holes 54
prairie 34–35, 124, 127
precipitation 48, 117
pyramid peaks 70
quarry 163
quotas 168
rain 117
raised beaches 98
rapids 53
recycling 157, 183
relief rainfall 117
renewable resources 143, 167
reservoir construction 63–64
resources (see renewable and non-renewable resources)
resurgence 85
revetments 101
ria 97
ribbon lakes 73
Richter scale 12
river basins 39, 46–47
river system
    definitions 48
    investigating 39
    management 40–42
    surveys 49–50

INDEX

roches moutonnées 72
rocks 6–8
Sahel 139–141
savannah 133, 138
San Andreas fault 14
San Francisco 12
sand dunes 28–29
sand and gravel extraction 163–166
scars 84
SEA, Section 5 90–107
sea walls 101
sediment cells 101
sedimentary rocks 6
slash and burn 140
slip-off slopes 54
Snowdonia (land use & management) 77–79
soil
   erosion 34–37
   investigating 31–32
   properties 30–31
   survey 33

solar power 143, 158–159
solution 21, 84
source (of a river) 39
spits 96
stalagmites 84
stalactites 84
stewardship 181
strata 7
stream order 46
striations 72
subduction zone 17
sustainable development 181–184
swallow holes 84
synoptic charts 122
temperate forest 126
temperate grassland 127
terraces 57
throughflow 48
tidal power 158–160
till 75
tombolo 96

transpiration 48, 126
transportation 25
tributaries 39
tropical rain forest 125, 176
truncated spurs 71
tsunamis 13
tundra 135
U-shaped valleys 71
undernourishment 180
V-shaped valleys 52
vegetation
   savannah grassland 133, 138
   temperate forest 126
   temperate grassland 127
   tropical rain forest 125, 176
   tundra 135
   world distribution 124
volcanoes
   cause 10–11
   distribution 15

   prediction 14
WATER, Section 2 32–65
waterfalls 53
water supply
   England and Wales 60
   Kenya 60–62
waves 26
wave-cut platforms 91
weather
   definition 109
   measuring 109–113
   survey 114
weathering
   biological 22
   chemical 21
   physical 20
   surveys 23–24
WEATHER, CLIMATE AND VEGETATION, Section 6 108–141
wind 28, 111, 118, 132
wind power 158–160

ACKNOWLEDGEMENTS

The author and publishers thank the following for permission to reproduce photographs, diagrams and statistical information in this book:

Cambridge University Press, J Allen, *Energy Resources*, Fig 317; *The Guardian*, 14/9/92 Fig 305, undated Fig 354, 31/3/92 Fig 355; Longman Group UK, Knox et al, *The United States: A Contemporary Human Geography*, Fig 237, J Knapp, *Challenge of the Natural Environment*, Fig 303; *The Observer*, 15/4/90 Fig 366; Ordnance Survey, 1:50 000 Middleton-in-Teesdale, Crown Copyright, Fig 132, 1:50 000 Snowdon, Fig 175; Robert Harding Picture Library – cover; Fig 7 Ted Harvey: Chapter Head 1.1 Colin Hoskins/Sylvia Cordaiy Picture Library; Fig 23 USGS Picture Library; Fig 24 Japan National Tourist Organisation; Fig 67 Nick Britton/Suzy Skevington; Fig 77 The Hulton-Deutsch Collection; Fig 78 ASAP/Robert Harding Picture Library; Chapter Head 2.1 Raj Kamal/Robert Harding Picture Library; Fig 116 Aerofilms; Fig 127; Fig 129 Alison Kings; Fig 130 Northumbria Water; Fig 138 British Antarctic Survey; Chapter Head 3.1 Dizzy de Silva/Sylvia Cordiay Picture Library; Fig 152 Still Moving Picture Company; Fig 159 British Geological Survey; Fig 169 The J Allan Cash Photolibrary; Fig 170 Forest Life Picture Library; Fig 171 Celtic Picture Library; Chapter Head 4.1 E. Rostom/Sylvia Cordaiy Picture Library; Chapter Head 5.1 Chris North/Sylvia Cordaiy Picture Library; Fig 208; Fig 211 Aerofilms; Chapter Head 6/1 A Felix/Robert Harding Picture Library; Fig 247 HMSO Copyright Section; Fig 280 Stan Osolinski/Oxford Scientific Films; Fig 297(i) T. Bølstad/Panos Pictures; Fig 297(ii) Tropix/M & V Birley; Fig 299 Geoscience Features Picture Library; Fig 309 Oxfam Picture Library; Chapter Head 7.1 John Farmon/Sylvia Cordaiy Picture Library; Fig 312 ZEFA Picture Library; Fig 336 David Houghton/Oxford Scientific Films; Chapter Head 8.1 Nick Pains/Sylvia Cordaiy Picture Library; Fig 323 Topham Picture Source; Fig 325; Fig 327 Press Office, Britishy Petroleum; Fig 332 ZEFA Picture Library; Figs 346, 347, 348 & 350 Steve Dann Fig 356 Robert Harding Picture Library; Fig 359 Greenpeace/Pickaver; Fig 360 Greenpeace/Mortimer; Fig 369 Panos Pictures; Fig 373 Tony Morrison/South American Pictures; Fig 375 Sue Cunningham Photographic; Fig 381 Oxfam Picture Library; Fig 383 SIPA–Press/Rex Features.

All other photographs supplied by the author.

Every effort has been made to trace and acknowledge correctly all copyright holders but if any have been overlooked the publishers will be pleased to make the necessary arrangements at the first opportunity.